Endorsements

"*Igniting Your Life* will kindle your innermost desires and rouse the passionate fire that has been smoldering within you."

– **Cherie Soria**, author *The Raw Food Diet Revolution*. Founder and director Living Light International. RawFoodChef.com

"This journey of remembering is constant throughout this book, an uplifting and empowering collection of worldy work. Inspiring conversations arise from those in earshot as you read."

– **Sheridan Hammond**, Australia. Founder and director Samudra Yoga Surfing & Food 4 Life. Samudra.com.au.

"We defy you to not be inspired by this book! *Igniting Your Life* is overflowing with both practical information and motivational messages that are clearly the result of a lifetime's worth of research and practice. *Igniting Your Life* is a book that really enables one to 'start where they are' and begin to incorporate its ideas for change immediately. Never before has a 21st century writer combined so eloquently a vision with a tangible blueprint for the holistic healing of the human body and spirit."

– **Matt Amsden**, author *RawVolution*, and **Janabai Amsden**, ELR restaurant, Santa Monica, CA. EuphoriaLovesRawvolution.com

"An impressive collection of eclectic quotations and thoughtful commentary. Inspiring and motivating… I'm reading your book again and really enjoying it. You've certainly captured the wisdom of the ages."

– **Victoria Moran**, author *Living a Charmed Life: Your Guide to Finding Magic in Every Moment of Every Day*. VictoriaMoran.com

"In this book McCabe encourages readers to recognise their true potential and work towards a better way of living and being, so all may benefit."

– **Sienna Blake**, Australia's *Vegan Voice* magazine: Veganic.net

"A powerful book full of quotations about all aspects of life. A great compilation that shouts inspiration from every page. You can simply flick to any page and you get some supercharg'n info. The more I read it, the more I can relate to it. Gold stuff!"

– **Harley Durianrider Johnstone**, Australian Division One biking athlete and co-founder of 30BananasADay.com

"An Amazing book!"

– Gl**len Colello**, Catch a Healthy Habit restaurant, Connecticut, USA; CatchAHealthyHabit.com

"John has collected wisdom from hundreds of people from many centuries. He has organized this and added his own wisdom to create a manual for changing your life for the better. This is a practical book with tasks which, if followed, will improve your life. After only a few hours of reading, I was already writing life plans and lists of things I needed to change in my life."

– **Rob Hull**, publisher, London's *Funky Raw* magazine: FunkyRaw.com; RawRob.com

"*Igniting Your Life* is a book written by an independent thinker for independent thinkers. Or, chances are, you will certainly be one by the time you have finished reading it. John has a penetrating and comprehensive view of the numerous ways in which we can all safeguard not only our own health but also, by extension, the health of the environment and the other people and life forms we share it with. To put it simply, he knows what really matters. The huge collection of great quotations that fill his latest book are reason enough to read it, but if we choose to actively ignite our lives in the ways that John suggests, our enhanced energy and clarity will enable us to do more good in this world and also to be a lot happier in the process."

– **Angela Starks** and **Michael Stein**, New York. YogaInTheRaw.com

"Where we place our attention determines our experience. If we focus on the news and mainstream media we get negativity, death, and destruction. On the other hand, if we focus on uplifting our spirit and mind we create a completely different reality. To this end I highly recommend that you turn off the TV and read John McCabe's *Igniting Your Life*; it is pure gold! If you are looking for inspiration to improve or change your life, this book is an invaluable companion on the journey. John weaves a commentary full of practical hints, tips, and insight with uplifting quotations from some of humanity's greatest souls."

– **Anand Wells**, Australia's RawPower.com.au and LiveFoodEducation.com

"I have been involved with the raw food movement for over 12 years and I've seen and heard a lot of things. My experiences with raw foods have been amazing over the years, and just keep getting better. I am thankful for John McCabe and his extraordinary work. He has gone above and beyond in his research, some of the best I've seen actually - especially since there are so many books on the subject. John is a great writer who passionately exposes truths. He is a breath of fresh air!"

– **Angela Elliott**, Author of *Alive in Five*; She-ZenCuisine.com

"After a few days of reading and being completely inspired, I wanted to say a huge THANK YOU! Every quote, every paragraph, made me think, 'I want to add this to my next blog' as they resonated so profoundly within me. This book is about to become the first book in the cafe! To ignite everyone's life!"

– **Maya Melamed**, Sydney, Australia. ChangingMaya.com.au

"I love your book. Your book has also changed my mum's life. She is now searching for her purpose more than ever. Thank you so much. X"

– **Freelee Love**, Australia; 30BananasADay.com

"An enjoyable read with a common sense approach. Gets to the point in a basic, matter-of-fact way."

– **Michelle Premura**, Turquoise Barn, New York; TurquoiseBarn.com

"Your book is really marvelous. Once again, I hit a quote that jumped my DNA to full attention, and I appreciated it so much I wanted to tell you that you have done a very good thing. I hope your book sets the world on fire. In a good way."

– S**ara Honeycutt**, artist proprietor of New Gallery Studio, Taos, New Mexico; NewGalleryStudio.com

"A wonderful book, one you can resource over and over again for eternity."

– **Hugh Cruickshank**, Raw-Foods-Diet-Center.com

"John McCabe has written a comprehensive guide to bringing yourself into alignment with your higher being. *Igniting Your Life* is essential reading, for those looking to evolve in all areas of life. I have this book on my nightstand, to inspire me before I sleep and when I awake."

– **Steven Prussack**, RawVeganRadio.com

"In *Igniting Your Life*, John McCabe weaves his own insightful narrative in and among some of the most soul-stirring and evocative quotes from notable people around the world, past and present. Open any page, anytime and become inspired to live the life of your dreams."

– **Rhio**, author of *Hooked on Raw*, New York; RawFoodInfo.com

For the love of books.

"We read to know we are not alone."
– C. S. Lewis

"I suggest that the only books that influence us are those for which we are ready, and which have gone a little farther down our particular path than we have yet got ourselves."
– E. M. Forster

"It was books that taught me that the things that tormented me most were the very things that connected me with all the people who were alive, or who had ever lived."
– James Baldwin

"When I look back, I am so impressed again with the life-giving power of literature. If I were a young person today, trying to gain a sense of myself in the world, I would do that again by reading, just as I did when I was young."
– Maya Angelou

"Books are the carriers of civilization. Without books, history is silent, literature dumb, science crippled, thought and speculation at a standstill."
– Barbara Tuchman

"He that to what he sees, adds observation, and to what he reads, reflection, is in the right road to knowledge."
– Caleb Colton

"Science is a wonderously successful way of knowing the world, but it isn't the only way. Knowledge also derives from other sources, such as common-sense experience, imaginative literature, music, and artistic expression."
– Francisco Ayala

"From your parents you learn love and laughter and how to put one foot before the other. But when books are opened you discover that you have wings."
– Helen Hayes

"We defy you to not be inspired by this book!"
– Matt and Janabai Amsden
EuphoriaLovesRawVolution.com

Igniting Your Life

Pathways to the Zenith of Health and Success

John McCabe
Author of
Sunfood Living: Resource Guide for Global Health
Sunfood Diet Infusion: Transforming Health Through Raw Veganism
and *Sunfood Traveler: Global Guide to Raw Food Culture*

Foreword by
Cherie Soria
Author of *Raw Food Revolution Diet*
Founder and director of Living Light International

Carmania Books
Santa Monica, California

Igniting Your Life: Pathways to the Zenith of Health and Success
by John McCabe, IgnitingYourLife.com
$20.95 U.S.

Disclaimer:

This book is sold for information purposes only. How you interpret and utilize the information in this book is your decision. Neither the author nor the publisher and/or distributor will be held accountable for the use or misuse of the information contained in this book. This book is not intended as medical advice because the author and publisher of this work are not recommending the use of chemical drugs or surgery to alleviate health challenges. It also does not stand as legal advice, or suggest that you break any laws. Because of the way people interpret what they read, and take actions based on their own intellect and life situations, which are not in the author's, publisher's, and/or distributor's control, there is always some risk involved; therefore, the author, publisher, and/or distributor of this book are not responsible for any adverse effects or consequences from the use of any suggestions, foods, substances, products, procedures, or lifestyles described hereafter.

ISBN: 978-1-884702-15-0
Library of Congress Control Number: 2010920345
Dewey CIP: 158.1. **OCLC:** 24218880
First Edition: 2010
Graphics by: Steve Minard: MinardSteve@yahoo.com
Editing by: Brenda Koplin: BrenKo2@aol.com
Published by: Carmania Books, POB 1272, Santa Monica, CA 90406-1272, USA
IgnitingYourLife.com.

Acknowledgments

Thank you to those who encouraged me throughout the years to finish this task, including Daniel and Ninaya Laub, Daniel and Sydney Morello, William Fedasko, Diane Ballou, Victor Zolfo, Nick Pemble, Vivian King, Rich Marchewka, Phillip Landry, Deven Allyn Michaels, Susan Nowak, Erika Willhite, Sheri Sibiski, Laura Hemmer, Andrew Koenig, Lukani Hutaff, Brian Tillis, Kevin Redmond, Willow Evans, Jim Abbot, Adam Daniels, Cheryl Lake, Sarah Honeycutt, Tracy Larkins, Michael Zeno, Dr. Lorin Lidnder, Joseph Narvaez, Chari Birnholz, Julie Tolentino, Dr. Barbara Foley, Tony Amara, Patricia Meisels, and Susan Landau. And also the readers that have responded so positively to my earlier writings.

Thank you to Eileen Zeber, Peggy Lee, Doris Duke, Susan Iddings, and Marian Cole.

I must thank those who read early versions of the manuscript as I was writing it and gave me helpful feedback, including Sheridan Hammond of Australia's Samudra.com.au; Rob Hull of England's FunkyRaw.com; Victoria Moran of VictoriaMoran.com; John Robbins of FoodRevolution.org; Sienna Blake of Australia's *Vegan Voice Magazine*; Angela Starks and Michael Stein of YogaInTheRaw.com; and Matt and Janabai Amsden of EuphoriaLovesRawvolution.com.

I'd like to give special acknowledgment to Cherie Soria of the Living Light Culinary Institute in Fort Bragg, California. She is exactly who I wanted to write the foreword, and I was very pleased that she responded so positively when I got up the nerve to ask her — after she had read the manuscript three times and kept saying such positive things about it. (Sign-up for her enewsletter by going to RawFoodChef.com.)

And, thank you to Brenda Koplin, the editor. Without her work this book would not be what it is.

> "A teacher affects eternity; he can never tell where his influence stops."
>
> – Henry Brooks Adams

Books by John McCabe

Igniting Your Life: Pathways to the Zenith of Health and Success
Sunfood Diet Infusion: Transforming Heatlh Through Raw Food Veganism
Sunfood Traveler: Guide to Raw Food Culture, Restaurants, Recipes, Nutrition, Sustainable Living
Hemp: What the World Needs Now
Sunfood Living: Resource Guide for Global Health
Surgery Electives: What to Know Before the Doctor Operates

Table of Contents

"The lure of the distant and the difficult is deceptive. The great opportunity is where you are."
– John Burroughs

Foreword

By Cherie Soria

Life is filled with experiences ... some good, some bad, and some that are positively joyous. This opportunity to write a few words about my friend John McCabe and the transformational process he describes in *Igniting Your Life* definitely falls happily into the third category.

John and I share the belief that those who succeed in life — truly succeed in all aspects, mentally, physically and spiritually — learn from and model themselves after people they admire, and set intentions to take action so their goals can reach fruition. Successful people have developed a strong sense of positive self-identity that enables them to continue to work on their weaknesses without judging themselves or their past for not being "perfect." They do not allow their weaknesses, fears, or past experiences to run them. The material in *Igniting Your Life* is all about these issues. It is a vibrational match with my truth. It changed my life and I believe it can change yours, too.

When I was in my twenties, I read dozens of books and spent thousands of hours studying self-improvement techniques. The profound wisdom, inspiration, and motivation I received as a result of those years had a huge impact on my life and the vision I carried of myself in the world. If *Igniting Your Life* had been available, however, I would have saved a lot of time trying to piece together the different things I was learning into a single, cohesive design for living.

Igniting Your Life contains what I had been searching for in other books. It provides an integrated approach to achieving a balanced, meaningful, and prosperous life, and is for anyone and everyone who knows there is something more to life than what they are currently experiencing. *Igniting Your Life* explores the mind-body-spirit connection and touches on all levels of being so that you can stop struggling, let go of fear and limitations, focus on possibilities, and overcome obstacles that otherwise might threaten your ability to become all that you are capable of being. In these pages, you will find the secret to achieving your goals in life by addressing critical issues of money, relationships, health, security, and peace of mind.

John McCabe's book, *Igniting Your Life,* is both timeless and timely. I believe it holds the promise of being a limitless resource of hope and inspiration. It is a diversion from John's previous books that deal more with healthful living from a physical perspective. It includes vital information about how to create optimal health, of course — that cannot be ignored; but it also addresses the importance of mental, emotional, and spiritual well-being, without which true happiness cannot be achieved. These various aspects of us are inseparable. To attain balance, we cannot ignore the physical body while putting all of our attention on our spiritual growth, nor can we expect to be happy and fulfilled by focusing only on health. John is keenly aware of this and uses the voices of many people throughout history as inspirational guidance concerning all aspects of human experience.

John's own life experience, coupled with his fascination and research on the subject of human triumph, provide the rich foundation upon which this book is written. Like many of us, John had much to overcome in his life. He was the product of a dysfunctional and violent household of many misfortunes, could barely read until he was a teenager, and received a public school education that was both inadequate for life needs and could leave a person on the path to a low-quality existence. Aware of being unprepared for the next step in his life, John knew he had come to a crossroad. Wanting to avoid the future of failure laid out for him, he began to study what makes some people succeed while others fail. He made the world his teacher while collecting words of wisdom from the most inspiring scientists, philosophers, poets, authors, artists, and teachers the planet has ever known. Essentially, John made these into his mentors, and now they can become yours. Nowhere else, to my knowledge, will you find the wealth of inspirational quotations contained on the pages of *Igniting Your Life*!

Studying the wisdom in the words of these masters of life uplifted and motivated John to experience a renewed confidence and spirit. Over time he has been able to achieve a more balanced, fulfilling life. The boy who was set on a path to failure overcame adversity and became a man choosing to follow a path to success. John continues to take actions in tune with making his dreams come true.

What are *your* dreams? John's book can help you achieve them. *Igniting Your Life* contains what he considers to be the most powerful, inspiring, transformative, and life-altering of his collection of "wisdom quotations." Together they are a kind of Cliff Notes for a Successful Life that you can use to get out of your rut, change your life, and become all that you have the potential to be.

This is a singular moment in your life. It's time for you to step into your joy and allow your life to unfold, revealing layer after layer of that which you have the potential to be. With *Igniting Your Life* as your guide, you'll find yourself steadily moving in the direction of improved selfesteem, better relationships, a greater sense of security, and a willingness to risk in order to achieve fulfillment.

But be prepared. As you delve into *Igniting Your Life*, you'll begin to take a look at your self-imposed limitations, start to understand why you may be stuck, and gain an understanding about why situations continue manifesting in your life as they do. *Igniting Your Life* will kindle your innermost desires and rouse the passionate fire that has been smoldering within you.

While you may consider yourself to be past your zenith, taking actions in tune with the wisdom of the ages gathered within *Igniting Your Life* will rekindle your enthusiasm for life, and help provide a foundation of appreciation for where you are now, as you take steps to create the life you want.

Congratulations. You are at the beginning of a new journey. The destination is joy, peace, health, and prosperity.

Cherie Soria
Author, *Raw Food Revolution Diet*
Founder and Director of Living Light International
RawFoodChef.com

"If one advances confidently in the direction of his dreams, and endeavors to live the life which he has imagined, he will meet with a success unexpected in common hours."
– Henry David Thoreau

"One who meets the true reality is transformed into gold."
– Guru Granth Sahib

Introduction

> "Tell me, what is it you plan to do with your one wild and precious life?"
>
> – Mary Oliver

Are you allowing places, things, events, and people to toss you around because you are not taking control of your life? Or are you accessing and using your intellect, instinct, talents, skill, abilities, and other graces to make your life form into what you want it to be?

Your future does not have to be some random spec that falls out of the cosmos. You also do not have to settle for a low-quality life.

> "It is never too late to be what we might have been."
>
> – George Eliot

If you are not experiencing the life you want, there is one person to whom you can turn to change your life, and that person is you.

Your life is not going to stay the way it is. Instead, it is going to change in some way regardless of what you do. But if your life is going to reflect what you wish it to be, it is up to you to transform your wishes into reality.

> "Thought is cause: experience is effect. If you don't like the effects in your life, you have to change the nature of your thinking."
>
> – Marianne Williamson

If you are reading this type of book, it is likely that you are not satisfied with what you see as your life.

Maybe you are at some level of dissatisfaction of how you have spent your life, and have decided that you do not want to waste one more moment replicating the results you have been experiencing.

Maybe you have reached what you feel to be the end of your rope and have made the decision that you do not want to go through another year, or even another day, without seeing your life improve.

> "The truth is that our finest moments are most likely to occur when we are feeling deeply uncomfortable, unhappy, or unfulfilled. For it is only in such moments, propelled by our discomfort, that we are likely to step out of our ruts and start searching for different ways and truer answers."
>
> – M. Scott Peck

Your life does not have to be guided by the formula of the myth in which your strongest life-altering revelation arrives at your darkest moment. A great change in your life also does not have to be spurred by a cataclysmic event. You also do not have to depend on others or on events for inspiration. The personal revelations and inspirations that trigger improvement in your life can arrive at any time when you open your thoughts to their possibility.

> "Every exit is an entry somewhere else."
> – Tom Stoppard

Maybe you are at the point of feeling as if your life has been shattered. But instead of thinking of it as shattering apart, consider that it may finally be coming together. You may simply be going through a major life cleanse as you are shedding what truly is not you and taking on a new understanding and form.

> "Storms purify the atmosphere."
> – Henry Ward Beecher

You might be going through a life storm, even deluged by a typhoon of issues. Storms are ways Nature rearranges and clarifies, renewing energy, opening new pathways, and infusing patterns of growth.

> "Sometimes a breakdown can be the beginning of a kind of breakthrough, a way of living in advance through a trauma that prepares you for a future of radical transformation."
> – Cherrie Moraga

What you may be going through may be some level of what some call a shamanic conversion — or enlightenment — as you discover what it is you are truly about.

> "Sometimes our fate resembles a fruit tree in winter. Who would think that those branches would turn green again and blossom, but we hope it, we know it."
> – Johann Wolfgang von Goethe

> "There is a life-affirming spark within you which constantly nudges you towards saying yes to life."
> – Linda MacDonald

> "The world is round and the place which may seem like the end may also be the beginning."
> – Ivy Baker Priest

> "For last year's words belong to last year's language. And next year's words await another voice. What we call the beginning is often the end. And to make an end is to make a beginning."
> – T. S. Eliot

I have read a lot of books on the topic of life change. I found some that were helpful, and some that were not so helpful. In particular, I think a book that would be most helpful in manifesting a truly healthful life would be one that helps determine the difference between the authentic traits of a person and the personality someone has tried to become so that they better fit into what they have perceived to be acceptable society.

Considering that many of us do conform to what we think is the most acceptable way of being, maybe it is the conformity that is holding us back, and which may have placed limits on the expression of our intellect and talents. The conformity may also have played a part in the feelings of awkwardness that crushes potential. In a good way, this may lead to the introspection that can bring about healthful life changes by doing away with the false self and allowing people to identify and cherish their true beneficial qualities.

> "I have always believed, and I still believe, that whatever good or bad fortune may come our way we can always give it meaning and transform it into something of value."
> – Hermann Hesse

Perhaps you feel that your life has been injured, and that what you desire and need is to undergo healing. Understand that you have power within you to heal your wounds. You can use your desire as motivation to make the changes that direct your healing.

Maybe you are tilting on the edge of the life you have been leading and want to change course. Through changing your patterns of thinking, eating, exercising, and time management you can follow a different path that will bring you into a more satisfactory situation.

Maybe you are seeking options that can lead to a more satisfying life. The options you need may be right inside you, and these include thinking differently, which leads to taking actions that give you different experiences from those you've been having.

"Every human being is a problem in search of a solution."
– Ashley Montagu

If you want to change your life, and no matter what step of life you are in, it is good to remember that people can rise out of their former ways of living and take charge of becoming what it is they want to be. They can become more of an expression of their true selves. They can do away with the things holding them back. They can bring in the things that will propel them toward health, happiness, and satisfaction. They can change the way they perceive things, and they can do so in ways that are more healthful.

"The world is but a canvas to the imagination."
– Henry David Thoreau

This book mentions a lot about thoughts, because if you want dramatic changes in your life, you need to equally change the way you conduct your thoughts. Changing your patterns of thinking is the major key in life change and transformation.

"Change your thoughts, and you change your world."
– Norman Vincent Peale

What you see around you partially consists of your thoughts made visible.

What you think, as in how you perceive things, is what may determine your future more than anything else. Your actions are the result of your thoughts. What you have accomplished, or failed to accomplish, has often been the result of your thinking. If you want a future that is very different from your past, start turning your thoughts into actions that make things happen in your favor.

"Life is not a 'brief candle.' It is a splendid torch that I want to make burn as brightly as possible before handing on to future generations."
– George Bernard Shaw

Future generations were in my thoughts as I was putting this book together. But I also know that it could be a book for anyone of any age who desires to have a more satisfying life.

Some of those who have read my previous writings have encouraged me to produce a book like this. Rather than writing an instruction manual, I was aiming for something that was exploratory in nature.

"If you have knowledge, let others light their candles in it."
– Margaret Fuller

My approach to this topic of changing thought to create life change was to write a book that I could give my children in the hope that it might help guide them in their lives. I also aimed to write for people who have been through any number of life situations. I'm especially interested in motivating people who have been trampled down, or who otherwise come from troubled backgrounds, including people who have been neglected, abused, homeless, addicted to substances, or have been imprisoned. My aim also is to motivate people to live in ways that are more environmentally sustainable and universally healthful.

Writing this book also has provided me with the opportunity to use many of the quotations I've been collecting throughout my adult life. I use quotations from other people because I don't want the book to consist only of my thoughts. I want it to include the thoughts of many, and to inspire readers to have their own so they infuse their dreams into their lives with parallel actions creating the improvements they wish to be.

"The best of a book is not the thought which it contains, but the thought which it suggests; just as the charm of music dwells not in the tones but in the echoes of our hearts."
– Oliver Wendell Holmes

Many books about motivation are so scrubbed and polished that they seem more like corporate handbooks. Creating a book like that was not my goal.

I wanted to write a book to enliven people and to motivate them away from being anywhere within that description F. Scott Fitzgerald used in *The Great Gatsby*: "He's so dumb he doesn't know he's alive."

While writing this book, I aimed to get away from the sort of self-help mysticism that some success and positive-thinking gurus seem to dwell in, and that I find hard to relate to. Instead, I aimed to write plainly with wording that I hope to be accessible, and without grand dressing.

"A good coach will make his players see what they can be rather than what they are."
– Ara Parsegian

When I've looked at other motivational books, I have found that I can't relate to many of them. The authors seem to project a spiffy image of a person who lives a life of opulence while focusing on extreme abundance. That is hardly what most people can relate to, and is also the type of lifestyle that isn't sustainable, nor does it appeal to those of us who like to live simply, and who like to keep our hands in the soil.

> "When we stop working with our hands, we cease to understand how the world really works."
> – Clive Thompson

I'm more of the hands-on person, like to dig my own garden, bury my own kitchen scraps, and am not interested in a lifestyle surrounded by technological spectacles. Nor am I interested in pretending to have the perfect life, nor in setting myself as an example of a flawless specimen.

Because of numerous circumstances, many people don't have the type of situation that gives them access to the so-called perfect life idealized in some of the most popular success books. And, even when they do, they may harbor no desire to live that type of life.

What many people desire isn't about luxury and posh living. Instead, most people simply want to experience happiness, health, and satisfaction while maintaining loving relationships. As I see it, none of the things that people truly want have anything to do with the materials that make up the corporate imagery seen in advertising, which is of huge financial wealth.

Many people do not care to make their lives into the apparently flawless images seen in commercials, but would like to own a life that is more in tune with true happiness.

No matter what life presents to them, in managing their lives, many people unfortunately choose what they may consider the easiest route, which may actually turn out to be the most difficult. It is likely that if people really did put themselves to work making their lives into what their potential can present when it is truly used, they would find that the more healthful life in which they do wisely use their resources, intellect, and talents would be much less troublesome.

> "Let him who would move the world first move himself."
> – Socrates

I hope this book speaks to those who are living lives that are based on self-sufficiency while they work on becoming more sustainable and a part of the solution, rather than participating in what many people consider success: a money-hoarding, mansion-dwelling, and unsustainable lifestyle of high maintenance and luxurious excess.

"Try not to become a man of success. Rather, become a man of value."
– Albert Einstein

As you read through the book, realize that the repetition is intentional. That is because people often need to hear the same message repeatedly before they grasp a concept. This can be especially true if they are going to take the concept to heart and apply its principles to their life.

Repetition of the knitting needle creates the sweater. Repetition of a bricklayer's hands creates a structure. Repetition of a swimmer's movements creates fitness. And repetition of messages creates a learned mind.

"Self-education is, I firmly believe, the only kind of education there is."
– Isaac Asimov

I don't think a book like this could ever be finished. This is especially so because the book covers such a broad range of issues that are not the same for each person. The subject of personal fulfillment is also a rich one that cannot be explored within one book.

"Discovery consists of seeing what everyone else has seen and thinking what no one else has thought."
– Albert Szent-Gyorgyi

"The whole idea is to earn the flavor. No one gives it to you."
– Jamie Oliver

"To read without reflecting is like eating without digesting."
– Edmund Burke

Readers of books about personal growth can more effectively apply what they learn by making notes as they read, exploring their thoughts and options, then acting upon what they discover.

With this book, the process may be brought about more effectively if you:

A) Use a notebook to take notes and record thoughts relating to the parts of the book that most strongly speak to you.

B) Write out a game plan that applies your goals to your thought patterns.

C) Act upon the information.

D) Keep a journal detailing the changes and successes you have made happen in your life.

E) Review and adjust your goals every morning so that you begin each day focused on what you wish to attain.

Do all of these things with the goal of improving your situation on every level.

> "The thirst after happiness is never extinguished in the heart of man."
> – Jean Jacques Rousseau

While there are millions of people ready to sell others something that they claim will improve their lives, there also seems to be an endless parade of people ready to purchase the products, which often do not hold any of the promises contained in the advertising.

I have no products to sell, nor is this book about marketing things based on claims that they will improve your life. The initial tools you need to improve your life can't be purchased. They are what you already have, and that is the desire and drive to become more healthful and satisfied with your life. Value your self.

> "If I am not for myself, who is for me? And if I am only for myself, what am I? And if not now, when?"
> – Hillel

This book, *Igniting Your Life*, is about restructuring your being through excellent nutrition, exercise, positive-thinking, visualization, and goal setting in tune with continual actions and intentional living. It is about accelerating your actions to propel your life toward happiness and self-fulfillment in the best way you can while using what is available to you.

The nutrition aspects of this book largely focus on what is called Sunfood nutrition. As is covered later in the book, the Sunfood diet has been around for a very long time. It is a plant-based, nearly vegan diet that is largely uncooked. When you consume a diet that consists of what Nature provides, and the closer it is to its natural state, the nearer your body will be to its natural, healthful state.

Humanity has survived for thousands of years on a natural diet. It is only in the last century that humans have consumed unnatural substances containing synthetic chemicals that have proven to contribute to birth defects, learning disabilities, developmental disorders, depression, cancers and degenerative diseases, and in damage to the environment, the death of wildlife, and a tainted Earth.

"We are living in a world today where lemonade is made from artificial flavors, and furniture polish is made from real lemons."
– Alfred E. Newman

Inadequate nutrition and the consumption of junk food contribute to everything from skin problems to obesity, from heart disease to visual impairment, from depression to blood disorders, and from the inability to concentrate to a weakened immune system.

Eating whole foods, such as unprocessed fruits and vegetables, provides the body with important nutrients, including vitamins, minerals, essential fatty acids, amino acids, enzymes, and health-inducing phytochemicals, such as isoflavonoids and lignans.

A raw food nearly vegan diet that is rich in fresh fruits and vegetables is also rich in biophotons, an often overlooked true nutrient of light energy that is produced, emitted, and absorbed by the cells of plants and animals. Biophotons are in our DNA and in the nucleus of all our cells. Biophoton meridian fields run through our cells and body structures. Biophoton light energy fields are one way our cells communicate. The presence of biophotons and photoreceptor proteins within our tissues allows for our cells to communicate, vibrate, and otherwise function. A diet that consists largely of uncooked plant matter is rich in antioxidants and biophotons, and helps the body to function at a higher level.

As explained later in the book, those who are truly interested in experiencing vibrant health should banish fried foods; synthetic food additives; MSG (monosodium glutamate); hydrogenated oils; processed sugars, including corn syrup; processed salts; bleached grains; and other low-quality foods and nonfood substances from their diet. They would greatly benefit by following a fresh-food diet consisting of a rotation and variety of raw fruits, berries, vegetables, nuts, seaweeds, and germinated or sprouted seeds and legumes, and by getting daily exercise.

When you consider that your body is constantly replacing its cells, that your blood cells only live a little more than a week before they are replaced with new cells, and that your muscle cells live about three months before they are replaced, you can begin to understand how nutrition plays a major role in creating and recreating your life.

While your body cells today may have been constructed of the substances of the low-quality foods you have consumed, understand that you can transform your body structure in a matter of months by consuming a diet that consists of high-quality, plant-based nutrition, and especially a diet that consists largely or entirely of fresh, unheated fruits and vegetables. It is these fresh plant substances that carry truly living enzymes; high-quality essential fatty acids; bioavailable amino acids; and a full spectrum of vitamins, minerals, and trace nutrients, including antioxidants and biophotons.

> "To keep the body in good health is a duty, otherwise we shall not be able to keep our mind strong and clear."
> – Buddha

I include the Sunfood diet as the basis for the best nutrition because I believe it is a major key in experiencing the highest levels of vibrant health. As Dr. Edward Howell explained in the 1940s, edible raw plant matter provides the nutrients we need, including life force energy.

The natural state of the body is to be healthful and free from toxins and disease. The keys to health are a proactive thought pattern, a daily exercise regimen, a plant-based diet, a regular sleep pattern, and a healthful atmosphere. It also can be of great help to well-being to be in uplifting, loving relationships, including a nurturing relationship with self.

> "If you want to meet someone who can fix any situation you don't like, who can bring you happiness in spite of what other people say or believe, look in a mirror and say this magic word: Hello."
> – Richard Bach

You can begin to improve your life at any moment. It is largely your decision. If you are to experience satisfaction, it is more likely to happen if you take the actions that create it. Know that it is within your power and ability to do so.

> "The value of achievement lies in the achieving."
> – Albert Einstein

You can work to make all parts of your being function in ways that are more beneficial to you. At the same time, you can begin to pull the things into your life that will build it into what you want it to be. You can also begin to turn away those things in your life that do not harmonize with the way you want your life to be.

> "Most powerful is he who has himself in his own power."
> – Lucius Annaeus Seneca

There is no better time to begin improving your life than the present.

Now is the time to take control of your existence so that you can begin leading the best life you possibly can.

> "A moments insight is sometimes worth a life's experience."
> – Oliver Wendell Holmes

You can decide at this very moment that you will change your life for the better.

You can decide right now that you will no longer settle for the qualities and standards you have been experiencing.

You can decide as you read this that you will achieve your goals.

> "The greatest revolution of our generation is the discovery that human beings, by changing the inner attitudes of their minds, can change the outer aspects of their lives."
> – William James

The ancient peoples of the world, the cave dwellers on every continent, the originators of religious teachings and philosophies, the creators of mythological stories that have been handed down for generations, everyone from the Aztecs and Buddhists to the Egyptians, Eskimos, Hebrews, Hindus, Hopi, Mayans, Polynesians, Sumerians, and every other group of people have shared the message that a person's happiness in life greatly relies not on government or industry, but on the choices of the individual to use his or her power.

Throughout this book I use quotations from a wide variety of people. I did not pay attention to their religion, race, nationality, gender, sexuality, political leanings, or even to their history of purity or corruption. I simply sought to use quotations that spoke what I felt was truth, and I did so with one goal: to motivate the reader.

> "Change will not come if we wait for some other person or some other time. We are the ones we've been waiting for. We are the change that we seek."
> – Barack Obama

As a human being, you are meant to be healthful and satisfied. Health and happiness is what we naturally desire.

You can choose to keep following a pattern of dissatisfaction, or you can get busy creating a new pattern.

This book is the invitation to aim for and go toward that which makes you healthful and satisfied.

"We learn wisdom from failure much more than from success. We often discover what will do by finding out what will not do; and probably he who never made a mistake never made a discovery."
– Samuel Smiles

Get busy doing what you want to do.

"Skill to do comes of doing."
– Ralph Waldo Emerson

One hundred percent of the rest of your life starts right now.

Ending or Beginning Results

If you are not doing what you want to do, consider that you may be doing what you don't want to do.

"Action may not always bring happiness, but there is no happiness without action."
– Benjamin Disraeli

Many people say that they don't have time in their day to accomplish the things they want to do. But they may be overlooking the fact that they are not managing their time as wisely as they could.

"We have more possibilities available in each moment than we realize."
– Thich Nhat Hanh

Everyone on this planet has the same number of hours in the day. Some accomplish great things, while others watch TV, become obsessed with celebrity culture, and/or otherwise engage in wasteful and slothful activities.

What you do with your life is up to you. You can either let the whimsy of whatever happens create your life, or you can become proactive in forcing the creation of a more desirable life.

"What you are is a question only you can answer."
– Lois McMaster Bujold

Decide right now to spend your time more wisely.

Stop drifting in the ocean of dissatisfaction. Instead, revive and nurture your ambitions. Live with aim. Develop and follow a plan to get you to a desirable destination.

> "All serious daring starts from within."
> – Harriet Beecher Stowe

Three things you can manage include what you eat, your attitude, and what you engage in. You can immediately begin to select only the highest-quality foods available to you. You can immediately decide to think in a way that is more conducive to a healthful life. You can decide from now on to set goals and be involved in activities that will bring you what you want. As you do this your body and life will begin to function at a level equal to the food and mind fuel you are feeding on.

Whether you like it or not, there are outside influences that impact your life. Luckily you can have some power over how they do so.

Consider that you may be treating your life the way society collectively reacts to its own problems, and that usually means lazily, without the most helpful solutions, and while doing things that will lead to similar unsatisfactory conditions.

Your surroundings are impacting you. You absorb the energy that surrounds you. The people and things in your atmosphere affect you. These can have a positive impact, or they can have a negative impact. You can learn to have more control over these things.

Each person is a power source. Each body is generating energy that is manifested in its thoughts, actions, words, relationships, and results. By plugging into your potential, using your talents and skills, guiding your thought processes, and actively choosing what to do with your energy and time, you can fuel a life that you want to lead. Or, like many people, you can do none of it, and end up in a life that you may not care to have.

> "Some men see things as they are and say, 'Why?' I dream of things that never were, and say, 'Why not?'"
> – George Bernard Shaw

Many people live their days reacting to things that have already happened with energy that has already been spent to form those things.

Much of the activity you see around you, including on the daily news, may consist of people reacting to things that have happened, getting dulled by and lost in results, and doing what amounts to taping bandages on societal wounds that continue to hemorrhage because the underlying thought processes, actions, and issues that are causing the problems have not been changed in a way that would bring more satisfying results.

Presently, you can decide to live your days working for a better future by making better choices in all areas of your daily life.

> "A life of reaction is a life of slavery, intellectually and spiritually. One must fight for a life of action, not reaction."
> – Rita Mae Brown

Many people trip and stumble over the constant concern and worry about finances. But finances are the end result of thoughts and actions. Many people also continue to stumble over issues that are the result of unwise decisions that continue to be followed even though the very same people hate the results of those decisions.

Reacting to secondary causative factors is how many people lead their lives. They don't take action to rule their lives. Instead, they allow themselves to be ruled and formed by what has been expressed or is being expressed by others.

Focusing on end results prevents you from creating solutions and taking actions that lead to better results and greater satisfaction.

> "There is nothing as easy as denouncing. It don't take much to see that something is wrong, but it takes some eyesight to see what will put it right again."
> – Will Rogers

No longer allow yourself to get tangled in end results. They are unraveling before you and the energy that led to their manifestation has already been spent. Instead, be involved in actions that get the results you want using the energy you have now.

> "The sole purpose of human existence is to kindle a light in the darkness of mere being."
> – Carl Gustav Jung

What drives your actions are your thoughts, and those are driven by your soul. The real power is not that of wealth, but it is the power of thought. The power of your thought is guided by your belief in what you are capable of doing mixed with the level at which you have tapped into the power of your essence and spirit, which is the dwelling of your intellect, talents, instinct, abilities, elegance, and other graces that fuel your potential. The real power is in how enlightened you are combined with how you choose that enlightenment to guide your being.

> "You must live in the present, launch yourself on every wave, find your eternity in each moment."
> – Henry David Thoreau

Your anticipatory behavior is something that defines you. Anticipatory behavior is a constant, and it has to do with every action you take.

> "I always entertain great hopes."
> – Robert Frost

> "To the question whether I am a pessimist or an optimist, I answer that my knowledge is pessimistic, but my willing and hoping are optimistic."
> – Albert Schweitzer

> "Hope is a waking dream."
> – Aristotle

Behavior reveals what you hope for, or your lack thereof. It reveals intention and attention. It displays how deeply you are tuned into your graces. And it shows what you are conscious of, what you desire, and your passions.

> "Every decision you make — every decision — is not a decision about what to do. It's a decision about who you are. When you see this, when you understand it, everything changes. You begin to see life in a new way. All events, occurrences, and situations turn into opportunities to do what you came here to do."
> – Neale Donald Walsch

Through your actions you are revealing what you think of yourself, and whether you believe in your attributes enough to use them to better yourself. Your actions not only reveal who you are, they also determine what you will become.

> "What disappoints me the most is somebody who can do something well and does not do it."
> – Sean Penn

What I am talking about is not about limiting yourself. It is about opening yourself up to what could be yours: health, satisfaction, happiness, and loving relationships. It is about discovering new foods, new energy, new thought processes, and a level of vibrant health you have not experienced. It is about accessing and utilizing your talents, intellect, and potential.

> "By sowing frugality we reap liberty, a golden harvest."
> – Agesilaus

When I am speaking of improving your life, I'm not talking about increasing your material possessions, which are a façade. I am not about hoarding wealth and trying to impress people with money and expensive stuff, which is silly and wasteful nonsense. If anything, I'm talking about having fewer things than what commercialized and greed-driven culture grooms us to believe in as a validation of a successful life.

> "We can only be said to be alive in those moments when our hearts are conscious of our treasures."
> – Thornton Wilder

I am advising that you get involved in having a bigger, more satisfactory, and more sustainable life saturated with health and the true expression of the good things about you.

> "Everything can be taken from a man but one thing: the last of the human freedoms — to choose one's attitude in any given set of circumstances, to choose one's own way."
> – Victor Frankl

I'm advising that you get involved right now in making your better life happen through the wise use of your intellect and talent, time and graces, and the passion of your spirit, which are your treasures.

> "How can you follow the course of your life if you do not let it flow?"
> – Lao Tzu

Set a course for your life that will reveal all that you wish your life to be.

Tune yourself to continually anticipate good things happening in your life. Plan on them happening. Visualize them happening. And work and love to make them happen.

Consider the Possible

"Granted that I must die, how shall I live?"
– Michael Novak

"The most important thing in life is to stop saying 'I wish' and start saying 'I will.' Consider nothing impossible, then treat possibilities as probabilities."
– David Copperfield

On some level, and probably at a higher level than you have considered, you are in charge of how happy and healthful you can be.

If you do not like the health you are experiencing, you can change it. If you do not like the thoughts and visions in your mind, you can change them. If you do not like the atmosphere you are living in, you can change the scenery. If you do not like the type of life you are leading, you can lead it onto a more satisfying path.

"Each of us has much more hidden inside us than we have had a chance to explore. Unless we create an environment that enables us to discover the limits of our potential, we will never know what we have inside of us."
– Muhammad Yunus

Changing your life takes work. And I mean work in a good way, because it fuels growth toward the expression of potential. It means working to access the inner wealth of character resources to create a better outside. It means exploring our options and making our favorite ones happen. It means working to create an environment that is in alignment with how we wish our life to be. It means considering, planning, working toward, and expressing the possible.

"My grandfather once told me there are two kinds of people: those who do the work and those who take the credit. He told me to try to be in the first group; there is much less competition."
– Indira Gandhi

"Opportunity is missed by most people because it comes dressed in overalls and looks like work."
– Thomas Alva Edison

Some people say it is too difficult to work on changing their life. Instead of working toward creating an amazing life, these types of people are more likely to conform to the mundane and less vibrant. Little do they seem to understand that their choice also takes time, energy, resources, and effort as they are still maintaining a life, but a life that won't give them as much satisfaction as the life they truly desire.

You can either work toward improving your life, or work toward giving into whatever happens. I believe it is easier and more enjoyable to work toward improving your life.

> "Hope is passion for what is possible"
> – Soren Kierkegaard

> "The very least you can do in your life is to figure out what you hope for. And the most you can do is live inside that hope. Not admire it from a distance but live right in it, under its roof."
> – Barbara Kingsolver

Whether a person succeeds or continues to succeed, experiences health or sickness, enjoys life or grovels in despair often depends on what happens within. And it depends on if there is hope, and if the person engages in actions to manifest the hope.

> "Hope is beautiful, and so are those who have it."
> – Cathy Rowland

If you are living a life that is not desirable to you, it is time to explore solutions and work toward the life you want to have. It is time to make plans in alignment with what you hope for, to turn those hopes into possibilities, and to convert those possibilities into your reality. As you do this, you will be engaging the innermost faculties of both your mind and brain.

In his book *Curious? Discover the Missing Ingredient to a Fulfilling Life*, psychologist and George Mason University professor Todd Kashdan writes that scientists have found that anticipating satisfactory things to happen in your life activates the nucleus accumbens in the ventral striatum region of the brain, which is known as the pleasure center. The simple contemplative and curiosity thought processes of considering the possible increases both the dopamine neurotransmitter activity between the nerve cells and the opiate neurotransmitter presence within the brain, preparing our body to experience what we are expecting to happen. It is then, when we feel the motivation to make our expectations form into our reality, that we are daring enough to take action.

As we continue to visualize and then attain our goals through intentional actions, the hippocampus region of the brain, which is involved with thoughts of curiosity and imagination, and with memory, will get accustomed to the patterns of visualizing and attaining success, and help form it into our habits.

> "The moment of enlightenment is when a person's dreams of possibilities become images of probabilities."
> – Vic Braden

It appears that working with the thought processes that create the body chemicals in relation to those thoughts, and to do so in an uplifting, anticipatory manner that will stimulate actions, and then specifically and intentionally taking those actions in alignment with the set goals will be what gives you the most fulfilling feeling of satisfaction. Getting your self to actively and knowingly participate in this process by setting goals and achieving them through intentional actions will instill a habit of the process that will involve many areas of your brain, which always is involved in wiring and rewiring itself in tune with the your habits. As Norman Doidge explains in his book, *The Brain That Changes Itself: Stories and Personal Triumph from The Frontiers of Brain Science*, what we think and what we do plays a large role in the formation of the network of nerves in our brain. These processes, and how being actively aware of and engaged in using them can play a large role in changing your life, are also explained in the book, *Buddha's Brain: The Practical Neuroscience of Happiness, Love, and Wisdom*, by Rick Hanson and Richard Mendius, and in books by Daniel Goleman, such as *Social Intelligence: The New Science of Human Relationships.*

Either you are visualizing the life you want, and working toward that vision, or you are not. Either you are creating the life that you want, and forming habits that create the neuro pathways in tune with the activities of the life you want, or you are not. There is no in-between.

Begin now to think in a way that brings about actions that create satisfaction and achievement.

Take time today to consider the things you can succeed in, and decide that you will experience success. Then, become devoted to making this success your reality and your common way of functioning.

> "People think I'm disciplined. It is not discipline. It is devotion. There is a great difference."
> – Luciano Pavarotti

Successful people know what it is they want to do. They know where they want to land. They know what they want to get. And they continually work to get it.

Successful people seek information that will help them. They research and prepare and practice for getting the things they want. They work to transform themselves into their vision of how they see themselves living. They are actively engaged in manifesting their goals. In doing so, their brains are in the habit of functioning at the level of their success.

You can do the same. And you can begin doing it now with everything you think, plan, say, and do.

> "The happiness of your life depends on the quality of your thoughts."
> – Marcus Aurelius

What is being advocated here is improvement in any and every area possible. This is about being proactive in sculpting your life, and it is about continually applying your mind to do it.

You can be what you desire to be if you take the steps to be what you want to be.

> "In psychotherapy, enthusiasm is the secret of success."
> – Carl Gustav Jung

The concept I am advocating is one I believe in. It is that anyone can take the lessons presented to them in their life and use them to improve their life. The goal is to create not only long-term improvement, but also to force immediate improvements that will build upon one another like brickwork to construct a more healthful and satisfying life.

> "We know what we are, but know not what we may be."
> – William Shakespeare

> "Do not follow where the path may lead. Go instead where there is no path and create a trail."
> – Ralph Waldo Emerson

> "We do not need magic to change the world. We carry all the power we need inside ourselves already: We have the power to imagine better."
> – J. K. Rowling

"Most people are other people. Their thoughts are someone else's opinions, their lives a mimicry, their passions a quotation."
– Oscar Wilde

Stop listening to commercialism that broadcasts falsities, and that formulates the agreement that you will be happy only when your life resembles a TV commercial or a magazine advertisement.

Make your life become what you want it to be. Understand that nobody can do it for you. You have to do it for yourself. Visualize it. Plan it. Nurture it. Do it. Become it. Live it. Love it.

Be your original you.

"The work will teach you how to do it."
– Estonian proverb

The Condition

"We fear our highest possibility (as well as our lowest one). We are generally afraid to become that which we can glimpse in our most perfect moments."
– Abraham Maslow

"The first step to getting the things you want out of life is this: Decide what you want."
– Ben Stein

If you are waiting around for your life to begin, for things around you to change, for your days to be more to your liking, and to be in company that you would better enjoy, then it is likely that you will be waiting a very long time. What you see around you is your life. If you don't like it, stop waiting for it to change, and start making it change.

"I am a part of all that I have met."
– Alfred Tennyson

"If you gaze for long into the abyss, the abyss also gazes into you."
– Friedrich Wilhelm Nietzsche

The way your life has turned out up to this point is not something that simply happened. Consider that there is a chance that it has largely been formulated by the things you have done, said, worn, accumulated, sought, and eaten, and the people with whom you have associated, the places you have gone, and especially the things you have thought.

> "If you wish to make an apple pie truly from scratch, you must first invent the universe."
> – Carl Sagan

> "You can count how many seeds are in the apple, but not how many apples are in the seed."
> – Ken Kersey

The tools to plant the seeds of a vibrant life exist within each person at every moment. However, it is up to each person to discover, access, and use those tools, to manage how they are used, and to apply them to the areas of life that need the most improvement.

> "There's a lot happening in many of us. I think you have to celebrate every part. It's what you are. You have to try to find all of those secret names."
> – Cassandra Wilson

As you continue to read further into this book, and make notes about what you read, you will find that *Igniting Your Life* is about a complete health transformation that begins with clarifying the interaction of body and mind, and using intentions combined with actions to get them to work the way you desire.

> "The whole problem is to establish communication with one's self."
> – E. B. White

Through high-quality nutrition, combined with thoughts and actions that attract health, you can activate an intentional, conscious, proactive energy within you that leads to a more satisfying expression of your being. To get those things working in your life you must truly desire them and bring them in. This too is of your working. It takes mental conditioning that you will understand once you begin to experience it and begin to create the circumstances and take the actions that lead to satisfaction.

> "Don't compromise yourself. You are all you've got."
> – Janis Joplin

"The potential of the average person is like a huge ocean unsailed, a new continent unexplored, a world of possibilities waiting to be released and channeled toward some great good."
– Brian Tracy

Begin now to look at your life as though it were a garden. Eliminate that which chokes the beauty and damages the harvest of good things that you want from life. Continually plant the seeds and nurture them to get the harvest you desire.

"When you examine the lives of the most influential people who have ever walked among us, you discover one thread that winds through them all. They have been aligned first with their spiritual nature and only then with their physical selves."
– Albert Einstein

Changing your life from what it is to what it can be, especially if the change is radical, may require strengths you never have exercised, and perhaps powers you never knew you possess. Improving your life takes a continual expression of bravery, courage, focus, and intentional thoughts and actions.

"I now see my life, not as the slow shaping of achievement to fit my preconceived purposes, but as the gradual discovery of a purpose which I did not know."
– Joanna Field

Many people spend years maintaining an unhealthful lifestyle. They feed themselves with unhealthful foods while entertaining low-quality thoughts that result in passive or self-loathing actions while utilizing little of their faculties to get through their days. And they do so over and over again in a pattern that builds the life they do not desire; thus, by default, the unsatisfying life they end up with is quite literally the life they worked for.

"We either make ourselves happy or miserable. The amount of work is the same."
– Carlos Castaneda

If people have become lazy in their lives, breaking away from their common patterns of thought and behavior while putting their intellect to work may feel incredibly satisfying and amazingly liberating.

"If you want to build a ship, don't herd people together to collect wood and don't assign them tasks and work, but rather teach them to long for the endless immensity of the sea."
– Antoine de Saint-Exupery

Perhaps one of the main motivators in changing your life will come from the realization that you can make your life happen the way you want it to happen. You do not have to collapse under whatever weight you perceive is being forced onto you; instead, you can rise up, use your power, and build the life you want. You don't have to conform to conditions others have created, but can form your own conditions. Educate yourself, align your situation, create the conditions you want, and otherwise do what you can to capture the vision of what you want your life to be, and then work every day toward creating that vision.

"The higher education so much needed today is not given in the school, is not to be bought in the market place, but it has to be wrought out in each one of us for himself; it is the silent influence of character on character."
– William Osler

We all began our lives with nothing at all. Some of us have been provided with material possessions, and some of us have been lucky to have been nurtured by parents, or parent figures, who somehow helped to bring out our best characteristics.

Some people are born with that euphemistic golden spoon in their mouth, and go on to live a life where they seem to be handed everything. Others are born into the most unfortunate conditions, and go on to a life of discouragement, regret, and misfortune. Sometimes it works the opposite way in which those handed everything end up in tragedy, and those born into tragedy go on to live a life of health and satisfaction.

"Failure is the condiment that gives success its flavor."
– Truman Capote

In a way, it seems that those who are handed everything are the unfortunate ones. They might never experience the exhilarating satisfaction of succeeding from the depths of miserable circumstances that children born with next to nothing may experience. Challenges are opportunities.

However, even those who appear to be handed everything are also faced with the choices that could result in a reversal of fortune.

We cad all penetrate through challenges to better our situation.

"People who have attained things worth having in this world have worked while others have idled, have persevered while others gave up in despair, and have practiced early in life the valuable habits of self-denial, industry, and singleness of purpose. As a result, they enjoy in later life the success often erroneously attributed to good luck."
– Grenville Kleiser

"Let me tell you the secret that has led me to my goal: my strength lies solely in my tenacity."
– Louis Pasteur

No matter what conditions you were born into, please recognize your talents and strengths and use your intellect to create the life that is part of the sustainable solution.

"I wasn't exactly brought up in one of those Norman Rockwell paintings you used to see on the cover of the *Saturday Evening Post*."
– Reggie Jackson

No matter what your background has been, you have to take what you have and make the best of your life. Otherwise you stagnate and often devalue your life and the lives around you through not trying, not exercising your talents, not using your intellect, and not contributing to the solutions the world needs.

"If you don't take chances, you can't do anything in life."
– Michael Spinks

Whether people are rich or poor, old or young, living in the north or south, east or west, they are depending on the same thing for their survival: environment, air, water, food, thought, movement, and love. The quality of each one of these plays a part in the level of life they get to experience.

"Winners have simply formed the habit of doing things losers don't like to do."
– Albert Gray

Work the things into your life that you need for accomplishing the life you want to have.

"There is no chance, no destiny, no fate, that can hinder or control the firm resolve of a determined soul."
– Ella Wheeler Wilcox

"With our minds we can make anything happen. I believe in immersion — it's one thing to know the principals and it's another thing to live it day to day so it becomes a pattern"
– Anthony Robbins

"No matter who you are, we are creatures of habit. The better your habits are, the better they will be in pressure situations."
– Wayne Gretzky

Your Filter

"A human being is a part of the whole, called by us, 'Universe,' a part limited in time and space. He experiences himself, his thoughts and feelings as something separated from the rest — a kind of optical delusion of his consciousness.

This delusion is a kind of prison for us, restricting us to our personal desires and to affection for a few persons nearest to us. Our task must be to free ourselves from this prison by widening our circle of compassion to embrace all living creatures and the whole of nature in its beauty.

Nobody is able to achieve this completely, but the striving for such achievement is in itself a part of the liberation and a foundation for inner security."
– Albert Einstein

People build their mental landscape out of what they think, study, feel, hear, see, smell, do, and the ways in which others treat them. They apply it to the things they think, study, see, hear, smell, feel, and do, including how they treat others. This landscape, which is your filter, can be limited by the life experiences that formulated it, including the limits that you and others have placed on your life.

The early humans applied their mental landscape to everything, including the planets and stars they saw in the sky. They looked at the various terrestrial groupings and named them after familiar shapes, such as creatures of the land, air, and sea.

Consider what your mind filter consists of, how it was formulated, how you apply it, and how you allow it to alter and guide you. Your mind filter is something that began to form at the earliest stages of your life, and it is something that continues to form, even now.

> "Human beings are perceivers, but the world they perceive is an illusion created by the description that was told to them from the moment they were born."
> – Carlos Castenada

Fetal programming is what happens to you before you were born, and it can play a part in what you feel and respond to after your birth.

Parents often talk to their babies as the babies sleep. This plays into the subconscious mind of the child, often suggesting how successful the child will be, and how much the child is loved. These early interactions, even if only amounting to a simple comprehension of sound tones, help formulate the child's filter.

The uterus and placenta are not impervious barriers. Scientists have learned that fetuses are sensitive not only to sounds, but to the foods their mothers eat, smells their mothers smell, and the emotions their mothers experience.

While science mostly has concentrated on fetal exposure to Industrial pollutants, bacteria, fungi, and parasites, and on the genetic expression factors of what forms and affects fetuses and newborns, it is increaseingly being recognized that everything the fetus and a newborn is exposed to can impact a child, both in the fetal and infancy stages. This includes the mother's health, diet, mental state, living arrangement, relationships, workplace, and lifestyle issues. It also includes the conditions of other parent figures who nurture, or neglect, the infant and child.

Because fetal conditioning has an influence on gene expression, it may help determine what sort of health the child experiences throughout life, and also may have an impact on the next generations. This is called *epigenetics*.

Scientists have recognized that certain drugs that have had damaging effects on fetuses can also cause the next generation to have birth defects. They also know that children born to parents who are obese are more likely to have children who experience weight and blood sugar issues, and that people who have diabetes are more likely to have children who become diabetic. I theorize that a number of things that can impact a fetus can play a part in future generations. Some of this has to do with learning and conditioning, and also with what the mother chooses to keep as a part of her life, thought, activity, relationships, and dietary patterns.

This does not mean that an expectant mother should go into a cocoon away from every thing that could bring about an emotion, or that she should hide from sounds and smells and people. It is important for expectant mothers to remain physically and socially active as well as intellectually engaged while following a regular sleeping pattern and a healthful, balanced, plant-based diet. The variety of chemical changes occurring in sync with the expectant mother's emotions in a healthful environment are helpful to the formation of a healthy baby.

As an adult, your filter partially consists of both sense-perceived memories that have tuned you as well as the chemicals surrounding you, the foods you have been exposed to, the sounds you have heard, the smells you have smelled, the sights you have seen, the textures you have felt, the words that have been spoken to and by you, and the emotions and health of the people who birthed and raised you.

In addition to foods, smells, and emotions, certain words, sounds, colors, textures, flavors, shapes, temperatures, and even shades of light can bring about memories that affect your cell structures, tissue function, and hormonal production.

Your experiences in life create a filter in your mind through which you judge all that is presented to you. Your filter will determine what things, colors, shapes, textures, foods, smells, sounds, and people you like to have in your life.

> "Habits of thinking need not be forever. One of the most significant findings in psychology in the last twenty years is that individuals can choose the way they think."
>
> – Martin Seligman

Your filter is not permanently fixed in its present state. It continues to change throughout your life. Luckily, you have some control over your filter and over how you reconfigure your logic in that you can decide and reformulate how you factor and react to things.

People hold prejudices and desires developed in their minds based on their experiences. They may not like to be around people who resemble, or who sound or act similar to certain unhelpful or undesirable people from their past. These are examples of how their filter was shaped by their experiences.

All of this does not mean that you need to remain susceptible to your past, or that you should be freakishly fanatic about understanding and deciphering the impact of every little thing about your past. I'm not suggesting that you should be obsessed about your epigenetics. I am mentioning how your past shaped you because it is part of understanding who you are and what you respond to, and this can give you ideas about what you can do to change into what you want to become.

While considering these angles about your filter, it may be interesting to observe how people live their lives and to listen to what concerns them, what interests them, what they complain about, and what they cherish.

> "If you want something you've never had, you have to do something you've never done."
> – Kimnesha Benns

Many people are so caught up in the mess that has become their life that they lose sight of what it was they wanted out of life in the first place. They become so burned out that they do things that allow them to escape into a life that is not their own. They eat foods they know are not good for them, spend time doing things they know are not best for them, watch too much television, do too much shopping, don't get enough exercise or movement, and somehow end up being surrounded by people who zap their energy, negate their goodness, and blur their focus. They don't get the things done that they know they need to do. Altogether they don't advance toward where they want to be in life. Their filter is broken down, clogged, neglected, frazzled, and in great need of repair, restructuring, and nurturing.

Your filter can be as rigid or as fluid as you allow it to be. This has to do with having a closed or open mind, and how you allow yourself to perceive what life presents to you — and what you present to life.

> "The future is not some place we are going to, but one we are creating. The paths to it are not found, but made — and the activity of making them changes both the maker and the destination."
> – John Schaar

Your perceptions play a part in how you deal with your past and present, and what you agree to do based on your calculations of these in the present. Perceptions play so much a part of you that they might be considered to be one of the senses. This is why I refer to them as sense perceptions.

Sense perceptions are continually in play as you survey what is presented to you and then compare these things to derive a conclusion of how the things act or react, consider what they can do, and if you can use them in ways that will satisfy you, benefit you, or help you to attain a goal. The calculation process of your sense perceptions may have as much to do with your past as it does your present.

"Look at the past as a bullet. Once it's fired it's finished."
– Catherine Bauby

Your past isn't as spent as the above quotation may lead you to believe. But you can reinterpret, reconfigure, and realign the filter created by your past so that it works better for you in the present and future.

All of us are somewhere between the extremes of complete amnesia and a condition named hyperthymestic syndrome, in which a person remembers impeccably accurate details of their life, including dates, times, and sequences. Most of us are some blend of the two conditions, wherein we don't remember anything about certain things, but remember great details about others.

You can reshape how you react to memories, and use them to bring forth good for the present and the future.

"Make not your thoughts your prisons."
– William Shakespeare

If you had a sad or unsatisfactory past, and want a happy future, choose not to dwell in the past. Decide for yourself that you will not be a walking wound. Look forward, not backward. Be constantly involved in creating a better future.

"People who look ahead are very rare. Most people look to the past. We walk backwards, we back our way through life. We move forward but always while looking backwards. People who envision their future and more toward it, peering ahead are incredibly rare."
– Henri Langlois

"Even a happy life cannot be without a measure of darkness, and the word 'happy' would lose its meaning if it were not balanced by sadness. It is far better to take things as they come along with patience and equanimity."
– Carl Gustav Jung

You can play a large role in how limiting or broadening your ability to experience life will be. It can be largely up to you if you are being held back from or moving forward toward the life you want. It is largely up to you if you are healing your life or are enabling an unhealthful lifestyle to dominate you. It is up to you if you are going to be welcoming to the things, people, thoughts, activities, and love that can benefit you. In the long run, it is most likely that it will be largely up to you if your joy is being limited or broadened.

It is up to you to construct and reweave your filter and exercise your sense perceptions to help you factor and formulate the conditions you need to experience the life you want.

> "You have powers you never dreamed of. You can do things you never thought you could do. There are no limitations in what you can do except the limitations of your own mind."
> – Darwin P. Kingsley

I don't think it is any coincidence that the word life is so similar to the word love. If you want to experience the best life possible for you, lift yourself up through love, which is the real power that can create miracles in and around you.

> "Where there is great love there are always miracles.
> – Willa Cather

Let love be the filter through which you see the world.

What Is Your Truth?

> "All truth is an achievement. If you would have truth at its full value, go win it."
> – Munger

People can choose to believe whatever they want. But belief does not always jive with reality. You can believe the sky is made up of psychedelic orange gas with green polka-dotted blue cows floating in it, but this does not mean it is true.

The longer you live, the more likely you will realize that not everything you consider to be true actually is. It is also likely that you will recognize this condition as being common among humanity.

> "There is great hunger and thirst in all of us for the truth whether we are aware of it or not. There is no-one unfeeling or unseeing. To think ourselves unique is the height of ignorance."
> – Agnes Martin

"Truths are universally and not individually rooted; a truth cannot be created, but only perceived."
– Paramhansa Yogananda

Those who base their conclusions of human life wholly on the "findings" of the so-called intellectuals of the science world are constantly having to adjust their beliefs because the scientists are forever "discovering" something different that shatters what they had formerly believed and set forth as truth. In the same way, we are continually re-evaluating our conclusions and often factoring other conclusions, which are essentially agreements with ourselves based on what we believe to be true, and perhaps what we wish to be true.

"My greatest challenge has been to change the mindset of people. Mindsets play strange tricks on us. We see things the way our minds have instructed our eyes to see."
– Muhammad Yunus

"All truths are easy to understand, once they are discovered; the point is to discover them."
– Galileo Galilei

As humans have progressed in their understanding of things, they have disposed of inaccurate past beliefs. Where once they believed that exposing wounds to air was what caused infection, they now understand that tiny things called "germs" grow and multiply in moist, warm wounds, and that this germ colony and how the immune system responds to it is what has been named *infection.*

There is a long list of falsehoods that humans believed, and they have based much of their life choices on these falsehoods.

"The real does not die. The unreal never lived."
– Nisargatta Maharay

For a long time many people believed that Earth was the center of the universe. In the 1600s Galileo Galilei argued with Catholic Church leaders over their insistence that Galilei was wrong in his belief that Earth revolved around Sun. His 1632 work, *A Dialogue Concerning the Two Great Systems of the World*, included his theory. Galilei had to go to Rome to plead with Catholic leaders not to ban his teachings. He was tried on suspicion of heresy and ordered to recant his theory, was put under house arrest, and the publication of any more of his ideas was banned.

Galileo Galilei's concepts furthered the theory of Nicholas Copernicus, who lived from 1473 to 1543, and who also concluded that Earth revolves around Sun. Copernicus was hardly the first to believe in that reality. Ancient drawings found on various parts of Earth reveal that many people who lived long before Galilei and Copernicus had real-ized Earth revolves around Sun.

Remarkably, it wasn't until 1992 that the Catholic Church officially conceded that Earth revolves around Sun.

Even though many people before Galilei had realized that Earth revolves around Sun, Galilei's predicament stands as an example of how people, including many so-called authority figures, refuse the truth and choose to continue living in and promoting ignorance.

> "The mind can assert anything and pretend it has proved it. My beliefs I test on my body, on my intuitional consciousness, and when I get a response there, then I accept."
> – D. H. Lawrence

No matter what people believe or do not believe, there are basic fundamental truths that exist. False beliefs do not change the truth. There are many things that people believe, but which are not reality. Even after they learn that something isn't how they thought it had been, they may continue to try to hold onto their disproved beliefs, and drift into denial. Many people refuse to change behavior associated with former false beliefs and end up in unfortunate situations because of that.

> "God is near me (or rather in me), and yet I may be far from God because I may be far from my own true self."
> – C. E. Rolt

False beliefs are limiting in that they can block you from accomplishing what you are capable of becoming and reduce you to less than what you are capable of being. You may believe in something about yourself falsely, and that limits you.

> "The difference between what we do and what we are capable of doing would suffice to solve most of the world's problems."
> – Mahatma Gandhi

You may think that you cannot accomplish something that you are perfectly capable of accomplishing. The simple process of thinking that you are only capable of a certain level of something will likely limit you to that level — or to less.

> "We need limitations and temptations to open our inner selves, dispel our ignorance, tear off disguises, throw down old idols, and destroy false standards. Only by such rude awakenings can we be led to dwell in a place where we are less cramped, less hindered by the ever-insistent External. Only then do we discover a new capacity and appreciation of goodness and beauty and truth."
> – Helen Keller

False beliefs in health are limiting. Believing in something that doesn't work for the body, even though it may provide some good, limits your ability to experience better health. Doing something that you believe is good for the body, even though it is damaging, reduces your potential.

> "This above all: To thine own self be true, for it must follow as dost the night the day, that canst not then be false to any man."
> – William Shakespeare

Your truth already exists within you. You simply need to exercise the tool to bring out your truth. The tool you need is something you already have. It is your spirit.

Work to do away with the false beliefs you carry about yourself. Recognize that your frustration with others not believing in your capabilities may be because you falsely and fearfully believe that you are not capable. Consider that others may be reflecting back to you what you project about your belief in yourself. Realize that they may also be displaying their own fears, self-doubt, and lack of self-esteem: a lack of belief in their own intellect, talents, craft, abilities, potential, instinct, and love.

> "Fears are educated into us, and can, if we wish, be educated out."
> – Karl A. Menninger

Many people live their lives by fear. They are fearful that they are not going to succeed, are not going to be able to pay their bills, are not going to keep their loves, and are going to lose any security they may be experiencing. Their fears may become their driving force, and bring them into the energy of desperation, which can fuel irrational thought patterns that create unfortunate consequences.

> "I saw a study that the more television people watched, the more afraid of their neighbors they became. The researchers called

> it 'the dangerous world syndrome.' The mathematical correspondence was compelling. The more television people watched, the more crime they thought there was in their neighborhood, and the more exaggerated their belief about how many murders and burglaries were taking place."
>
> – John Robbins

When we live while ruled by fear, we are more likely to live dishonestly, to rob others of their energy and resources, to eat unhealthful foods, to entertain low-quality thoughts, to engage in risky behavior, and to partake of damaging substances. When we allow ourselves to live by fear, we doubt others because we doubt ourselves.

> "We tell lies when we are afraid — afraid of what we don't know, afraid of what others will think, afraid of what will be found out about us. But every time we tell a lie, the thing that we fear grows stronger."
>
> – Tad Williams

When we doubt ourselves, we are more likely to lie to others, and to ourselves. When we fear, we are more likely to lie. When we lack confidence, we are more likely to lie. When we aren't truthful to ourselves, we are likely to be untruthful to others.

> "As we are liberated from our own fear, our presence automatically liberates others."
>
> – Nelson Mandela

Confidence is the opposite of fear. It challenges and disperses fear. And it has to do with people knowing that they are capable of improving and carrying on with their life in a way that utilizes their intellect, talent, craft, abilities, potential, instinct, and love.

> "Perhaps the most important thing we can undertake toward the reduction of fear is to make it easier for people to accept themselves, to like themselves."
>
> – Bonaro W. Overstreet

When we live confidently, we have hope and faith in ourselves and in others. In this way being confident is charitable as it spreads confidence into those around us. When we live confidently in tune with our natural attributes, we take care of ourselves, we have heart, and we are less likely to allow ourselves to drag our chins on the floor. When we live confidently we naturally bless the lives of those around us and contribute to a positive energy that can spread into our atmosphere.

> "As we let our light shine, we unconsciously give other people permission to do the same."
> – Marianne Williamson

If you want to be aligned with a manner that is more conducive to improvement, you might wish to especially work to do away with the energy of fear and doubt. They are not what you want to be your truth or your reality. They are of the dreadful victim mentality consisting of energy that opposes faith and hope.

> "Everything that happens in all material, living, mental, or even spiritual processes involves the transformation of energy. Every thought, every sensation, every emotion is produced by energy exchanges."
> – J. G. Bennett

> "Each of us makes his own weather, determines the color of the skies in the emotional universe which he inhabits."
> – Archbishop Fulton J. Sheen

> "Life is the sum of what you focus on."
> – Winifred Gallagher

Isn't it interesting that many so-called elected officials continually focus their attention and words on fear, doubt, crime, and punishment? This is where many public servants fail the people. It also displays their concept of the world. Rather than recognizing problems and creating solutions that lead to better results, they are only focusing on the unsatisfactory end results, and fueling more of the same, thus perpetuating what they claim to be working to get rid of.

People who continually talk about fear and terror are all about fear and terror.

> "It is not whether your words or actions are tough or gentle; it is the spirit behind your actions and words that announces your inner state."
> – Chin-Ning Chu

Refuse to dwell in fear and doubt. Allowing fear and doubt to rule your thoughts and emotions weakens you and stifles your ability to succeed.

> "People deal too much with the negative, with what is wrong. Why not try and see positive things, to just touch those things and make them bloom?"
> – Thich Nhat Hanh

Build your inner state to consist of what you want by visualizing what you want, thinking about what you want, and acting on those thoughts to bring about what you want. Dwell in, live for, and rule your life by creating the life you want.

> "If we were logical, the future would be bleak indeed. But we are more than logical. We are human beings, and we have faith, and we have hope, and we can work."
> – Jacques Cousteau

Your belief helps formulate your reality. Your belief rules your reasoning, which is continually adjusted as you are exposed to different experiences, which helps you determine what is true or untrue, what to accept, and what to reject, and what you like and don't like, and this plays into the actions you take and words you speak.

Continually adjusting to simple truths can lead to great improvement in one's life. This includes the truth about your self.

> "Truth is a demure lady, much too ladylike to knock you on the head and drag you to her cave. She is there, but the people must want her and seek her out."
> – William F. Buckley, Jr.

> "Integrity is telling myself the truth."
> – Spencer Johnson

> "Our own life is the instrument with which we experiment with truth."
> – Thich Nhat Hanh

> "If you cannot find the truth right where you are, where else do you expect to find it?"
> – Dogen Zenji

Dream Another Dream

"All that we see or seem, is but a dream within a dream."
– Edgar Allan Poe

"Cherish your visions and your dreams, as they are the children of your soul, the blueprints of your ultimate achievements."
– Napoleon Hill

Consider that you are living in a dream. You say that may be a silly thought. But, similar to a dream, many people lead their daily lives making decisions based on perceptions they believe to be true, but that actually are not. Some perceptions are formed in their minds, and some are taught to them by others who may have created them, or who have passed along myths formed over the years by their culture, or by those with an agenda.

"What gets us into trouble is not what we don't know. It's what we know for sure that just ain't so."
– Mark Twain

You know that there were things you believed that you eventually realized were untrue. Now think back and realize that you made decisions, and may have lived your days, based on those falsehoods. Consider that some of these falsehoods may have limited your joy and satisfaction in life.

Even when things are completely untrue, people can be brought to believe in them, and make life-altering decisions based on falsehoods.

Wars have been fought, people have been killed, many people have given up their lives, wildlife has been decimated, the planet has been damaged, and species have gone extinct based on false information spread by a few people. Often those people knew that what they were saying was not true.

People once believed certain people were evil witches. Because of this, many people were killed in horrible ways simply because they were believed to be witches. Many people have also been killed by other people believing they were carrying out the will of God, but who were only acting on delusional concepts created in the minds of power-hungry religious leaders.

Another example of what people are capable of doing based on false information occurred on October 20, 1938. That was the day Orson Welles broadcast a reading of H.G. Wells's *The War of the Worlds* on

Mercury Theatre Radio. Many thousands of people who heard this broadcast believed that Martians were attacking the world. People became engulfed in fear. Massive panic took place in and around New York City. People frantically ran from their homes, abandoned their workplaces, and clogged the streets to escape the Martians. Their decisions were based on imagination.

Consider that you are currently making decisions in your daily life based on fallacy.

> "The eye sees only what the mind is prepared to comprehend."
> – Henri L. Bergson

Consider the possibility that all you believe about the past, from what you think you know about world history, to what you think to be the truth about the people around you, and even about yourself, may largely consist of created perceptions not based on reality.

What you conceive to be true may be a figment of somebody's imagination. Even the most intricate details of what you consider to be reality may be falsehoods. This includes everything from the so-called old wives tales to what you have read in books and heard in the media, at school, or from the mouths of others.

Many people have realized that what they learned about history from textbooks when they were schoolchildren was largely fictionalized, romanticized, and filled with lies. Often, this is done for political reasons, such as to build blind national patriotism. For instance, here in the United States, many students were taught that Christopher Columbus both "discovered" America and was the first to find that Earth is round. Columbus has also been portrayed as a heroic figure who brought civility to the heathens.

In truth, Columbus didn't discover America in 1492. Many people from other continents, including Africa and Asia, had already been to what became known as the American continents. The Americas were named by German cartographer Martin Waldseemuller in about 1507. Waldseemuller may have used the name of the Welsh merchant, Richard Amerike, who sponsored John Cabot's 1497 boat rides to what is now known as Newfoundland. Waldseemuller also may have used the feminized name of Italian explorer Amerigo Vespucci, who traveled with a group exploring the coasts in 1499; or the name of the gold-rich Amerique district of Nicaragua, which may have been visited by both Vespucci and Columbus. Millions of people were already living on what became known as the American continents before Columbus made his famous boat ride. Columbus landed on an occupied island that is now part of the Bahamas, thus the teaching that he landed on a continent is also flawed. Columbus and his group also went on to other islands, including what are now Cuba, Haiti, Jamaica, and Puerto Rico.

In reality, for thousands of years before Columbus there were people who knew the world is round. Evidence of this can be found in ancient drawings and literature from every continent, including in navigational maps and on cave walls.

Columbus was also not a flawless and heroic figure. He and his group of thugs were homicidal rapists who robbed, enslaved, and tortured the indigenous people of the islands where Columbus' fleet of ships had landed. Who else would be more suitable to expand an imperialistic empire than a group of cold-hearted thugs?

In truth, the island people were better off without Columbus. The islanders had their own culture, which was much more peaceful and civil than the practices Columbus and his group introduced, which involved cutting off the hands of those who were believed to be lazy, or who were otherwise viewed as uncommitted to following the dictates of Columbus's group. The "Columbus Day" holiday that is recognized in the U.S. is an insult to indigenous cultures, and it is based on lies. Columbus was not a figure to be admired; he was someone who should be abhorred and exemplified as a genocidal maniac.

Just as there are mistruths being taught to schoolchildren in the belief that they will be more dedicated citizens to the reigning government if they believe a certain whitewashed and fictionalized history, there are authority figures today working to groom their country's citizens to believe in lies that advance the careers of politicians, promote the monsters of the military, and lavish wealth on corporate giants.

Throughout history there have been those who have fashioned themselves as heroic figures. Their self-promotion has been accomplished through the sacrifice of many lives. Their activities involve sending forth their troops to rob, plunder, kill, and overtake.

Consider that there are people today who are in positions of so-called power who are doing great damage to Earth and it's life. Perhaps some of these people are those you have perceived as good and righteous.

Realize that the way you perceive other cultures, your government, your local community, and your life may be a part of the mistruths spread by others with unwise agendas that are not about improving your condition.

> "You cannot fix an illusion. You can only wake up from one."
> – Michael Beckwith

What if everything you have believed in and learned up to this point has been based on false information fashioned by the dreams or clever minds of others?

Maybe it is time to realign your perceptions.

Perhaps it is time to begin to dream another dream.

> "You are never too old to set another goal or to dream a new dream."
>
> – C. S. Lewis

> "The future belongs to those who believe in the beauty of their dreams."
>
> – Eleanor Roosevelt

> "All people dream; but not equally. Those who dream by night in the dusty recess of their minds wake in the day to find that it was vanity. But the dreamers of the day are the dangerous people, for they may act their dream with open eyes to make it possible."
>
> – T.E. Lawrence

> "In dreams begins responsibility."
>
> – William Butler Yeats

> "Re-examine all you have been told at school or church or in any book, dismiss whatever insults your own soul, and your very flesh shall be a great poem."
>
> – Walt Whitman

> "The courage to penetrate and power to see clearly the meaning of things hidden beyond the situation prevailing around us and to act up to the discovered meaning is what is known as revolutionary insight. Revolution can take place only where there is this power of penetrating insight."
>
> – Vinoba Bhave

> "Champions aren't made in the gyms. Champions are made from something they have deep inside them — a desire, a dream, a vision."
>
> – Muhammad Ali

> "Never underestimate the power of dreams and the influence of the human spirit. We are all the same in this notion: The potential

for greatness lives within each of us."

– Wilma Rudolph

"Dreams come in a size too big so that we may grow into them."

– Josie Bisset

"There is hope in dreams, imagination, and in the courage of those who wish to make those dreams a reality."

– Jonas Salk

"The most unrealistic person in the world is the cynic, not the dreamer. Hopefulness only makes sense when it doesn't make sense to be hopeful. This is your century. Take it and run as if your life depends on it."

– Paul Hawken

"If one advances confidently in the direction of his dreams, and endeavors to live the life which he has imagined, he will meet with a success unexpected in common hours."

– Henry David Thoreau

"Your imagination is the preview of life's coming attractions."

– Albert Einstein

"Dreams pass into the reality of action. From the actions stems the dream again; and this interdependence produces the highest form of living."

– Anais Nin

Bring Forth Good

"Goodness is the only investment that never fails."

– Henry David Thoreau

"The single largest pool of untapped resource in this world is human good intentions that never translate into action."

– Cindy Gallop

"There is a spark of good in everybody, no matter how deeply it may be buried, it is there. It's waiting to govern your life gloriously."
– Mildred "Peace Pilgrim" Norman

Improving your life is about tuning in to your potential and bringing forth good things. It is about preparing for and creating success, about taking care of your body through excellent nutrition and exercise, about awakening to and working with your intellect, and about using your talents and abilities to experience satisfaction.

"There is a you, lying dormant. A potential within you to be realized. It does not matter whether you have an intelligence quotient of 60 or 160, there is more of you than what you are presently aware of. Perhaps the only peace and joy in life lies in the pursuit of and development of this potential."
– Leo Buscaglia

Reiterating what I suggest earlier, and also going a bit further, as you read this book I encourage you to make notes in alignment with preparing yourself for a better life. Exercise your body and mind daily to build your mental and physical fitness level. Nurture your mind with that which uplifts you. Nourish your body with a plant-based diet that advances you toward experiencing vibrant health. Realize that a better future is within your grasp, and know that you can create it through intentional thoughts, planning, and actions.

"Success is simple. First, you decide what you want specifically; and second, you decide you're willing to pay the price to make it happen, and then pay that price."
– Bunker Hunt

"Do or do not. There is no 'try.'"
– Master Yoda

Your life is like a sculpture. You are either chiseling away at your life in a very specific manner to create something beautiful, or you are simply allowing life to batter away at you to become like a decomposing ship stranded on a rocky beach. It is your decision which of these scenarios your life resembles.

"If ya keep on doing what you've always done, you'll keep on getting what you've always got."
– Momma Turtle

Those who have greatly improved their lives will likely tell anyone wanting to do the same that experiencing successful change is like having a weight removed from the shoulders. They will also likely say that if you want desired changes to take place in your life, it is up to you to make them happen through planning combined with intentional action.

Everyone knows that there is always something that can be improved. As the saying goes, "The biggest room in everyone's house is the room for improvement."

Whether on a profound or subtle level, there is some area in each person's life that could be improved. Many of the answers of how to go about making the changes toward improving an individual's life lie within the person. Other answers may have to be found by study, by contemplation, and by utilizing outside sources.

When you review your life and scan it for areas that can be improved, at first you may not know what improvement is needed, or what the answer could be. But there surely is a way to improve it — no matter what your life situation may be. And there is a way to open doors of opportunity that you may have considered to be closed to you.

Many of the doors you wish to be open may already be, and they only may be closed to you because you have perceived them as being so.

> "Reflect upon your present blessings, of which every man has plenty; not on your past misfortunes, of which all men have some."
> – Charles Dickens

Many opportunities to improve your life have likely escaped you simply because you did not notice them, did not recognize them, believed you were not capable of attaining the betterment of them, and because you may have been preoccupied with focusing on what you don't want and don't like while you have loitered in places you would rather not be.

What you want to do is to focus on what you do want and what you do like, and to be involved in doing what you can do and what you see yourself doing in ways that will make your life better.

> "You are precisely as big as what you love and precisely as small as what you allow to annoy you."
> – Robert Anton Wilson

> "The only limit to our realization of tomorrow will be our doubts of today."
> – Franklin Roosevelt

Be brave and wise enough to face up to the tasks you need to accomplish, and to engage your mind in figuring out a healthful way of dealing with any issues that hold you back. Not only would it be helpful for you to figure them out, but it would be so to work them out through your actions.

Many people become so stuck in knowing that their life is a mess that the fact of knowing it becomes their main focus. It as if they are staring at an accident. The reality of their disaster leads to doubt that they can ever get out of their mess. Their doubts become their ruling factor while their vision becomes stalled at the site of the accident. Some have been staring at the accident so long that they got towed away with it to the junkyard, which is what their life resembles.

> "If one desires a change, one must be that change before that change can take place."
>
> – Gita Bellin

Stop believing in your doubts, and focusing on what you perceive to be the misfortunes of the past. Instead, believe in your future, and what you can make of it.

Choose right now to create and act on solutions that will place you in a more satisfactory life.

> "When I dare to be powerful — to use my strength in the service of my vision, then it becomes less and less important whether I am afraid."
>
> – Audrey Lorde

Listening to encouragement, and being encouraged is good, and refusing to listen to discouragement helps people to be invincible in their pursuits, but people who are undergoing intentional life change would likely benefit from remembering this: There is a difference between being reasonably optimistic about changing your life and being so extreme that your choices may create problems.

> "The differences between optimists and extreme optimists are remarkable, and suggest that over-optimism, like overconfidence, may in fact lead to behaviors that are unwise."
>
> – Manju Puri

While going about changing your life, it is important to remember that there are wiser choices and choices that aren't so wise. This is why you might consider reading a variety of books on self-improvement and about your interests; to be open to revising and redefining your plans; and to seek out professional help to make wiser choices.

There are numerous ways people may go about determining what they desire to change in their life. Through self-review and goal-setting you can help identify what may work best for you.

> "Possessions, outward success, publicity, luxury — to me these have always been contemptible. I assume that a simple and unassuming manner of life is best for everyone, best for both the body and the mind."
> – Albert Einstein

When people talk about improvement they often think of the word *success*. Often their definition of success involves money and material possessions.

When I talk about success, I am not speaking of mansions, expensive things; the most trendy labeled products; piles of money; the latest techno-gadgets; closets filled with expensive clothes; and material nonsense. I believe it is best to live simply. Rather than belongings and luxury, when I mention success I'm speaking more of satisfaction and comfort with self, including health; fulfilling, nurturing, and loving relationships; and responsible use of talent and intellect.

> "It is health that is the real wealth and not pieces of gold and silver."
> – Mahatma Gandhi

Consider what minimal belongings you would require to fulfill your needs. Make a list of these that you could configure into a workable plan if you needed or wanted to get rid of things.

> "Remember this, that very little is needed to make a happy life."
> – Marcus Aurelius

Along with a list of what it would require to fulfill your needs, make a list of actions you need to take to bring you closer to a satisfying lifestyle.

Along those lines, clarify what you want from life. Then, take action to implement it.

> "If you don't risk anything — you're risking even more."
> – Erica Jong

There are innumerable actions you might take that will result in a more satisfying life. It may involve new ways of dealing with belongings, education, career, professions, people, food, exercise, and community, or all of these. Whatever they may be, work them in ways that manifest satisfaction.

"The best way to predict the future is to create it."
– Peter F. Drucker

"Taking in the good is not about putting a happy shiny face on everything, nor is it about turning away from the hard things in life. It's about nourishing inner well-being, contentment, and peace — refuges to which you can always return."
– Rick Hanson

"What we do flows from who we are."
– Paul Vitale

"There is a redemptive power that making a choice has. Rather than feeling that you're an affect to all the things that are happening, make your choice. You just decide what it is going to be, who you are going to be, how you are going to do it. Just decide, and from that point, the universe is going to get out of your way. It's water. It wants to move and go around stuff."
– Will Smith

"Concerning all acts of initiative and creation, there is one elementary truth, the ignorance of which kills countless ideas and splendid plans: That the moment one definitely commits oneself, the Providence moves too. Whatever you can do or dream you can do, begin it. Boldness has genius, power, and magic in it. Begin it now."
– Johann Wolfgang von Goethe

Courage

"Whatever you do, you need courage. Whatever course you decide upon, there is always someone to tell you that you are wrong. There are always difficulties arising that tempt you to believe your critics are right. To map out a course of action and follow it to an

end requires some of the same courage that a soldier needs. Peace has its victories, but it takes brave men and women to win them."
– Ralph Waldo Emerson

"Life expands or contracts in direct proportion to one's courage."
– Anais Nin

Those interested in self-improvement are more likely to experience it if they are constantly involved in some sort of thought pattern fueling intentional activities result in improvement. This process will create patterns that bring more of the same.

"I'm not afraid of storms, for I'm learning to sail my ship."
– Louisa May Alcott

There is bravery, courage, integrity, and dignity in working to establish improvements in your life. Exercising these in ways that bring satisfaction will strengthen the resolve to create and experience more satisfaction. A key factor is to do it with a set plan with clear goals, and to do it consistently, responsibly, and wisely.

"The most glorious moments in your life are not the so-called days of success, but rather those days when out of dejection and despair you feel rise in you a challenge to life, and the promise of future accomplishments."
– Gustave Flaubert

Many people are afraid to face their problems. This is often true even when their problems are so obvious that their troubles overwhelm their life. This includes people who simply dig themselves into denial, and those who regret the fact that there are issues facing them.

"To live a spiritual life we must first find the courage to enter into the desert of loneliness and to change it by gentle and persistent efforts into a garden of solitude."
– Henri J. M. Nouwen

Ignoring problems does not make them go away. Instead, it may make them much worse. Like an infection, problems that go untreated can spread into other areas of people's lives, and into the lives of those with whom they associate.

"Every time I close the door on reality, it comes in through the window."
– Ashleigh Brilliant

"You cannot find peace by avoiding life."
– Virginia Woolf

People often spend lots of time doing things to delay having to face an issue. In the modern-day procrastination often involves watching TV; getting caught up in the web of the worldwide Web; obsessing about celebrity culture; and shopping to replicate images which commercials define as what happiness should consist of. But escapism can also involve substance abuse, consuming unhealthful foods, sleeping too much, wasting time doing meaningless things, pornography, anonymous and risky sex, and/or spending time with people who are also not dealing with their issues and who enable problems to fester and slothfulness to perpetuate. What some people are best at is achieving failure and regret.

"Most people spend more time and energy going around problems than in trying to solve them."
– Henry Ford

"Procrastination is the thief of time."
– Edward Young

"Nothing is so fatiguing as the eternal hanging on of an uncompleted task."
– William James

"Procrastination is the passive assassin of opportunity."
– Roy Williams

"A lot of disappointed people have been left standing on the street corner waiting for the bus marked perfection."
– Donald Kennedy

The sooner you take care of your problems, the better your situation will be.

Consider your hands, your feet, your lips, and your eyes. All probably are similar to any others of anyone who accomplished great things. Some were smaller, some were larger, some may have lost parts along their way. Some may have even been born without certain parts. But all made do with what they had. Some started out with little, and others with fancy things. You take what you got and make with it what you can. Some people with physical ailments certainly are disabled, and some use it as an excuse for just about everything, and some with more debilitating ailments succeed far beyond even those who could be considered the most physically ideal.

Certainly there are those who will never succeed at certain occupations or talents. A tone-deaf person will not become an opera star. A blind person will not become a professional baseball player. But if you can't build your house out of brick, build it out of bamboo. Do what works for you, and stop fighting against what is unlikely ever to work, and go with what will.

Use the mechanism of your mind to formulate the combination that will release you from any locks and chains that bind you down.

Do not allow your problems to overwhelm your life. Refuse to let past or present events own your soul. Absolutely do not let the past rob you of your future. Continually and intentionally live your days as they are golden, and not stolen.

> "I always wanted to be somebody, but I should have been more specific."
> – Lily Tomlin

Stop looking away from those parts of your life that need attention. Instead, courageously turn and face them. Create a plan and make the situation change in your favor according to what you want.

> "One of the great lessons I've learned in athletics is that you've got to discipline your life. No matter how good you may be, you've got to be willing to cut out of your life those things that keep you from going to the top."
> – Bob Richards

Do not give in to people who doubt that you are capable of succeeding. Never allow yourself to think that you are not capable or worthy of experiencing true health, kindness, joy, and love.

It is likely that three of the most helpful things you can do for yourself are to:

A) Stop feeling as if you need to explain yourself
B) Stop allowing yourself to react to other people's drama
C) Refrain from slandering other people

I mention slandering other people in that list because how you treat other people is reflective of the beliefs you hold within and in how you treat your self.

Be ambitious in creating the life you want, and do so with good manners. Do this even if you were raised by people who had neither ambition nor manners.

Completely overhaul the way you communicate with the people who are overly critical of you and/or who strongly doubt that you are going to succeed in improving your life. This may mean communicating with them less, or not at all.

> "As I grow older, I pay less attention to what men say. I just watch what they do."
> – Andrew Carnegie

People may doubt your words, but they can't doubt your actions.

Value your talents, intellect, and creations enough not to toss them around before people who would trash them, or who would devalue your intellect, belittle your character, undermine your goals, or otherwise drag you down.

Believe in your self, no matter what.

> "Use what talents you possess; the woods would be very silent if no birds sang there except those that sang best."
> – Henry Van Dyke

Do not spend your time or energy explaining your goals to the doubters, to the haters, to the underminers, or to the wasters of time. Instead, spend your time and energy planning for and working to improve and create the life you want.

> "You can't build a reputation on what you are going to do."
> – Henry Ford

Grab onto courage and build your confidence. Bravely take charge of your days by setting a plan to succeed, and then spending your days working toward it.

Be determined to rid yourself of that which clutters your path and holds you back.

Do not look back toward what you consider to be your failures. Instead, look forward to that which you can attain through perseverance.

"As for failures, I very, very rarely look back."
– Richard Branson

"Courage is not the absence of fear, but rather the judgment that something else is more important than fear."
– Ambrose Redmoon

As you go forward into a healthful life and learn of the benefits of the good things you are doing for yourself, you will be able to surpass the limits under which you once lived. You will be able to see that you are capable of attaining good things that truly improve your life. This will strengthen, edify, and motivate you.

"We must all suffer one of two things: the pain of discipline or the pain of regret or disappointment."
– E. James Rohn

"Believe in yourself and there will come a day when others will have no choice but to believe with you."
– Cynthia Kersey

"Obstacles don't have to stop you. If you run into a wall, don't turn around and give up. Figure out how to climb it, go through it, or work around it."
– Michael Jordan

Stop allowing anything that challenges you to push aside your focus or to dismiss your drive to succeed. Work to be invincible in practicing your intention to succeed at your goals through everyday action.

Be relentless in pursuing the life you want to have.

Command your thoughts and force your life to happen in your favor.

"Nurture your mind with great thoughts, for you will never go any higher than your thoughts."
– Benjamin Disraeli

Give energy to thoughts that get you to work toward your goals and let the vision of accomplishment drive you.

Like an athlete who constantly works toward victory, you too can surpass your records in ways that you never considered. Believe in and work toward experiencing this satisfaction.

Allow yourself to be propelled toward a better life by visualizing your life the way you want it to be and making it happen through intentional living.

> "Nothing is, unless our thinking makes it so."
> – William Shakespeare

Be courageous about and focus on your goals the way runners and bikers focus on the finish line, the way swimmers focus on form and speed, the way mountain climbers focus on the top, and the way ball players focus on upping the score. Work on creating your goals into reality the way classical musicians organize musical notes to make beautiful sound: That is, through thoughts and actions called *practice*. Within the bravery of courage in action is the beauty of elegance in practice.

> "Dreams are renewable. No matter what our age or condition, there are still untapped possibilities within us and new beauty waiting to be born."
> – Dale E. Turner

> "You may be whatever you resolve to be. Determine to be something in the world, and you will be something. 'I cannot,' never accomplished anything; 'I will try,' has wrought wonders."
> – J. Hawes

> "Fortune sides with him who dares."
> – Publius Vergillus "Virgil" Maro

> "Chained by their attitudes, they are a slave, they have forfeited their freedom. Only a person who risks is free."
> – Anonymous

> "That is will never come again is what makes life so sweet."
> – Emily Dickinson

> "Let me not pray to be sheltered from dangers, but to be fearless in facing them. Let me not beg for the stilling of my pain, but for the heart to conquer it."
> – Rabindranath Tagore

> "Courage is never to let your actions be influenced by your fears."
> – Arthur Koestler

"You miss 100 percent of the shots you never take."
– Wayne Gretzky

"Man cannot discover new oceans unless he has the courage to lose sight of the shore."
– Andre Gide

"Each person has inside a basic decency and goodness. If he listens to it and acts on it, he is giving a great deal of what it is the world needs most. It is not complicated but it takes courage. It takes courage for a person to listen to his own good."
– Pablo Casals

"Life shrinks and expands in proportion to one's courage."
– Anais Nin

"The fact is, that to do anything in the world worth doing, we must not stand back shivering and thinking of the cold and danger, but jump in and scramble through as well as we can."
– Robert Cushing

"It is courage the world needs, not infallibility. Courage is always the surest wisdom."
– Wilfred T. Grenfell

"With courage you will dare to take risks, have the strength to be compassionate, and the wisdom to be humble. Courage is the foundation of integrity."
– Keshavan Nair

"Everyday courage has few witnesses. But yours is no less noble because no drum beats for you and no crowds shout your name."
– Robert Louis Stevenson

Plan Your Life

"Twenty years from now you will be more disappointed by the things you didn't do than by the ones you did do. So throw off the bowlines. Sail away from the safe harbor. Catch the trade winds in

your sails. Explore. Dream. Discover."
– Mark Twain

"The more severe the pain or illness, the more severe will be the necessary changes. These may involve breaking bad habits, or acquiring some new and better ones."
– Peter McWilliams

"People who say that life is not worthwhile are really saying that they themselves have no personal goals which are worthwhile. Get yourself a goal worth working for. Better still, get yourself a project. Always have something ahead of you to look forward to, to work for and hope for."
– Maxwell Maltz

"When plans are laid in advance, it is surprising how often the circumstances fit in with them."
– William Osler

"If we do not know what port we're steering for, no wind is favorable."
– Lucius Annaeus Seneca

Many people reach a breaking point where they declare, "I can't live my life like this." But their intention to carry out their declaration has no definition because they have no plan. By not having a set plan they are committed to nothing. Rather than a declaration that they are going to change, their words are simply commentary.

"The man without a purpose is like a ship without a rudder — a waif, a nothing, a no man. Have a purpose in life, and having it, throw such strength of mind and muscle into your work as God has given you."
– Thomas Carlyle

If you are going through life without an idea of how you want it to be, you are spending your days aimlessly. If you have an idea of what you want your life to be, but aren't spending your days both planning and working for it, you are only fantasizing. But if you have the idea of how you want your life to be, and are actively spending your days not only planning it, but also working toward it, that is your life, and how it will become.

"The vision must be followed by the venture. It is not enough to stare up the steps — we must step up the stairs."
– Vance Havner

"Reach high, for stars lie hidden in your soul. Dream deep, for every dream precedes the goal."
– Pamela Vaull Starr

The mind works in accordance with the influences that are suggested to it. To get your mind to work in your favor, define your intentions.

"People who do not see their choices do not believe they have choices. They tend to respond automatically, blindly influenced by their circumstances and conditioning. Mindfulness, by helping us notice our impulses before we act, gives us the opportunity to decide whether to act and how to act."
– Gil Fronsdal

As an example of what people become based on their thoughts, consider those you can think of who have accomplished amazing things. Realize that the reason they are likely to have experienced such success is that they set goals for themselves and combined their intention with their intellect, talents, abilities, and instinct to accomplish those goals through everyday actions.

"You have got to know what it is you want, or someone is going to sell you a bill of goods somewhere along the line that can do irreparable damage to your self-esteem, your sense of worth, and your stewardship of the talents that God gave you."
– Richard Nelson Bolles

Many sports events have been won through the power of suggestion from coaches, cheering fans, and cheerleaders. The players also did it because they had a plan to win and a vision to win, and they acted out those plans and visions.

"How do you go from where you are to where you want to be? I think you have to have an enthusiasm for life. You have to have a dream, a goal, and you have to be willing to work for it."
– Jim Valvano

"Our goals can only be reached through a vehicle of a plan, in which we must fervently believe, and upon which we must

vigorously act. There is no other route to success."
– Stephen A. Brennan

Sports teams work with game plans. Architects work with plans called blueprints. Corporations function under corporate plans. Farmers run their farms by following plans of what to plant and where and when to plant it. People who knit blankets do so with plans. Take these examples of having and working with plans to obtain goals. Make a game plan for your life to improve, write it out on paper, and read it every morning.

"The greater our awareness of intentions, the greater our freedom to choose."
– Gil Fronsdal

Keeping a list of goals and priorities and reading it every morning is one of the most powerful tools you can use to help you focus on what you want to accomplish, and on accomplishing your goals.

"The term 'power' comes from the Latin posse: to do, to be able, to change, to influence or effect. To have power is to possess the capacity to control or direct change. All forms of leadership must make use of power. The central issue of power in leadership is not will it be used? But rather will it be used wisely and well?"
– Al Gini

There is power in suggestion — in suggesting things to others, and especially in suggesting things to yourself. Repeated suggestion is particularly effective. Making a list of your goals and reading them every morning to focus your mind is using the power of suggestion.

"Don't let the fear of the time it will take to accomplish something stand in the way of your doing it. The time will pass anyway; we might just as well put that passing time to the best possible use."
– Earl Nightingale

"Don't be fooled by the calendar. There are only as many days in the year as you make use of. One man gets only a week's value out of a year while another man gets a full year's value out of a week.
– Charles Richards

Many people use suggestive or self-affirming notes to motivate them toward succeeding at goals. These notes are often as simple as, "You can do it," or "Believe in yourself." Or the notes may be task-specific, such as, "I will spend less money, and save more," or, "I will finish [name of project]."

Daily affirmations may also include chanting, repeating motivational thoughts, writing uplifting and encouraging thoughts, and by literally defining your path by both mapping it and verbally proclaiming intentions.

Reading and writing daily affirmations helps to set energy patterns in your thoughts that travel throughout your brain and body tissues, which work as one. I suggest that you use both daily affirmations and reading of your specific written plan every morning to set your mind on a path at the start of every day to improve your life.

> "What I do today is important because I am exchanging a day of my life for it."
> – Hugh Mulligan

To experience great improvement in health and mind you have to make the decision to do so, and act on that decision every day.

If you don't have a plan that you are continually working with, you are simply bumping into life, people, experience, and things as if you are in a bumper car with a broken steering wheel.

Starting today, chart out a plan, and begin taking the steps necessary to get yourself to where you want to be with your health and life. Plan out your way to live by making a plan, and then live out your plan to live by continually taking actions manifesting that plan.

> "One person with a belief is equal to a force of 99 who have only interests."
> – John Stuart Mill

Make a list of what changes are necessary in your life to make it what you want it to be. This will be the beginning of your strategy for life change.

Keeping a "journaling" notebook of your thoughts regarding your concepts, intentions, observations, progress, nutrition, experiences, and dreams can help guide you along in your process of self-improvement. Slowly allow it to be a workbook that will assist you in leading a more healthful and intentionally satisfying life. Write down what inspires you. Write down the thoughts that motivate you. Write down what you desire to overcome and provide some detail on how you plan to overcome it.

> "Time is an equal opportunity employer. Each human being has exactly the same number of hours and minutes every day. Rich people can't buy more hours. Scientists can't invent new minutes. And you can't save time to spend it on another day. Even so, time is amazingly fair and forgiving. No matter how much time you've wasted in the past, you still have an entire tomorrow."
> – Denis Waitely

Once you have your game plan you can go about exploring different ways of how to make the plan happen. In tune with that plan, study and strategize in ways that mold your thought patterns to be in alignment with what you want your life to become.

> "Learning to understand our dreams is a matter of learning how to understand our heart's language."
> – Anne Faraday

> "I am a writer who came from a sheltered life. A sheltered life can be a daring life as well. For all serious daring starts from within."
> – Eudora Welty

In your notebook, detail the things you want from life; the helpful things you dream about at night; and the positive thoughts you have regarding these issues. But don't get so obsessive about journaling that it takes away time and energy that would be more helpful to spend on accomplishing your goals. To make your life change you must be actively engaged in actions that make it change, and not just in dreaming of or fantasizing about them.

The journal you keep of your goals, priorities, wants, dreams, and positive thoughts will be a "before and after" snapshot of your thought processes. Your actions will create the "after" picture.

> "Think clearly and deeply, go into the structure of your desires and their ramifications. They are a most important part of your mental and emotional make-up, and powerfully affect your actions."
> – Nisargadatta Maharaj

When you see a list of what you want written on paper it helps you to visualize what you want. Going through the list every morning helps you keep the life changes you want at the forefront of your mind. Thinking about the positive changes you want is the process that drives the actions that manifest your goals into your reality.

"Remember, you cannot abandon what you do not know. To go beyond yourself, you must know yourself."
– Nisargadatta Maharaj

Journaling exercises that will help you discover your passions and achieve goals. This is to explore thoughts, to trigger self-invention, to awaken creativity, to define your character, and to begin the exploration and consideration of the possible.

1. Make a list of a few things you were good at when you were a child. Or a short list of what you wished to be good at.

2. Make a list of several things you thought were interesting and caught your attention when you were a child. Specifically, these should relate to what you would like your life to be.

3. Make a list of some things you did that gave you satisfaction when you were a child. Specifically, these should be accomplishments, such as in music, art, sports, or goal accomplishment.

4. Make a list of some of the memorable compliments you have received about your character, talents, and/or skills.

5. Make a list of some of your favorite things, such as colors, activities, hobbies, books, music, movies, flowers, plants, and wildlife. Maybe you will draw some of these in your journal.

6. Make a list of some of the things currently in your life that you do not want in your life.

7. Make a list of some of the things that you do not have in your life, and that you want in your life. You might also draw some of these in your journal, and do so without being critical of your artistic skills.

8. Go to a library and look for nonfiction books that interest you.

Keep in mind that you are looking for books that will teach you things that will improve your life, not books that are meant for entertainment and/or for leisure. For instance, look for books that will improve your skills and intellect, and/or that will help you to be more accomplished in your talents and craft.

9. Make a list of some of the things you are capable of doing in relation to skills and talents.

10. Make a list of some things you would like to do during your life.

"The secret of getting ahead is getting started. The secret of getting started is breaking your complex overwhelming tasks into small manageable tasks, and then starting on the first one."
– Mark Twain

Some people spend hundreds of dollars on planning calendars and fancy motivational calendar notebooks. While this may work for some people, you don't necessarily need a fancy binder to get your life together. All you need is one piece of paper, keep it updated and organized, and make it part of your mornings to guide your days.

Fold a piece of paper into four segments. Use color ink, because the mind tends to remember things that it reads in color more clearly than things it reads in black and white.

On the first segment: Write several things you want to be engaged in every day in relation to accomplishing your goals.

On the second segment: Write several things you want to accomplish this week.

On the third segment: List several things you want to accomplish this month.

On the fourth segment: Write down several things you want to accomplish in the next three months.

On the back of the page: Write down several things you want to accomplish during the year.

Write the date on it.

Remake this paper at the start of every week. Rewriting it every week will help you refine your plans while keeping them fresh in your mind.

Make this your game plan, day plan, intention, and a motivational tool. It is your contract with yourself. Let it guide your thoughts and actions from the start of every day so that you go about fulfilling the contract.

"Unless commitment is made, there are only promises and hopes; but no plans."
– Peter F. Drucker

"We are what we repeatedly do; therefore, excellence is not an act, but a habit."
– Henry David Thoreau

Working at improving your life every day is the key.

When things seem to be getting complicated, keep the basics of your list in mind. If you find that you are growing doubtful, go back to your list and work it out. Focus on those simple things that are the basics of your life, talents, intellect, abilities, skills, and needs. And be sure to read through your list every morning.

> "If you don't set a baseline standard for what you'll accept in life, you'll find it's easy to slip into behaviors and attitudes or a quality of life that's far below what you deserve."
> – Anthony Robbins

Each little item on your list is like a rudder in your life. They will be similar to the small rudders of a large ship that guide it across the vast oceans. A slight change in the angle of your intentions can guide you to a whole other destination.

> "Be faithful in small things because it is in them that your strength lies."
> – Mother Teresa

As you go through your day, keep a pen handy so that you can write down any ideas you may have on how you can improve your life. If you don't write down these ideas, you may forget them. So, write them down. Then add them to the larger list you are keeping of things you want to do to realign your life.

Make improving your life be your ruling habit.

> "You don't get to choose how you're going to die, or when. You can only decide how you're going to live. Now.
> – Joan Baez

> "Not choice, but habit rules the unreflecting herd."
> – William Wordsworth

> "Our challenge is to see beyond the world and invoke new beginnings."
> – Marianne Williamson

> "The final destination of a journey is not, after all, the last item on the agenda, but rather some understanding, however simple or provisional, of what one has seen."
> – Pico Iyer

"It is good to have an end to journey toward; but it is the journey that matters, in the end."
– Ursula K. Le Guin

"I would rather be ashes than dust! I would rather that my spark should burn out in a brilliant blaze than it should be stifled by dry rot. I would rather be a superb meteor, every atom of me in magnificent glow, than a sleepy and permanent planet. The proper function of man is to live, not exist. I shall not waste my days in trying to prolong them, I shall use my time."
– Jack London

Ignite Your Life

"Strong lives are motivated by dynamic purposes."
– Kenneth Hildebrand

"The best way to make your dreams come true is to wake up."
– Muhammad Ali

"Through fear of knowing who we really are we sidestep our own destiny, which leaves us hungry in a famine of our own making. We end up living numb, passionless lives, disconnected from our soul's true purpose. But when you have the courage to shape your life from the essence of who you are, you ignite, becoming truly alive."
– Dawna Markova

If you are tired of leading a life that does not satisfy you, change it. Move the obstacles out of your way. Do not dwell on what you perceive to be the unfortunate or unfair things that may have happened to you, and refuse to allow them to shade your world or halt your progress. Refuse to be held bound by things, events, situations, and/or people that you perceive as working against you. Do not make any time for self-pity in your days. Do not let your talents be caged in by the bars of regret. Remove the walls and chains that hold you from what you want. Awaken your life from any slumber.

Look for the good in things, and build upon the good. Start with whatever good you have and use it to bring yourself closer to the person you want to be. Work at this every day from the moment of awakening.

Do so in a calm and determined manner that will propel you toward being the person you wish to become.

> "Realize that if you have time to whine and complain about something, you have time to do something about it."
> – Anonymous

> "When you complain, all you do is broadcast, 'There's a victim in the neighborhood.'"
> – Maya Angelou

> "Continuous effort — not strength or intelligence — is the key to unlocking our potential."
> – Winston Churchill

> "Don't be disquieted in time of adversity. Be firm with dignity and self-reliant with vigor."
> – Chiang Kai-Shek

Refuse to be overthrown by any problem that faces you.

The message that transcends generations is that you are to decide which of your dreams becomes reality.

Just as your grandest successes may be self-created, so too may be much of what you consider to be your greatest failures. It is likely that it is largely up to you to decide which one of these possibilities may be realized.

> "We carry within us the wonders we seek without us."
> – Thomas Browne

> "Deep within man dwell those slumbering powers; powers that would astonish him, that he never dreamed of possessing; forces that would revolutionize his life if aroused and put into action."
> – Orison Swett Marden

Don't think of creating your life as a way of finding it. Creating your life is not about finding it, it's about opening it. What you become is nurtured from within you. What moves you is your spirit. It is there. It is real. And you can use it any way and at any time you wish.

> "You must be lamps unto yourselves."
> – Buddha

"If you have built castles in the air, your work need not be lost. Now put foundations under them."
– Osa Johnson

It is taking actions in tune with the power to believe in yourself that can work miracles in your life.

Surround yourself in all ways with what motivates you and brings out your best qualities.

Make the positive, uplifting, nurturing, loving, and kind substances of your life the most vibrant and present in a way that they will continually capture and hold your attention. The strongest vibrations will always win, just as when listening to two voices at the same time, it is the loudest that will get your attention.

"A man's life is what his thoughts make it."
– Marcus Aurelius

Decisions are seeds of the mind. Decisions that receive nurturing thought patterns will grow. Make your most helpful decisions grow into reality through actions as you would grow seeds into an orchard to produce fruit.

Being proactive in changing your life is about nurturing your most helpful decisions, creating positive thoughts, and taking actions in alignment with these that lead to satisfaction.

"To see things in the seed, that is genius."
– Lao Tzu

As your thoughts are known to affect your tissues, thoughts can be compared to the seeds of events that spread their roots into your tissues, and out into the atmosphere through your words and actions.

Uplifting thoughts lead to uplifting words, actions, and events. When uplifting thoughts lead to uplifting words, they can uplift you and those around you. When uplifting thoughts are combined with uplifting words, vibrant foods, exercise, and goal-oriented actions, transformative vibrant health can be experienced in all areas of your life.

"The first step to becoming is to will it."
– Mother Teresa

Because you are a manifestation of what your thoughts are, you are a being that is reflective of what enlightens you. Because of this, your words and actions are continually revealing the level of your enlightenment.

The positive life change you are undergoing is equal to your level of enlightenment combined with your determination.

The essence of truth in enlightened teachings is that enlightenment inspires people to conduct themselves wisely, to respect and believe in themselves and others, and to respect animals and wildlife. It instills a belief in power — the power to overcome, and the power to push forward and to improve.

> "You can't wait for inspiration. You have to go after it with a club."
>
> – Jack London

Make common practices of the persistent actions toward achieving your goals and the sustained focus on your enlightened decisions, until the behaviors become both a habit and your normal way of conducting your life.

> "Energy and persistence alter all things."
>
> – Benjamin Franklin

> "When you acknowledge the obstacle you give it power by the acknowledgement of it. I'm going to walk over it. I'm going to walk around it.
>
> I would say that my preoccupation is with the power that we all possess individually and I refuse to relinquish my power. So my preoccupation with that happening is that the belief in possibility is our power. And don't give it away for anything.
>
> I believe very strongly that we are who we choose to be."
>
> – Will Smith

The more persistent you are in accomplishing your goals, and the more sustained your focus on your enlightened decisions, the more you will see and realize that it is possible to do what you want to do, and the more you will find yourself making a habit of healthfulness in your life.

If you do anything habitually, make it the constant wise use of your time, resources, talent, abilities, skill, craft, intellect, and love.

> "Without heroes, we are all plain people and don't know how far we can go."
>
> – Bernard Malamud

By doing all of these things while trusting in your heart, you will see that you are capable and worthy of changing your life. While you once may have given up on attaining your goals, as you go about accomplishing them with a renewed and continually intentional focus you will be your own witness to the truths that lie within you.

> "The simple act of caring is heroic."
> – Edward Albert

Care about yourself so much and so consistently that you become your own hero.

> "Heroes take journeys, confront dragons, and discover the treasure of their true selves."
> – Carol Pearson

> "His high endeavors are an inward light, that makes the path before him always bright."
> – William Wordsworth

> "We can be drones addicted to crap, destruction, and material possessions we gather to impress upon people we don't even really like, or we can make our life count for something real and meaningful and make it count that we graced the planet at all.
> Life is either a dance to remember or a dance to forget. Let's make it one to remember. Let's make it elegant, honorable, and saturated with truth."
> – Harley "Durianrider" Johnstone

> "Every aspect of our lives is, in a sense, a vote for the kind of world we want to live in."
> – Frances Moore Lappe

> "When you are inspired by some great purpose, some extraordinary project, all your thoughts break their bonds: Your mind transcends limitations, your consciousness expands in every direction, and you find yourself in a new, great, and wonderful world. Dormant forces, faculties and talents become alive, and you discover yourself to be a greater person by far than you ever dreamed yourself to be."
> – Patanjali

"Go confidently in the direction of your dreams. Live the life you've always imagined."
– Henry David Thoreau

Intentional Living

"Regret for the things we did can be tempered by time; it is regret for the things we did not do that is inconsolable."
– Sidney J. Harris

The way you perceive things has to do with your life experiences, including with whom you have spent time, how you have been treated, what you have been taught and told, where you have gone, what you have done, what you have read, and the pattern of thinking with which you have allowed yourself to align.

How you go about changing your life to have experiences that are different from your past is to choose to do so, focus on doing so, and continually take actions to make it so.

"First say to yourself what you would be; and then do what you have to do."
– Epictetus

Some people get caught in a cantankerous way of thinking that continually considers the problems, irritants, and drama — or what they can perceive as these. It is likely that their attitude helps to attract or create more of the same. Other people seem to glide along while continually focusing on the positive, acknowledging what makes them glad, and on creating the life they wish to have. Perhaps the greatest difference between these two types of people is that they consider and treat their issues differently, with a different way of calculating what could be perceived as problems, and a different way of finding and working on solutions.

"Three rules of work: Out of clutter find simplicity; From discord find harmony; In the middle of difficulty lies opportunity."
– Albert Einstein

Perhaps one way of looking at the issues that face you is to do what many positive-thought coaches suggest, and that is not to think of them as problems. Instead, think of them as lessons and as opportunities to achieve. They may be challenges, but that is not necessarily a bad thing. The difference between a problem and an opportunity may often be a matter of perception, and what you choose to do about the situation.

> "I discovered I always have choices and sometimes it's only a choice of attitude."
> – Judith M. Knowlton

> "Could we change our attitude, we should not only see life differently, but life itself would come to be different. Life would undergo a change of appearance because we ourselves had undergone a change of attitude."
> – Katherine Mansfield

Some say that you only experience the things that will bring you the lessons you need. While that concept may be debatable, perhaps it can be helpful to form an attitude of conducting yourself in such a way that you can learn from your experiences, use them to make better decisions, and hopefully avoid repeating the unwise decisions of your past.

> "I really do think that any deep crisis is an opportunity to make your life extraordinary in some way."
> – Martha Beck

Through the power of thought it is likely that you can transform many of your otherwise unfortunate experiences from those that may be damaging into those that can be beneficial.

> "Reality is like a bud that keeps opening. The petals keep revealing themselves. It's not as if that bud becomes something that it wasn't before. It just keeps showing its potential."
> – Adyashanti

> "The good life is a process, not a state of being. It is a direction, not a destination."
> – Carl Rogers

The line of progress toward the life people want is often largely determined by their thoughts and actions, which are driven by the internal. In that way, the path of their progression is up to them to create, and that has to do with their intentions, drive, focus, and determination, or lack thereof. The level of intention is defined by their priorities combined with the intensity of their desire mixed with their determination and potential. How these transition their life has to do with their thought choices playing out in their words and actions.

> "Choose your intention carefully and then practice holding your consciousness to it, so it becomes the guiding light in your life."
> – John Roger

A key to all of this is to keep the body and life tuned and more organized so that your intellect, talents, abilities, passions, and other graces may be accessed as you need them. The more you sustain these practices the more available and common they will become. And the more you do so in alignment with your goals, the more your life will become what you want it to be.

> "I never suspected that I would have to learn how to live — that there were specific disciplines and ways of seeing the world I had to master before I could awaken to a simple, happy, uncomplicated life."
> – Dan Millman

As suggested earlier, mastering your life includes not only thought and action, but also diet and environment. The issue of nutrition and how important your food choices are in the function of your body, mind, and brain are covered later in the book. Diet is linked with environmental issues. Your food choices are the number-one way in which you interact with Earth. Your role in creating a healthful planet is in alignment with how healthy you can be.

> "You are a product of your environment. So choose the environment that will best develop you toward your objective. Analyze your life in terms of its environment. Are the things around you helping you toward success — or are they holding you back?"
> – W. Clement Stone

Purifying your life through getting rid of clutter, through self-sufficiency, through following a plant-based diet, through daily exercise, through clarifying and keeping focused on your list of goals and priorities, and through not buying into commercial nonsense will allow you to stay on the path of your intentions. It will keep your mind clear for what you need to learn and do to achieve the radiant health and more vibrant, successful life you intend to create.

Arrange your life in every way possible that will allow your intentions to be fulfilled.

> "Ya gotta be ready for the fastball."
> – Ted Williams

> "Somebody should tell us, right at the start of our lives, that we are dying. Then we might live life to the limit, every minute of every day."
> – Michael Landon

> "Do not wait for extraordinary circumstances to do good action; try to use ordinary situations."
> – Jean Paul Richter

> "The purpose of life is a life of purpose."
> – Robert Byrne

Intentional living is defining your path, focusing on it, and following it every day.

If you want your life to be reflective of the good things inside you, you must work to reveal those.

If you want good in your life, you must bring good into it and create the good.

If you want love, kindness, and gratitude in your life, you will be more likely to obtain these if you are a projector of love, kindness, and gratitude.

> "Kind words do not cost much. They never blister the tongue or lips. They make other people good-natured. They also produce their own image on men's souls, and a beautiful image it is."
> – Blaise Pascal

If you want good people in your life that will uplift you, remember that you are more likely to have them present if you uplift those around you.

If you want to stop living in denial and get your life in order, you have to continually face and figure out your situation, factor solutions, and always work to create a better reality.

If you want your life to be less cluttered, you have to unclutter it.

> "A man cannot be comfortable without his own approval."
> – Mark Twain

If you are tired of seeing through tired eyes and living in a stale life, you must revive the way you factor things and revitalize your life through more motivating conclusions and helpful actions. Key to this is cutting out foods that muffle your health. Instead, choose a plant-based diet that is alive with the vibrant nutrients of raw fruits and raw vegetables. Doing so will help you to exper-ience a more vibrant life.

> "If we wait for the moment when everything, absolutely everything is ready, we shall never begin."
> – Ivan Turgenev

If you want the spiritual presence in your life, you must bring it forth.

If you want a stronger spiritual consciousness, you must recognize that your spirit is already there, and that it is up to you to tune into it.

If you want to reveal your true talents and intellect, then you must live your truth, stimulate your intellect, and make your talents fully functional through your actions.

If you want satisfaction to dominate your life, then you must decide what would satisfy you and work every day to bring it about.

> "The best way out is always through."
> – Robert Frost

If you want to get through the unfavorable issues veiling you from living a favorable life, you must work through them.

> "For the things we have to learn before we can do them, we learn by doing them."
> – Aristotle

If you want to have mental power to change your life, you must exercise your power to bring about a strong determination in the same way you exercise your body to make it stronger.

The reservations to attend more favorable life events are always made, but you have to take the steps to arrive at the venue.

> "If you have a great ambition, take as big a step as possible in the direction of fulfilling it. The step may only be a tiny one, but trust that it may be the largest one possible for now."
> – Mildred McAfee

Decide today to live more intentionally. Envision your life the way you want it to be. Learn what you need to learn to bring about that life. Work to create that life by spending your time accomplishing the goals that will make that life happen. Dominate your thoughts with what it is you need to focus on to realize your ideals. And do not settle for anything less than wholly creating your life through intentional living.

> "Emotions reflect intentions. Therefore, awareness of emotions leads to awareness of intentions."
> – Gary Zukav

> "The great and glorious masterpiece of humanity is to know how to live with a purpose."
> – Michel Eyquem de Montaigne

> "Action is the foundational key to all success."
> – Pablo Picasso

Expecting and Experiencing

> "Most of us serve our ideals by fits and starts. The person who makes a success of living is the one who sees his goal steadily and aims for it unswervingly. That is dedication."
> – Cecil B. De Mille

Many people get caught up in expecting life to happen in a certain way that is in tune with conditions they wish to be exposed to. Unfortunately, what they may be doing is experiencing their life opposite from the way they wish it would be. And often they are caught up in not living anything resembling their ideal life because they are stalled in a pattern of what they have been experiencing while thinking the same thoughts that brought about the life they don't want. They may be living in a way that simply happened without much use of their intellect, talents, or skills. They may be living in a way that is more in tune with how they believe others are expecting them to live, which could be the direct opposite of what would be most satisfying to and healthful for them.

> "What we achieve inwardly will change outer reality."
> – Otto Rank

When I was nineteen, I was in less than an ideal life situation, and most of the people in my life were also far from living up to their potential. Many were damaged, damaging, and slathered with failure. One day I sat in my apartment having a conversation with a friend about how it seems that the difference between people who are happy and successful and those who are not happy and not successful is simply how they allow themselves to think. We spoke about how it seemed that if you simply change the way you think, you could change your life.

As years passed, my life changed and I lost touch with most of the people I knew when I was younger. Later I learned that one became a successful maker of surf boards, one became a movie star, some lead more traditional lives, some of them died, a couple were murdered, others went to prison, and I had no idea what happened to the rest.

Years later I was at a friend's home and her television was on. I don't watch television, which leaves me pretty much detached from a lot of what is featured there. But this caught my eye. Appearing on the screen was the friend with whom I once had a conversation about the topic of thinking. He was talking about how you can change your life by changing your mind, and he had written a book about awakening the giant within. Apparently he had forced dramatic changes to take place in his life, and was in a tremendously different situation from the one he was experiencing when I had briefly known him. He had also become a successful life coach.

> "Prosperity is a way of living and thinking, and not just money or things. Poverty is a way of living and thinking, and not just a lack of money or things."
> – Eric Butterworth

Do you want to succeed? Then stop conforming to what you think others may or may not think you should be. Stop trying to fulfill the expectations of others, and start experiencing what you expect your life to be.

Stop paying attention to whatever holds you back from having the life you want, especially people who don't believe in you.

Stop entertaining thoughts that bring about the same actions that create the same experiences that you don't like to have.

> "No one knows your capability as well as you do. No one knows how big you can dream and no one knows how far you can go. You, like water, can seek and reach your own level."
> – Lynne Cox

Some people say that they don't succeed because they have no support system of people who believe in them. To allow people to believe in you, you have to believe in yourself. To allow people to see that you are capable of accomplishing something, you have to accomplish it.

> "Poor is the man whose pleasures depend on the permission of another."
> – Madonna Ciccone

Don't get caught up in being a praise junkie. Accomplish your goals without expecting praise from anyone. The achievement is the reward, not the acknowledgment from others. Force your self to achieve.

> "Real integrity is doing the right thing, knowing that nobody's going to know whether you did it or not."
> – Oprah Winfrey

> "Let me listen to me, and not to them."
> – Gertrude Stein

> "Why are women immobile? Because so many feel they're waiting for someone to say, 'You're good, you're pretty, I give you permission.'"
> – Eve Ensler

Seeking the approval and validation of others is really a desire to get yourself to approve of you — to validate yourself. You validate yourself by accomplishing your goals, and you do that by wisely using your resources, intellect, talents, and passions with integrity, and not wasting them on nonsense.

> "I think you have to take charge of your own life and understand that you're either going to live somebody else's dream or live your own dream."
> – Wilma Mankiller

> "Stop looking outside yourself for your substantiation. Learn to love who you are."
> – Alan Arkin

> "When you take charge of your life, there is no longer need to ask permission of other people or society at large. When you ask

permission, you give someone veto power over your life."
– Albert F. Geoffrey

Have you never experienced success? Consider that experiencing success depends more on what you think and do than on anything or anyone else. Perhaps you have utilized your innate abilities most effecttively to keep you in the ghetto victim mentality and in being a pushover. It is up to you to change this.

Stop fantasizing about the life you want to lead. Start living the life you want. By continually and intentionally being involved in doing what you want to do, and not just thinking about it, or talking about it, you will build your confidence through accomplishments.

"Great things are not done by impulse, but by a series of small things brought together."
– Vincent Van Gogh

"We can usually tell the quality of our subconscious mind by looking at the quality of the life we are living. If we are not pleased with our life, we must look at the content of our mind to discover how we have been programming our existence to meet our belief structure."
– Dudley Evenson

Just as a riverbed is created by water constantly flowing over it, you can embellish your mind with thoughts that improve your life by constantly thinking about and acting on what improves your life. Your body can get accustomed to performing certain tasks as you keep doing them. This includes the practice of eating a healthful, plant-based diet; thinking and planning with the intention of improving your life; focusing on the things you need; forming a routine of exercising regularly; and by continually doing the things that need to be done to create a healthful life.

"The thing always happens that you really believe in; and the belief in a thing makes it happen."
– Frank Lloyd Wright

The practice of improving your life is just that, a practice, which results in achievement. As you bring your mind, body, and life to be more in tune with that which is most pleasing to you, the more you will recognize your potential, and the more you will achieve what you want. This can be accomplished just as the musician must continually practice to be able to play music the way they want it to sound.

"Yesterday is a canceled check; tomorrow is a promissory note; today is the only cash you have — so spend it wisely."
– Kay Lyons

Many people allow themselves to be easily and repeatedly distracted from accomplishing their daily goals. This can be so common in their daily life that it has become their practice to fail at meeting their most basic daily goals by using the excuse that other matters needed their attention. Some may say that things keep happening that are less than ideal than what they expected. If you relate to this scenario, realize that some of the less than ideal situations may be of your making, and many may occur because you allow them to occur. As you are presented with situations throughout your day that may be less than ideal, look toward ways of remaining calm and dealing with them in a way that will bring about benefits. Also, realize that you may benefit more by staying focused on and remaining active in attaining your daily goals than by taking care of whatever matter it is that may be tempting to sway you.

"I am more and more convinced that our happiness or our unhappiness depends far more on the way we meet the events of life than on the nature of those events themselves."
– Wilhelm von Humboldt

As an exercise in staying focused, take a piece of paper and write down a bunch of actions you can take to improve your life. Start each sentence with the words "I will make myself…" It is important that you write it rather than type it. This is because the act of writing tends to connect more clearly with the subconscious mind. This exercise can help work your thoughts out of a rut, motivate you to pinpoint and act on what it is you want to do, and provide a stream of thought that you can explore to better understand what it is you want and how you are going to go about getting it. Try this exercise now by opening your journal and writing at least several sentences that begin with the words, "I will make myself…"

"If you lose hope, somehow you lose the vitality that keeps life moving, you lose that courage to be, that quality that helps you go on in spite of it all. And so today I still have a dream."
– Martin Luther King, Jr.

Self-hate, Self-deceit, and Self-sabotage

Perhaps you have been living under the shadow of not feeling worthy of having your dreams come true. Now is the time to start feeling worthy. It is the time to make your dreams come true.

> "The worst tyrants are those which establish themselves in our own breasts."
> – William Ellery Channing

If you never have experienced success, consider that you might benefit from exploring the possibility that you are in a habit of having self-deceptive thoughts.

Self-deceptive thoughts often revolve around believing you are not capable. They may be about continually remembering negative and discouraging words others may have said to or about you.

> "Fundamentally the marksman aims at himself."
> – Eugen Herrigel

Self-deceptive thoughts may also be about thinking the discouraging words of others are about you.

Something to be considered when people say lousy things about you is that they may be revealing more about their own condition while aiming their comments toward you. You just happened to be the target at which they could toss their darting words of self-hate.

People often accuse others of what the accuser truly is. I know someone who is forever accusing others of spreading gossip, when he is truly the town gossip broadcast system. I once knew a woman who continually accused others of being liars, when she was quite skilled in lies and deception, including misleading the people who put trust in her. I once knew a woman who habitually accused others of being jealous, when she was very much a person driven by jealousy. I once knew a businessman who was continually suing people for dishonest business dealings, and he certainly was no example of honesty. This sort of behavior sometimes plays out in the media, such as the famous minister who always preached against homosexuality and drug use, but who was found to be leading a closeted life that involved hiring male prostitutes, taking drugs, and pressuring his subordinates into sexual situations. He was certainly filled with self-deception and self-hate, and projected it onto others. It is also likely that he had been around people who taught him to hate himself, pressing him into hiding his true sexual identity because he was so needlessly ashamed of it.

Self-deceptive thoughts often reflect your own ideas of how others are being judgmental of you. Self-deceptive thoughts can be agreements you have made with yourself to allow the negative comments of others to impact you in a negative way, thus enabling others to define you.

> "When a person drowns himself in negative-thinking he is committing an unspeakable crime against himself."
> – Maxwell Maltz

> "Anger and hardness is a shield, it masks other things."
> – Mickey Rourke

Self-deceptive thoughts are often of your own making, and can also be created by damaging, negative, neglectful, or otherwise unhealthful relationships. They consist of unfairly judging and unwisely limiting your self. They are about you agreeing to whatever it was that could be viewed as negative about you, and allowing the energy of that to alter your thoughts, decisions, actions, words, relationships, and life.

Self-deceptive thoughts fuel self-sabotage, doubt, low self-esteem, limiting beliefs, fear, awkwardness, insecurities, procrastination, damaging emotions, worry, junk diets, laziness, and failure.

> "Don't worry about the future. Or worry, but know that worrying is as effective as trying to solve an algebra equation by chewing bubble gum."
> – Mary Schmich

> "The most exhausting thing in life is being insecure."
> – Anne Morrow Lindbergh

Self-deceptive thoughts perpetuate guilt, shame, inadequacy, insecurity, and the feelings, emotions, and activities associated with self-hate.

Self-hate spurs you to dwell in ignorance. When dealing in self-hate you create and feed your fear, doubts, and worries, and/or you agree to accept the fear, doubts, and worries others have projected onto you. In the energy of self-hate, you wallow in these creations and drop below your abilities while accomplishing little of your potential. While dwelling in self-hate, you go along with anything that works against you while permitting low-quality communication and damaging relationships to continue.

> "Our doubts are traitors, and make us lose the good we oft might win by fearing the attempt."
> – William Shakespeare

If you are hosting self-deceptive thoughts, self-hate, self-sabotage, and low self-esteem, it is likely that you have been around damaging and damaged people who are unhealthful and who are hosting the very same issues. One thing these people are very good at is abundantly spreading around their unhelpful energies. They are really good at wasting their time, and the time of others who participate in their club of failure that is forever accepting new members.

Continually receiving negative messages from damaging people lowers your self-esteem and creates a belief that you are incapable of attaining your goals. It may stop you from setting goals, and may instill a sense that you are and always will be a failure, which is the energy of defeat. Refuse to eat from that buffet.

> "You must fight off a 'bad luck' way of thinking as if you were dealing with an invasion of hostile forces — for that is precisely what you are dealing with."
> – Maxwell Maltz

Your thoughts help create your body chemistry. By thinking you are going to fail makes you more likely to fail, and creates a body chemistry of failure. On the other hand, thinking of yourself as succeeding is more likely to bring about that experience. In other words, thoughts are self-achieving and trigger the body to act in relation to the thoughts.

Through low-quality thoughts, foods, and actions, you are creating and are in perfect alignment with the energy of failure.

By choosing to consume high-quality foods, getting daily exercise, and guiding your actions with goal-oriented thinking in accordance with a list of priorities, you are creating a body chemistry aligned with health and success.

> "It is well known that panic, despair, depression, hate, rage, exasperation, frustration all produce negative biochemical changes in the body."
> – Norman Cousins

To fracture a pattern of self-defeat and to get into a more healthful energy pattern, continually work toward thinking in a way that is more in keeping with a successful frame of mind. Don't allow yourself, or others, to fill your mind with negativity, hate, anger, fear, or other dramatic emotions associated with stress, worry, deception, slander, illness, and defeat. Exercise every day, preferably in the morning. Follow a plant-based diet rich in unheated fruits and vegetables; one that does not contain fried oil, sodas or colas, corn syrup or other processed sugars, processed salts, MSG (monosodium glutamate), bleached grains, or synthetic food chemicals. Set goals, read through them every morning, and work at accomplishing them from the start of every day.

Refuse to allow yourself to fall into the trap of making excuses that perpetuate a life of inconsistent commitments and failure.

> "Excuses are the nails used to build a house of failure."
> – Don Wilder

Often people who are timid, shy, and full of excuses have been subjectted to forms of neglect and abuse that result in low self-esteem, feelings of inadequacy, or full-fledged self-hate. Through the actions and words of others they have learned to hate themselves and/or feel that they are unworthy, dismissable, unimportant, and neglectable. If this defines you, it is time to get past the walls constructed by the mistreatment you have been subjected to. Do so without placing blame on others, and without dwelling on former relationships, which would keep you focused in the past. Instead, do so with an eye toward a better today and a more promising future, which you can intentionally create by staying in the present and focused on your intentions and goals. Do so while no longer allowing yourself to be guided by the negative words and actions of others.

Stop catering to the depths of self-hate that are filled with a lack of belief in your intellect and talents.

Do not listen to discouragement. Instead, treat discouragement like water and you are the buoy. Water can't sink a buoy, unless there is a leak. Positive thoughts, words, and intentional, goal-oriented actions combined with a healthful diet and daily exercise are what keep you up.

Stop hosting self-deceptive and self-hating thoughts. Instead of harboring negative thoughts, abhor them. Stop slandering and undermining yourself. Stop conforming to the limits you have placed on your life. Stop giving in to, rooting in to, and feeding off any unhealthful energy, thoughts, words, and actions of others — including in the past and/or present.

If you have been victimized, do not revictimize yourself by relishing in the unfortunate, by continually thinking about how you were victimized, by forever talking about how you were victimized, or by not gathering yourself up and moving on to some better way outside the path of your victimization.

Many, many people get caught up in continually thinking about who has betrayed them, and about how they have been betrayed. They constantly tell people about how they were betrayed. By doing so, they are dwelling in the energy of the betrayal — instead of learning, regrouping, and moving on.

> "We are the hurdles we leap to be ourselves."
> – Michael McClure

Most people need not even bother examining the way others may have betrayed them, because, truth be told, they themselves, not others, are likely to be the betrayers. They betray themselves by not living up to their intellect and talents; by wasting their time on frivolity; by practically discarding their talent and resources; by consuming garbage foods; by falling into laziness and not exercising; by diminishing themselves with their thoughts and conduct; and by staggering around in the low-quality situation they have settled into. Because of their actions, their life has aged into a fine patina of self-denial and wretched waste.

> "If we don't change the direction we're going, we're likely to end up where we're headed."
> – Chinese proverb

As I mention earlier, just as people are more likely to fail because they don't think they can succeed, those who believe they can succeed are more likely to do so. Either of these scenarios is simply a matter of which frame of mind a person chooses to hold, and what actions they take to manifest it.

> "If you doubt you can accomplish something, then you can't accomplish it. You have to have confidence in your ability, and then be tough enough to follow through."
> – Rosalynn Carter

You can either choose to believe you are going to fail, or you can choose to believe that you are going to succeed. Of course outside issues influence your frame of mind and surroundings. But you can also play a large role in both choosing and creating your surroundings, as well as in choosing how your surroundings affect you.

> "This above all, to refuse to be a victim. Unless I can do that I can do nothing."
> – Margaret Atwood

Do not get caught up in the degradation of negativity. Peel away the stifling feelings of anger, anxiety, hatred, loathing, jealousy, low self-esteem, fear, unworthiness, blame, and victimization.

Stop inflicting your life with limiting thoughts, absurdly critical comments, slander, stagnant energy, low-quality foods, and wasteful activities.

Stop talking yourself out of living your life.

> "Suffering can be our greatest asset. If we have the capacity to learn from our suffering we have the capacity to improve our lives, improve our families, and improve our communities."
> – Alexander McKinnon

Believe that you are unique, special, worthy, able, loveable, and have talents, skills, and craft that you can nurture. Realize this and start living your days knowing that you are a beautiful being capable of amazing things.

> "You can achieve anything you want in life if you have the courage to dream it, the intelligence to make a realistic plan, and the will to see that plan through to the end."
> – Sidney A. Friedman

Some people are so caught up in negative-thinking that they think the people around them are working against them. Think about the outcome these people would have if the opposite were true, that the people around them are hoping that the person becomes successful, healthy, and happy, and that loving relationships are strongly present in the person's life.

> "I am a kind of paranoiac in reverse. I suspect people of plotting to make me happy."
> – J. D. Salinger

Avoid feeling as if things and people are working against you, that you will not experience joy, or that your life will never improve.

> "If you seek love, appreciation, and affection, then learn to give love, appreciation, and affection."
> – Deepak Chopra

Rather than believe that others are thinking negatively about you, believe instead that they are working to do good to and wishing good for you. In doing so you will be doing the same for you.

> "If God be for us, who can be against us?"
> – Romans 8:31

There is absolutely not one truly healthy person who wants bad things for you. Instead, the enlightened people in life are wishing you health, kindness, and love. Be one of them – for you, and for others.

Stop living your life worrying about what other people think of you. Live your life knowing that what matters more is what you will think about yourself. What matters is what you do with the attributes of your character and the resources in your surroundings.

Stop resigning yourself to self-hate, which is overwhelming yourself with negativity. No longer slander yourself.

Your happiness depends on you, and not on others. You are capable of performing the tasks that need to be done to form your life into what you want it to be. And you don't need an authority figure to give you permission to do so.

> "Luck is what you have left over after you give 100 percent."
> – Langston Coleman

Do not get caught up in considering if you are lucky or unlucky. That is feeding into the self-deceptive thoughts of being worthy or unworthy.

We are all being given and are worthy of receiving amazing blessings. Choose to accept them.

You are an owner of intellect, a person of talent, and are worthy of experiencing happiness, health, and love. With integrity, think, plan, speak, and act in ways that reveal this honor.

> "Only when we are no longer afraid do we begin to live in every experience, painful or joyous, to live in gratitude for every moment, to live abundantly."
> – Dorothy Thompson

> "The difference between great people and everyone else is that great people create their lives actively, while everyone else is created by their lives, passively waiting to see where life takes them next. The difference between the two is the difference between living

fully and just existing."
– Michael E. Gerber

The Competition Myth

"You start getting into trouble in life when you start comparing and contrasting your life to anyone else's. You don't win when you do that."
– Jeremy Pivin

"We are raised on comparison; our education is based on it; so is our culture. So we struggle to be someone other than who we are."
– Jiddu Krishnamurti

Many people continually compare and judge themselves in relation to the next person. Often this is done believing in the concept that those who appear to have more material and monetary possessions have their lives together.

"The world I am trying to understand is one in which men think they want one thing and then upon getting it, find out to their dismay that they don't want it nearly as much as they thought or don't want it at all and that something else, of which they were hardly aware, is what they really want."
– Albert Hirschman

Some people seem to think that the more expensive things they accumulate and the more money they have, the better their life will be. Those of us who have been around wealthy people, as well as around those who have few possessions, know that money and material things do not hold an absolute promise of creating happiness, health, or love. Some of the wealthiest people I have known have been the most unhappy and lonely. Some of the poorest people I have known have been the most happy and content.

"I fear the popular notion of success stands in direct opposition in all points to the real and wholesome success. One adores public opinion, the other, private opinion; one, fame, the other, desert;

one, feats, the other, humility; one, lucre, the other, love."
– Ralph Waldo Emerson

"No man is more cheated than the selfish man."
– Henry Ward Beecher

"Greed is a bottomless pit which exhausts the person in an endless effort to satisfy the need without ever reaching satisfaction."
– Erich Fromm

There are many examples of those who basically hoard wealth, give little, and live selfish lives. Some are driven by unresolved issues relating to loneliness and the confusion about their existence. They may be acting to fill an empty void that never seems to be filled no matter what they do, where they go, how many things they purchase, or how successful they seem to be with their financial portfolios. When they experience empty feelings, they try to fill them by purchasing things — cars, homes, furniture, clothes, gadgets, and other stuff. They may try surrounding themselves with pretty people, or people they consider to be hip, which is a sure way to fill a life with fair-weather friends who vanish as soon as strength of character is needed. They may do so with the false belief that they think they need, or that they can't live without these things. They may be working to make their life resemble the so-called perfect lives they see in TV commercials and magazine advertising. In so doing they surround themselves with a lot of commercialized and mass-produced stuff. But it ends up simply being more stuff. Just as soon as they sell some of it, or throw it away, they are on to buying more stuff that they think will make their lives better. They may travel, visit places, and see things. And in the quiet times they talk about how they are lonely, bored, not happy, and feel the need for something, but they don't know what it is. They go through relationships like they do clothing. Just as soon as they think someone is the right fit, they start to look for the flaws while exaggerating what they see as the reasons they shouldn't be with the person. They can't communicate healthfully. Any problem they may have is blamed on another person. Through all of this it is likely that they are not accessing their intellect, talent, skills, truth, or love.

"One of the main reasons wealth makes people unhappy is that it gives them too much control over what they experience. They try to translate their own fantasies into reality instead of tasting what reality itself has to offer."
– Philip Slater

Even when people turn to self-help books they may be presented with the message that success in life is rewarded with and validated by ownership of material possessions, by the presence of pretty people, and by vast quantities of money. For instance, one author of positive-thinking books often mentions his resort-like mansion, as if that possession validates his belief that he is a success. I see his focus on wealth as a failure in that he appears to be idealizing an environmentally unsustainable life and is promoting that lifestyle as the ideal. Instead of being part of the solution, he has engaged in being part of the problem. I wonder if he feels as if his housekeeper, landskeeper, and other servants are failures in life because they don't own mansions. Maybe he pays well.

> "No richness is innocent. Richness around the world is the result of other people's poverty."
> – Eduardo Galeano

It seems that a lot of people who are successful at hoarding wealth do just that, become very good at it, and display it in extravagance. And where does it get them? There are people who have several mansions on various parts of the planet, and they spend their time shuffling between their homes. It is as if they are not content with anything, and they try to create the perfect resort homes to escape to when they want to escape from their other resort home. When they get more money they also get more stuff that accumulates to the point that they either have to hire someone to help get rid of it for them, or they spend more money to place it in storage units. I know of one person who owns several homes, and I have heard this person complain of being bored. Ruling over all of those possessions apparently has brought no meaning, and may have created a bigger quagmire.

> "Once you start to see through the myth of status, possessions, and unlimited consumption as a path to happiness, you'll find that you have all kinds of freedom and time. It's like a deal you can make with the universe: I'll give up greed for freedom. Then you can start putting your time to good use."
> – David Edwards

> "The poor man is not he who is without a cent, but he who is without a dream."
> – Harry Kemp

> "I have never been a millionaire. But I have enjoyed a crackling fire, a glorious sunset, a walk with a friend, and a hug from a child.

There are plenty of life's tiny delights for all of us."
– Jack Anthony

I have been around some of the wealthiest of the wealthy, and one thing that is noticeable is that they aren't a whole lot different from anyone else. They sleep, they eat, they have to take care of their basic needs, they tie their shoes, and, probably most of all, they want to be loved. They just happen to be surrounded by stuff that is more expensive than stuff that other people are surrounded by.

"Happiness resides not in possessions, and not in gold, happiness dwells in the soul."
– Democritus

"If there is to be any peace it will come through being, not having."
– Henry Miller

Among all the people I have been around, no matter if they are rich or poor, I have noticed that the people who have connected strongly with their talents are the happier ones, and more so if they have healthful relationships, follow a plant-based diet, and get regular exercise.

"Let your capital be simplicity and contentment."
– Henry David Thoreau

Avoid getting caught up in the symbols of wealth, symbols of success, and symbols of happiness. Just because the symbol exists does not mean that what it represents exists. Many people do get caught up in believing that if they surround themselves with certain things representative of wealth, success, and happiness, they are then truly wealthy, successful, and happy. That is one sure way to get into financial debt, such as by using credit cards to purchase things.

"True wealth is what you are, not what you have."
– Anonymous

Symbols don't always correlate with reality. This is especially true in a society reliant on loans and credit cards, and in which people have placed such financial burdens on themselves that they are working simply to maintain a life filled with mythological symbolisms of satisfaction in the form of possessions. They are using credit cards and bank loans to mask their true situation, which is that of someone not able to truly afford what they have fooled themselves into purchasing. What they may be most successful at is in creating a façade and in pretending that it is okay to have huge financial burdens to maintain an image of wealth and fake success. Not that they are able to enjoy their faux success so much, because they are too busy working to pay the bills and the lenders.

As I am writing this, the news is filled with stories of people who have overextended themselves, who are losing their homes and belongings, and who are having to face homelessness, unemployment, hunger, and destitution.

> "Why are you so enchanted with this world when a gold mine lies within you? Open your eyes and come. Return to the root of the root of your own soul."
>
> – Rumi

According to the United Nations, in 2007 the average worldwide income was under $8,000. That means approximately 3.6 billion people, or 60 percent of the global population, were living on less than $520 per year. On the other end of the spectrum are people who earn hundreds of millions of dollars per year. This includes those company leaders that have been widely criticized for accepting pay and bonuses that amount to several hundred times more than what is earned by the lowest paid workers in the company. It is the poorest of the poor who are working to maintain the lifestyles of the wealthy.

> "We need 'wake up economics,' where people value each other rather than the accumulation of wealth, power, and prestige."
>
> – Anna and Christine Rowinski

Financial wealth does not equal happiness or health. If it did, the newspapers wouldn't be filled with wealthy people experiencing torrential downpours of life problems, emotional breakdowns, and relationship meltdowns.

If you are constantly engaged in putting on the big façade that your life is royal when it is a big pit of debt, question why you are placing so much focus on appearance.

> "If you win, but don't help somebody when you should have, what kind of win is that?"
>
> – Bjoernar Hakensmoen

If you are a person with a lot of money, and you feel yourself getting too proud, go spend time volunteering for homeless groups, for abused women's shelters, for organizations helping teenage runaways, and for charities that work with those who are otherwise destitute. Help with inner-city reforestation and culinary gardening projects, with soup kitchens, with youth groups, and with animal shelters. Consider working with FoodNotBombs.net, which prepares and serves vegetarian meals to the homeless, poor, or anyone who is hungry. Pay for a student's tuition, books, food, clothing, and housing. Volunteer and/or donate money to groups working to protect the environment, such as The Natural Resources Defense Council, Earth Island Institute, EarthFirst, the Green World Campaign, or an organization that restores forests. And otherwise, be active in being a part of the solution to an ailing world.

> "Once the game is over, the king and the pawn go back into the same box."
> – Italian proverb

> "The essence of philosophy is that a man should so live that his happiness shall depend as little as possible on external things."
> – Epictetus

Competition for possessions and wealth, and the hoarding of these to ensure happiness and security is a falsehood.

While money can bring certain privileges and freedoms, it does not guarantee happiness, health, friendship, or love. Having money means only that you can buy stuff. For the wise, it means they can support organizations focused on improving the condition of wildlife, the environment, and Earth.

If you are one who has been caught up in hoarding money, or focusing on that as a goal, release the feeling that you need to judge yourself as successful or not successful based on money.

> "Enjoy the journey, enjoy every moment, and quit worrying about winning and losing."
> – Matt Biondi

> "There are two ways to get enough: one is to continue to accumulate more and more. The other is to desire less."
> – G. K. Chesterton

Free yourself of the false notion of competition.

Realize that there is no competition. You are only working to improve yourself, regardless of what others are doing.

> "I do not try to dance better than anyone else. I only try to dance better than myself."
> – Mikhail Baryshnikov

Stop comparing yourself to other people. It is a waste of your talents, intellect, time, energy, and resources. The competition mindset will distract your mind from what you need to focus on, and will drag you down below any fault you could possibly find in others. Comparing yourself to others is degrading to your spirit, and to others, and it weakens you.

> "Always dream and shoot higher than you know you can do. Don't bother just to be better than your contemporaries or predecessors. Try to be better than yourself."
> – William Faulkner

> "Each of us is meant to have a character all our own, to be what no other can exactly be, and do what no other can exactly do."
> – William Ellery Channing

> "Often people attempt to live their lives backwards: they try to have more things, or more money, in order to do more of what they want so they will be happier. The way it actually works is the reverse. You must first be who you really are, then do what you need to do, in order to have what you want."
> – Margaret Young

By working to develop your intellect, talents, and abilities, as well as your confidence, health, and level of standards, without feeling as if you need to keep up with anyone else, or compare yourself to anyone, you will be living your life.

> "We must break away from the widespread belief that bigger, faster, newer, and more is always better. We need to reconsider what constitutes 'wealth.'"
> – Greg Seaman

Set the pace for improving your situation and you may be surprised how you can help inspire others to do the same. Replace the false sense of competition with the real sense of inspiration and you will begin to feel a more healthful energy complementing your positive thoughts and actions.

> "No matter how much money you have, you can lose it."
> – Michael J. Fox

The world is filled with people who live their lives by the standards of other peoples' principles. And the world is filled with people caught up in paying attention to the way other people live – including fictional characters that appear in movies and TV shows.

Just as you don't have any competitors, you also don't have any enemies. There may be people that you don't care to be around, those who you would be better off avoiding, and some who you would be better off avoiding at all cost, but you don't need to think of people as enemies or competitors.

> "Your opponent, in the end, is never really the player on the other side of the net, or the swimmer in the next lane, or the team on the other side of the field, or even the bar you must high-jump. Your opponent is yourself, your negative internal voices, your level of determination."
> – Grace Lichtenstein

When you relieve yourself of the feeling that you are not competing with others, you will begin to understand the concept that there is no competition. All you are doing is working to improve your life regardless of what others are doing. Disconnecting from the competitive energy is liberating and empowering to your spirit.

> "A common conception of security is an achievement or possession on the physical plane. But an abiding sense of security can never come from possession or from achievement. Security comes only when we have established our constant oneness with our soul."
> – Sri Chinmoy

> "One characteristic of winners is they always look upon themselves as a do-it-yourself project."
> – Denis Waitley

> "Don't believe that winning is really everything. It's more important to stand for something. If you don't stand for something,

what do you win?"
– Lane Kirkland

"Success is the progressive realization of a worthy ideal."
– Earl Nightengale

"Since you are like no other being ever created since the beginning of time, you are incomparable."
– Brenda Ueland

Talent

"If you have a talent, use it in every which way possible. Don't hoard it. Don't dole it out like a miser. Spend it lavishly, like a millionaire intent on going broke."
– Brenda Francis

Imagine if there were a Black child from an extremely poor family living in a society largely prejudiced against dark-skinned people. Imagine if this Black boy had a most unfortunate thing happen to him, such as losing his sight at an early age. Imagine that instead of working through that problem, and putting it in its place, he instead spent his life in the depths of self-pity. Imagine if he never discovered and developed his talents. Imagine that if instead of trying to make his life work, he stayed in his parents' home, never went anywhere, and did nothing with his time because he was too busy dwelling in self-pity. Imagine if his parents then died while he was still a young boy and he ended up living on the streets doing nothing with his time, and only took the smallest bit of effort to get by in his blind and self-pitiful state. Furthering his difficulties, he allowed himself to be beaten down by the prejudices held by others who didn't like dark-skinned people and who didn't feel comfortable around blind people. Imagine if this boy grew into a man and never discovered what he could have become if he had discovered and used his talents.

"Things turn out best for the people who make the best of the way things turn out."
– Art Linkletter

Imagine a different set of life situations for that blind Black boy from the poor home. In this situation he had still lost both his sight and his parents at a young age. He also lived in a time when laws and people worked strongly against Black Americans. But this time the boy did not dwell in self-pity. Imagine that he went on to develop his talents, and despite some other life difficulties — including some of his own making — he broke through the obstacles that seemed to be chasing after him. Imagine that he used his intellect, talents, and abilities to become a very talented, world-famous musician who happened to be named Ray Charles.

> "Great talents, by the rust of disuse grow lethargic and shrink from what they were."
> – Ovid

Consider that you may have given up on some of the very best graces with which you have been blessed. Maybe you have buried what may be your most beneficial qualities beneath a pile of self-pity, repression, or denial. Perhaps your thinking has been altered to the point that there is a blackout of power in regions of your intellect in which your elegance dwells. You may have made the mistake of denying your abilities for so long that you forgot what they are. Maybe you are aware of this, and maybe you blame situations and other people. But who is it that really made the agreement to avoid nurturing your talents, craft, skill, and abilities? Is it you who continues to do so?

> "If you have made mistakes, even serious ones, there is always another chance for you. What we call failure is not the falling down, but the staying down."
> – Mary Pickford

Understand that the life of Ray Charles turned out to be so incredible because he used the power of his mind to make it that way. When he fell down, he got back up. He worked the patterns in his mind into patterns of sound that continue to entertain and inspire the people all over the planet who listen to his music.

> "I try to tell the young kids there are two cardinal rules: You should approach creativity with humility and have your success with grace. It's a gift from God. You don't deserve it. You are a vehicle of a higher power. Don't abuse it."
> – Quincy Jones

The successes experienced by people who have physical limitations is inspirational. They reveal that determination and persistence can pay off, that a healthy attitude is empowering, and that working to attain goals is dignified.

> "The only thing worse than being blind is having sight but no vision."
> – Helen Keller

Helen Keller is often given as an example of someone who overcame seemingly impossible odds to live an amazing life. When she was nineteen months old Keller became ill with what was possibly meningitis or scarlet fever. The illness left her both blind and deaf. She became an angry, frustrated child. Keller originally learned a way to communicate by feeling the hands of an incredible six-year-old girl named Martha Washington, who was the Keller family cook's daughter. It wasn't until Keller was nearly seven years old that she began to recognize the hand movements of her caretaker, Anne Sullivan, as being the alphabet she could use to spell out any number of words. By first learning to communicate by spelling out words with her hands, and feeling the hands of those spelling out words to her, Keller went on to learn Braille in several languages. By age 24 Keller had earned a Bachelor of Arts degree from Radcliff College. With various companions, Keller traveled the world and became a famous author and speaker who spoke out against war, and campaigned for women's rights and other humanitarian causes.

> "Just because a man lacks the use of his eyes doesn't mean he lacks vision."
> – Stevie Wonder

There is a long list of physically challenged people who have made great successes of their lives. Interestingly, an even longer list can be made of able-bodied people who have given into failure and defeat. There also are lots of people who have accomplished amazing things that many thought would be impossible. This reveals that many people are only limited with what they can accomplish by the limits they place on themselves through their beliefs.

> "Do not let what you cannot do interfere with what you can do."
> – John Wooden

In the lives of people throughout history, and in present-day people who have become greatly successful, it is often easy to recognize a pattern of persistence in action, and a sustained focus on goals. They had faith that they could accomplish their goals, then they demonstrated this faith through action that utilized their intellect. They didn't simply sit around talking and thinking about what they wanted to do, they went out and did it. Their concentration may have been broken on occasion, but they continued working on their goals and eventually experienced achievement.

> "The separation of talent and skill is one of the greatest misunderstood concepts for people who are trying to excel — for people who have dreams and that want to do things. Talents you have naturally. Skill is only developed by hours and hours and hours of beating on your craft."
>
> – Will Smith

Know that you can attain the rightful things in life that you want to attain. Go about your days knowing that you are a unique individual capable of using your talents, intellect, instinct, knowledge, power, faith, and energy to create a life that is right for you.

> "Tension is who you think you should be. Relaxation is who you are."
>
> – Chinese proverb

Know that you do not have to compete with anyone. You are a unique person with no need of comparing yourself to anyone but yourself, and that you are capable of attaining that which is right for you and nobody else.

> "Having talent is like having blue eyes. You don't admire a man for the color of his eyes. I admire a man for what he does with his talent."
>
> – Anthony Quinn

> "There is a fountain of youth: it is your mind, your talents, the creativity you bring to your life and the lives of people you love. When you learn to tap this source, you will truly have defeated age."
>
> – Sophia Loren

> "There is a vitality, a life force, an energy, a quickening that is translated through you into action, and because there is only one of

you in all of time, this expression is unique. And if you block it, it will never exist through any other medium and it will be lost. The world will not have it. It is not your business to determine how good it is nor how valuable nor how it compares with other expressions. It is your business to keep it yours clearly and directly, to keep the channel open."

– Martha Graham

"The real tragedy of life is not in being limited to one talent, but in the failure to use that one talent."

– Edgar W. Work

"You are the only person on earth who can use your ability."

– Zig Ziglar

"We can't take any credit for our talents. It's how we use them that counts."

– Madeleine L'Engle

"The real power behind whatever success I have now was something I found within myself — something that's in all of us, I think, a little piece of God just waiting to be discovered."

– Tina Turner

School Days

"A young child is, indeed, a true scientist, just one big question mark. What? Why? How? I never cease to marvel at the recurring miracle of growth, to be fascinated by the mystery and wonder of this brave enthusiasm."

– Victoria Wagner

"I have never let my schooling interfere with my education."

– Mark Twain

"The only thing that interferes with my learning is my education."

– Albert Einstein

When speaking with any group of people about their school days it becomes quite obvious that there is a wide variety of educational experiences. Some people had amazing teachers and excelled in every area they naturally tuned into. Some received better educations at public schools than some students received in what were considered to be the better, private schools.

Another thing that becomes obvious when speaking with people about their childhood education is that attitude and circumstances have much to do with what people learn, how they learn it, and what they do with it.

> "Education is too important to be left solely to the educators."
> – Francis Keppel

> "A teacher affects eternity; he can never tell where his influence stops."
> – Henry B. Adams

> "We are always too busy for our children; we never give them the time or interest they deserve. We lavish gifts upon them; but the most precious gift — our personal association, which means so much to them — we give grudgingly."
> – Mark Twain

> "Your children need your presence more than your presents."
> – Jesse Jackson

Some people grew up in what appeared to be so-called ideal neighborhoods where everything appeared to be proper and in its place, but where certain children were not in good situations because of various issues within their community, within their families, or within their schools. Their situations may not have been conducive to a healthful place for children to study, to learn, or to live. Many opportunities that could have been present for them were shut off in ways that may have had to do with their parents' choices; their school administrator's or teacher's choices; or the children may simply have been caught up in wasting much of their time; or they were not in a household with attentive parents or parent figures that would have nurtured a better learning environment.

> "You may have tangible wealth untold; Caskets of jewels and coffers of gold. Richer than I you can never be — I had a mother

who read to me."

– Strickland Gillilan

Other people may have grown up in households that were in the most undesirable neighborhoods, yet they may have been able to obtain an education far better than children living in the better neighborhoods with what appeared to be high-quality school systems. The children who lived in the worst parts of town may have had attentive parents or parent figures; teachers who cared; nurturing mentors; special school programs; healthful food that provided for high brain function; and probably most important of all, an attitude and curious mind that was open to learning and study. Even children who may have been in terrible neighborhoods and problematic households sometimes exceed far beyond what would be expected from a person in their situation.

"The mother's heart is the child's schoolroom."

– Henry Ward Beecher

It is unfortunate that people anywhere would allow a child to be living in a situation where they are endangered by, are abused by, or are otherwise treated badly by adults. Children growing up in households where abuse and/or neglect are present typically are not able to learn on a level equal to their age.

Stress, lack of sleep, and bad nutrition are three issues that directly impact the way the brain grows and functions. Continual stress and poverty have been found to hinder brain cell growth, and to impact thought and memory processes.

Children that are in terrible situations, including those related to bad diet, abuse, financial insecurity, feelings of helplessness, constant drama, chronic worry, and/or the continual presence of fear, can experience a sort of learning paralysis. Instead of being attentive, their minds may be so disturbed by their predicament that their attention level has broken down, impeding their ability to learn and progress. They may be hyperactive, which can be related strongly to the continual consumption of unhealthful food and lack of structure and meaning, or they may be so overwhelmed with their problems that they simply spend much of their time daydreaming, mentally escaping from their situations.

"It is easier to build strong children than to repair broken men."

– Frederick Douglass

If you grew up in a terrible situation and are troubled, do not give up on yourself or sacrifice your future to the combination of low-quality diet, thought, communication, or behavior. Know that you can use your body's amazing ability to heal and that you can transform into a much more healthful being. The depths of despair, anguish, sadness, and ruin you may have experienced are only examples of how far your life can advance in the other direction when you continually work to make the healing process take place in your life.

If you lacked the presence of responsible adults to nurture and foster your best qualities, recognize that you can become the responsible adult in your life who will bring out everything wonderful within you while maintaining a diet and schedule in which you can thrive.

Because the brain wires itself in accordance with our experiences, those who grow up under the constant threat of fear may have an abundance of neural growth in the amygdala region of the brain, which is the area that deals with anger and fear.

When those who have grown up in an extremely unhealthful household are exposed to healthful situations free of the presence of fear and danger, they can take awhile to begin to function more healthfully because the brain needs to learn how to deal with a new set of situations.

Low-quality nutrition and bad treatment are known to affect a person's voice quality, breathing, speech, eye movement, mannerisms, posture, sleep, and concentration. When low-quality nutrition is combined with stress and fear, which can trigger the brain to release the natural body chemicals, adrenaline and cortisol, which trigger defensive behavior, a child is not in a state of mind that is conducive to concentration, learning, or healthful growth.

> "Concentration is the secret of strength."
> – Ralph Waldo Emerson

If you grew up in a terrible situation, it is likely that your brain didn't have the opportunity to grow and function in the most healthful ways. Your ability to concentrate may not have been given an ability to blossom as you were too busy dealing with defending yourself, strategizing your safety, and worrying about your situation. Sleep deprivation also could have been a factor in your ability to function healthfully.

If you grew up in an unfortunate situation, it is likely that you did not have access to foods that provided the nutrients your brain needed for the most healthful growth. Unfortunately, and more commonly, even in households where money is abundant, children are often eating low-quality foods rich in processed sugars and salts, in bleached grains, in saturated fats, trans fats, fried fats, and in MSG (monosodium glutamate), synthetic chemical dyes, flavors, scents, and preservatives.

"Behaviors and thoughts that relate to hope, love, and happiness can change the brain — just as fear, stress, and anxiety can change it."
– Eric Kanel

Fortunately, the human brain can change with a change in diet, activities, and surroundings, and it can heal from damage and neglect. Through setting of goals, daily study, use of intellect, practicing of talents, regular exercise, healthful foods, and nurturing social interaction, the abilities in attention, memory, and sequencing can be improved, and people can reconfigure how to deal with life in a healthful environment in a way that advances their ability to prosper and experience satisfaction.

"Healing is not a matter of technique or mechanism; it is a work of spirit."
– Rachel Naomi Remen

All cells within the body continually work to eliminate waste products and toxins while taking in the better-quality nutrients they are exposed to while releasing lower-quality substances.

If you grew up eating the lowest-quality of food, your brain is in need of quality nutrients.

When you change your diet to one that is more healthful, and stick with it, you will begin to feel clarity of thought that you had not experienced. This is a sign that your brain has begun to heal and function at a higher level. You will likely also notice a drive to learn, to be more active, and to participate in activities where your talent and intellect can flourish, and where the graces of your spirit become more present and alive.

"And the day came when the risk to remain tight in a bud was more painful then the risk it took to blossom."
– Anais Nin

The brain works and grows in tune with what it is you are doing, hearing, saying, seeing, feeling, and experiencing. When you become involved in activities, your brain functions in tune with what you are doing. The more certain parts of the brain are used, the more neurons will wire into and function in those parts.

"We don't challenge kids in schools. We don't challenge them to think; we don't challenge them to create. We challenge them to get good enough grades to get into a good enough college."
– Bob Compton

Many of us were not intellectually challenged when we were young. What we were presented with may have bored us and set us in a pattern of being accustomed to the common and mundane. This may have been because it was not of our interest, or we existed in a situation that prevented us from being open to our interest. Peer pressure, low-quality nutrition, family drama, bad treatment, lack of nurturing, and lots of other aspects of our childhood may have interfered with our attitude and ability to learn what would have been most beneficial for us.

"We worry about what a child will become tomorrow, yet we forget that he is someone today."
– Stacia Tauscher

"That is the difference between good teachers and great teachers: good teachers make the best of a pupil's means; great teachers foresee a pupil's ends."
– Maria Callas

Some of us may have had teachers who were not at a level most helpful to our capabilities and talents. Some of us may have also been in school situations where resources were not available, or where, for any number of reasons, certain concepts that would have provided intellectual stimulation and that would have been most beneficial to us were not presented. We may have detected that what was being taught wasn't exactly the truth. This may ring true when common history books and their mythological and idealistically whitewashed hero aspects are taken into consideration. In certain ways, we may have functioned at a level that was above our age group while we were constantly presented with information that was below our level of learning.

"It is a miracle that curiosity survives formal education."
– Albert Einstein

"If I ran a school, I'd give the average grade to the ones who gave me all the right answers, for being good parrots. I'd give the top grades to those who made a lot of mistakes and told me about them, and then told me what they learned from them."
– Richard Buckminster Fuller

"Knowledge has to be improved, challenged, and increased constantly, or it vanishes."
– Peter F. Drucker

Many people grew up being taught at only a certain level of education that was based on what the typical person needed to know to function in that society. Many school systems are not funded sufficiently to allow for students to be nurtured in ways that would be most beneficial to their talents and intellect. Some school administrators and teachers may think that there is no use trying to excel in educating children because the children are most likely to follow their parents' footsteps, living lives far below their potential. Some teachers may even discourage students from learning. They may have done it purposefully and directly, or the teachers may not have known that they were stifling their students.

"We are each so much more than what some reduce to measuring."
– Karen Kaiser Clark

Some ways of teaching don't connect with students, don't speak to them, and have little or nothing to do with the reality in which the students are living. Some ways of teaching tell a child what to learn based on a certain ideal learning situation that often does not exist. Some schools teach mostly trivial things, which is excellent for giving good grades to students who are good at memorizing. But it doesn't work for students who may have high intelligence but who are not good at memorizing.

"The art of teaching is the art of assisting discovery."
– Mark Van Doren

Some teachers only pay attention to the students who are dressed and groomed in a certain way, while ignoring the students who are more unique, or who are from homes where resources are limited. Some teachers may have been interested in teaching in ways that would have been greatly beneficial for the students, but the teachers were bogged down by a school system that worked against any sort of genuine education. Some teachers may have been excellent, but the students were caught in the mindset of thinking it was cool to disregard authority figures.

"The aim of public education is not to spread enlightenment at all: it is simply to reduce as many individuals as possible to the same safe level, to breed a standard citizenry, to put down dissent and originality."
– Henry Louis Mencken

Some students never saw what they wanted to be. They had nobody to relate to, had no good examples, had no role models, and may not have had anyone capable of nurturing them in accordance with their intellect. Because of these situations, they may not have succeeded, and may have become lost in living far from what they would naturally have exceeded in. By their teenage years they may have gotten into mind-altering substances that played with their imagination that was otherwise never used, or used very little, or that was discouraged from being used. When they did express themselves, they may have been shamed as being eccentric, assuming, or outlandish. All of this may have brought them to live regretfully and to be filled with despisement and a jaded attitude.

"The important thing is this: to be ready at any moment to sacrifice what you are for what you could become."
– Charles Du Bos

It seems that people can decide at any moment to focus their thoughts in such a way that they may align themselves with being part of the problem, or choosing to be part of the solution. They may focus on complaining and pointing fingers to place blame and shame and spend their time responding to end results, or they may choose to get busy working to make the world into a place that is better for them and everyone around them.

"Education is not the filling of a pail, but the lighting of a fire."
– William Butler Yeats

At any time and in any part of the world there may be a child who is a potential prodigy. They may become one of those who revolutionize their culture, or who formulate an entirely unexplored aspect of humanity, of sciences, of arts, of agriculture, or of something else not previously discovered, and who transform society.

The potential of becoming incredible is not limited to children. At any age people may awake from slothful lives and excel at something that transforms not only their lives, but also the lives of many others.

"If a man does not keep pace with his companions, perhaps it is because he hears a different drummer. Let him step to the music which he hears, however measured or far away."
– Henry David Thoreau

As the saying goes, you can't help someone who doesn't want to be helped. No matter what our childhood situation was, our attitude may be the result of what level of education we received. Luckily for us, we can change our attitude.

The inner drive of the person may be what truly brings about a successful life. A healthful attitude may always have been a part of a person's character. If it isn't, the person can decide to change that at any moment.

Part of transitioning into a more healthful character may have to do with learning new ways of communicating, of conducting ourselves, of spending our time, of supplying ourselves with higher-quality mind and body nutrition, and of accessing our love.

Some people may have grown up in situations with everything good available to them, but they chose to be shut off from being healthful. Others may have grown up in troubling situations, but had an attitude that somehow was far more healthful than those of anyone in their presence.

"Men take on the nature, the habits, and the power of thought of those with whom they associate."
– Napoleon Hill

"Nothing of me is original. I am the combined effort of everybody I've ever known."
– Chuck Palahniuk

Just as we may have adapted to the manners of the people we were around when we were young, we also may adapt to the full spectrum of behaviors of the people who are presently around us.

Some of us may have been in childhood situations where we were regularly exposed to lying, stealing, slander, dishonesty, deception, violence, poverty, bad nutrition, substance abuse, and every manner of ruinous and terrible behavior. The unfortunate choices and behaviors of the elders may have been adapted into our common way of thinking. And these may be the first things from which we will need to educate ourselves away.

"Be an opener of doors for such as come after thee."
– Ralph Waldo Emerson

You can choose to educate yourself in any area of knowledge you are lacking. In today's world many people have access to all sorts of resources to learn about whatever their interests may be. By using information in books, libraries, and on the Internet, a person can receive an education that would likely be better than what was available to them when they were young.

The Internet has introduced a whole new opportunity for learning about everything from history to music, from health to economics, and from traditional topics to those that were not covered in school.

"There are two kinds of light — the glow that illuminates, and the glare that obscures."
– James Thurber

Unfortunately, many choose to use their time and resources to satisfy their most base desires, and they may choose to feed into the lowest aspects of life that they could possibly open for themselves — including through the blaring grotesqueness that can be found on the Internet.

Nowadays those people who feel they didn't receive the education they should have had can get busy educating themselves.

We are all educated, but in which way are we educated, and what can we do about it to educate ourselves in a more healthful way conducive to what we most need?

"I just wish people would realize that anything's possible, if you try; dreams are made, if people try."
– Terry Fox

Many people have been stuck in the bottomless grease pit of not exceeding in life, of not using their intellect and talents or of advancing their skills, of not taking advantage of their opportunities, and of not conducting their lives in ways that would be most beneficial to them. Many people have given up on their dreams, have settled into a life free of goals, have become slothful in every way, and have otherwise made decisions not in tune with what their life could be if they would instead tune into and use their intellect.

"Emancipate yourself from mental slavery. None but ourselves can free our minds"
– Bob Marley

Stop thinking that you are limited to the level of life that you have been experiencing. If you don't like the level of life you are leading, please use your power and whatever resources you have to bring yourself closer to the level of life you would like to experience.

> "You miss 100 percent of the shots you never take."
> – Wayne Gretzky

You can play a large role in creating your future. What will it be? That is the question. Your thoughts, words, actions, attitude, food choices, and how you spend your time and resources will create the answer.

Fathom your possibilities and become aligned with what you wish to be.

You may be young. You may be old. Whatever stage of life you are in, these are your school days.

Learn, live, labor, and love.

> "A world full of happiness is not beyond human power to create; the obstacles imposed by inanimate nature are not insuperable. The real obstacles lie in the heart of man, and the cure for these is a firm hope, informed and fortified by thought."
> – Bertrand Russell

You Are Not Here

> "I think I think, therefore I think I am."
> – Ambrose Bierce

> "In each of you are one quadrillion cells, 90 percent of which are not human cells. Your body is a community, and without those other microorganisms you would perish in hours. Each human cell has 400 billion molecules conducting millions of processes between trillions of atoms. The total cellular activity in one human body is staggering: one septillion actions at any one moment, a one with twenty-four zeros after it. In a millisecond, our body has undergone ten times more processes than there are stars in the universe — exactly what Charles Darwin foretold when he said science would discover that each living creature was a 'little universe, formed of a

host of self-propagating organisms, inconceivably minute and as numerous as the stars of heaven.'"
– Paul Hawken

"The fundamental delusion of humanity is to suppose that I am here and you are out there."
– Yasutani Roshi

Did you know that you can't be found? I mean, as far as what actually makes you form and grow and think and act and reason, you can't be found. Science can detect substances that interact with each other, such as chemicals and matter that are pretty much predictable. Scientists can look into the cells of the body and see what common substances they are made of, and they can see how the substances are arranged in various geometric patterns. They can use lenses to peer into the genes that play a role in determining how certain structures form and function. And they have some understanding of the biochemical interactions of the proteins. But other than understanding the human mechanism in an electro/chemical context, they can't figure out exactly what is the us that controls us. They can't even determine if what is us is even inside the structure that is us, or if we are outside of us.

"The nature of God is a circle of which the center is everywhere and the circumference is nowhere."
– Empedocles

"You live in illusion and the appearance of things. There is a reality, but you don't know this. When you understand this you will see that you are nothing. And being nothing, you are everything. That is all."
– Kalu Rinpoche

Another thing that is interesting about us is that nothing in our physical structures is touching. When we zoom into the smallest things that comprise us, we can see that there is space between the molecules, protons, electrons, atoms, and the finer particles and substances. There is so much space between the things that comprise us that there are very small substances traveling through the spaces within us, and they do this without our even knowing.

"Everything you've learned in school as 'obvious' becomes less and less obvious as you begin to study the universe. For example, there are no solids in the universe. There's not even a suggestion of

a solid. There are no absolute continuums. There are no surfaces. There are no straight lines."
– Richard Buckminster Fuller

Trillions of solar electron neutrinos are flowing through our bodies during every split second of every minute of every hour of every day. There is so much space between all the substances we are made of that the neutrinos have no problem traveling right through us. The solar electron neutrinos are produced by the fusion reaction occurring in the interior of Sun. As they travel away from Sun, the neutrinos travel through space and pass through ordinary matter, including people, plants, and Earth.

In addition to neutrinos, there are multiple types of other substances continuously making their way through us. Gasses consisting of millions of molecules are being absorbed by our lungs and skin during every second of every minute. Gasses consisting of millions of molecules are also being breathed out through our lungs and are evaporating through our skin, and even through our eyes and fingernails. We also, through drinking, are taking in water, and eliminating it both through our eliminative organs and through our lungs and skin. So much water is continually flowing through us that if we don't replace it every day, our health suffers.

Similar to a lake, you are a body that is a continuum of a flow. A lake may sit, but it is hardly still. It looks to be complete in itself, but there is always something entering, and something exiting. Without the flow, it would not be a lake, but would cease to exist as a lake. So are you.

"Water which is too pure has no fish."
– Ts'ai Ken T'an

All of us consist of a number of life forms, including bacteria. If it weren't for bacteria living around and within us, we would not be alive. Just as we are dependent on bacteria within us, the foods we eat are dependent on bacteria and fungi in the soil. When taken into consideration that our physical structure does not consist of only one organism, it is easy to understand that we are not a single life form, but many life forms. And we depend on many other forms of life to survive, including the plants, the soil organisms, and also the wildlife that helps nurture, fertilize, pollinate, and spread plant life.

"Every man is more than just himself; he also represents the unique, the very special and always significant and remarkable point at which the world's phenomena intersect, only once in this way, and never again."

– Hermann Hesse

There are spheres of energy surrounding the galaxy. There are also energy fields that connect between the planets and moons. And there are electrical currents traveling in and around the planets and their moons.

Scientists have been able to measure changes in the current of electricity flowing through Earth where it flows through the magnetic field in mantle rock. The current is formed when the stream of electrically charged atomic particles in the solar wind emitted by Sun interact with the magnetosphere within Earth. All life on Earth is dependent on the communication of this electrical magnetic field just as much as we are dependent on water, air, soil, plants, animals, insects, fish, bacteria, fungi, and all other life forms. And that magnetic field is part of what we are interacting with at all times along with all the substances that pass in and out of us.

"The invitation is about participation, not mere observation. We are not journeying in the universe but with the universe. We are not concerned about living in an evolving world but co-evolving with our world. We are parts of a whole, much greater than the sum of its parts, and yet within each part we are interconnected with the whole."

– Diarmuid O'Murchu

There is a flow of electricity passing through us, and a flow of energy being generated by us. We are generating electricity at all times within every one of our cells, and this electricity helps our body to function. Our actions, including our involuntary movements, generate electricity. Our thoughts affect the flow of electricity in our tissues and this thought-generated energy interacts with the energies of the substances around us.

Our thoughts are also producing molecules. These molecules of emotion are created throughout all our living body tissues and they travel out of us and into our atmosphere, also saturating the substances around us.

"Once we recognize that all matter is actually energy, we can begin to form a new vision of ourselves and the world around us. We begin to realize that our surroundings are not what they seem."

– William Buhlman

Isn't it interesting that when you walk into an ancient building your body may be interacting with molecules that were once in the bodies of the people who lived in that building hundreds of years in the past? It is also interesting to consider that what we are thinking is creating substances that are saturating the structures around us and that what we think and say sends forth patterns of energy that become part of the cosmic sound.

Unfortunately, what many people are thinking and saying involves low-quality thoughts and words, such as those revolving around celebrity culture. One wonders what people in the future will learn about us, and if they will develop tools capable of reading the thought molecules we have left behind. They may think that our generation once thought so much of a certain celebrity that we considered the person to be some sort of guru or idealized figure, when in reality the celebrity was truly a tragic disaster obsessed with believing in their own publicity.

> "Keeping your body healthy is an expression of gratitude to the whole cosmos, the trees, the clouds, everything."
> – Thich Nhat Hanh

Knowing all this, and that you are actually a form of energy, consider your power and what you are doing with your power. Recognize your consciousness and that you are a consciousness of ability, creativity, potential, impact, and community.

> "The more science I studied, the more I saw that physics becomes metaphysics and numbers become imaginary numbers. The farther you go into science, the mushier the ground gets. You start to say, 'Oh, there is an order and a spiritual aspect to science.'"
> – Dan Brown

> "Every human being has etched in his personality the indelible stamp of the Creator."
> – Martin Luther King, Jr.

Know that you are a spirit. You hold within you sacred energy that formed not only your being, but also the substances around you.

> "No one can stand in these solitudes unmoved, and not feel that there is more in man than the mere breath of his body."
> – Charles Darwin

You are a divine expression of love. You may scoff at that thought, but if you are not the expression of what was a loving relationship, you can decide to be an expression of your own love.

> "Yes, I am me, but what animates me is what animates Uncle Bob, the cat, the tree, the rock, and all that is. We are packaged differently, but we share the same essence. There are many of us and we are not the same but we are all one."
> – Cheri Huber

> "When I look inside and see that I am nothing, that's wisdom. When I look outside and see that I am everything, that's love. Between these two my life turns."
> – Sri Nisargadatta

Just as the genes within us are a combination of the genes from our Earth parents, the spirit that is truly us is the substance of spiritual genetics which originated from the masterful spirits of Divinity. Recognize that it is so and accept it. Although we may not always succeed in living up to such an honorable spiritual heritage, it is something we can strive for.

> "All of life is interrelated. We are all caught in an inescapable network of mutuality, tied to a single garment of destiny. Whatever affects one directly affects all indirectly."
> – Martin Luther King, Jr.

> "We see men haying in the meadow, their heads waving like the grass they cut. In the distance, the wind seemed to bend all alike."
> – Henry David Thoreau

Faith

> "Let no one be deluded that a knowledge of the path can substitute for putting one foot in front of the other."
> – Mary Caroline Richards

Do you want satisfaction? Then determine what will satisfy you and work to design your life to bring it about. To do so, utilize your faith.

Open your mind to possibilities and write down the things about yourself that you have faith in and or wish to have faith in. Include in these your talents, skills, and abilities, which some people call, *your graces*. They are your refining qualities, and are what present your elegance.

> "Imagination is the beginning of creation. You imagine what you desire, you will what you imagine, and at last you create what you will."
> – George Bernard Shaw

Believe in the power of your self to change into what you want to be. Know that you have access to tools that can adjust and tune you to be more in alignment with those things that will help you create your desired life. Three of these tools are free to you, and they are your instinct, creativity, and talent.

> "Some of the world's greatest feats were accomplished by people not smart enough to know they were impossible."
> – Doug Larson

When I speak of faith, I'm not speaking of an organized religion, but of faith in things that are, that may be, and that can become.

> "My goal in life is to be as good of a person my dog already thinks I am."
> – Author unknown

I don't follow or practice any one religion and am not a member of any organized religion. I have visited many types of churches, consider a lot of theories, find much of them to be interesting, and try to live by what I feel to be true. However, I'm also not one to sit around repeatedly reading scriptural writings, nor am I into regularly sitting around listening to preachers or ministers dictate their interpretation of theories they think they recognize in the various writings they consider sacred. Not that I am the perfect example of anything, but I seem to have done enough of reading various religious texts to satisfy me, and would prefer to get out and live and be involved in life rather than just think about it, or sit around listening to people talk about it.

> "Some people regard themselves as perfect, but only because they demand little of themselves."
> – Hermann Hesse

Many people seem to be caught up in following various preachers, ministers, or other guru types. They dedicate large amounts of money and time to listen to someone preach, perhaps hoping for enlightenment. But what is enlightenment if you aren't getting out and using it? What is so important about being sure to spend hours every week sitting around listening to someone speak, and more hours working to make the money to donate to the speaker, and perhaps even more time volunteering to help run the organization? Is that continual service to a leader truly enlightenment in action, or is enlightened action more defined by being engaged in using your talents, skills, craft, intellect, and other graces?

Why do people give up so much of their power by having someone tell them what to think and how to pray and what to hope for, especially when they end up not having much of a life because they are so involved in the so-called worship? Could it be that they don't have enough faith in themselves, or that they have given up their power? Could it be that the religions are holding the people back?

It is easy to understand that people feel a community and fellowship in their religious gatherings. And it is understandable that they can feel uplifted by associating with people of like mind. I can understand going to church to get uplifted when feeling down or lonely. What I don't get is the sitting around and listening for hours every single week. I also don't get into the man-made theatrics that really have nothing to do with much of anything other than mythology. And the whole concept of donating so many resources to support a concept that has nothing to do with eternity and everything to do with making money and vainglory does not seem like a reasonable way to spend energy. It seems as if those folks are waiting for something and trying to find something. Maybe they are the ones they are waiting for, and they are the ones they seek, and they don't know it. Maybe what they themselves need is what they already have, but they don't understand that it is already there. Maybe by getting active in creating the life they want by using their talents and intellect they would seek less, live more, be more satisfied, and understand that they can be their own guru that will bring them joy, health, satisfaction, and love.

> "I shall tell you a great secret, my friend. Do not wait for the last judgment. It takes place every day."
> – Albert Camus

Instead of using up days every week and a large chunk of their income dedicated to a church, what if people spent their time developing their talents, becoming active in environmental causes, and helping organizations that restore and protect trees, forests, and wildlife? This would do more to help the sacredness of life than supporting a church that does nothing to protect sacred Earth, but does everything to make sure that the financial books of the church are in order.

> "An ounce of practice is worth more than tons of preaching."
> – Mahatma Gandhi

I had a conversation about this with someone who spends large amounts of her time and income on her church. She said I wouldn't understand because I'm not a spiritual person. She claims that churches stop people from being involved in bad things because the churches take the people out of their lives that would otherwise be ruinous. I think that is an interesting concept that is also wasteful, tragic, weak, and ruinous.

> "The ultimate result of shielding men from the effects of folly is to fill the world with fools."
> – Herbert Spencer

If there is some sort of judgment gate, there will likely be a lot of people being asked why they didn't use their talent and time to improve life, and to do anything to protect wildlife and Earth. Their honest answer will be that they were too busy sitting in church and making money to donate to church. Others will say they were too busy playing video games, watching TV, playing on the Internet, shopping, or working to pay off the debt they got into to purchase stuff to replicate the images seen in corporate advertising, or to buy things they thought would make them happy.

> "The world is a dangerous place, not because of those who do evil, but because of those who look on and do nothing."
> – Albert Einstein

I encourage people to get out and live. It is through doing and experiencing that you will know life. Sitting around believing in something is having faith without works. Your actions are your intentions taking place, and are truly the practicing of your faith.

> "What sort of God would it be who only pushed from without?"
> – Johann Wolfgang von Goethe

Whether or not you believe in Buddhism, in Hinduism, in Jainism, in Christianity, in Judaism, in Islam, in Hopi wisdom, or in other popular or unpopular religious or spiritual beliefs, you can recognize goodness. Rather than sit around building your life philosophy, get out and live it, and construct it by practice.

Inspire your self. Use your talents. Play your skills. Engage in your craft. Stimulate your intellect. Manifest your divinity through good works.

Feed off the knowledge you get by living your life and building goodness in your life. Take good from wherever it may flow and use it in your life to fuel faith in your self and protect the sacredness of Earth by creating a more sustainable culture.

> "People are hungry for messages of hope and life."
> – Morgan Brittany

The difference between those who achieve great things and those who don't is most often a very simple process. Those who do achieve great things don't sit around thinking about it without taking action. They both believe they can accomplish the tasks, and consistently work with intention while staying focused on accomplishing their goals through actions.

> "Acting on a good idea is better than just having a good idea."
> – Robert Half

Many people believe they can accomplish something, but their belief is lost in fantasy — because they take no action to accomplish the imagery that is stuck in their mind because of inaction.

Belief combined with planning and intentional action results in accomplishment of goals.

> "I have been impressed with the urgency of doing. Knowing is not enough; we must apply. Being willing is not enough; we must do."
> – Leonardo da Vinci

There is a current of electricity in your body. The level of its vibrancy depends on what you think, what you do, what you are planning to do, how you spend your time, what you say, what you read, how you treat others, how you treat animals, the people with whom you spend time, the music you listen to, the environment in which you spend your time, and the quality of food you put into your body. The current responds to the level of your determination, intention, and faith.

Whether you choose to be ruled by faith or by doubt is a matter of which energy you choose to plug into. You can focus on good and invigorating energy that uplifts and builds faith in living. Or, you can tune into that which is negative, overly critical, and unaccepting of the gifts that can be found throughout your days, and simply leave your life up to whimsy.

Consider that a person who is ill may get well with the assistance of various therapies, and that perhaps one of the most important of all matters in healing is the person's state of mind, attitude, and will. It may be most helpful for those people to have a belief that their health will improve. But it will be more helpful if they work to recover and rehabilitate themselves. Instead of allowing frustration turn into stress, which can degrade health even more, they can spin that frustration into helpful actions.

How well people accomplish their desires may be determined by how much work they carry out in alignment with their want. Those who really want something, and work for it, are more likely to accomplish their desires.

> "Hope is itself a species of happiness, and, perhaps, the chief happiness which this world affords."
> – Samuel Johnson

Have faith in both your self and in others. By showing your faith in others you show faith in your self. By believing in the power of others, you believe in the power of your self.

Go about your days with grace and faith while knowing that you are capable of becoming a successful and happy person surrounded by the good that can manifest around you through your actions.

Embrace the concepts of positive-thinking, of building strength in a person, of the ability to master talents, and of fine tuning your being as an instrument filled with faith that you can attain that which is good, positive, and satisfying in your life.

If you want your life to improve, be determined to improve it. Intentionally act to improve it. Have faith that you can improve it. Use self-discipline combined with actions to make it improve.

> "Some people regard discipline as a chore. For me, it is a kind of order that sets me free to fly."
> – Julie Andrews

Be brave, caring, driven, kind, gallant, and active in changing your life. Intentionally create a nurturing atmosphere of prosperity, clarity, and self-awareness where the strengths of your spirit will prosper.

Defy fear with your faith. Refuse to accept doubt in your life.

Believe in your self. Believe in your power. Believe in your divine energy. Have faith in your self and build your faith in your self.

Work with your instincts, talents, and abilities. Build your strengths to fine-tune your self as an instrument that can be conducted by the thoughts of your mind to bring your life into that which it is capable of being.

What you do is the example of what you are.

> "My life is my teaching."
> – Mahatma Gandhi

Words

> "Kind words are a creative force, a power that concurs in the building up of all that is good, and energy that showers blessings upon the world."
> – Lawrence G. Lovasik

Words are the expression of thoughts and they plant the seeds of other thoughts in the minds of the people who hear them.

Words are powerful. Just as others can say things to you that limit or motivate you, you can say words to yourself and to others, which motivate, encourage, strengthen, and bring about improved relations and conditions.

Words play into the collaboration of the conscious mind with the subconscious mind. Words can create energy signatures in the minds of people who hear them. They can bind people into believing things, even when the things that are said are not true. For instance, many people have heard negative things about themselves and then alter their behavior according to those unfortunate words.

> "Language exerts hidden power, like a moon on the tides."
> – Rita Mae Brown

Have you ever heard or read words that make you feel a certain way, such as motivated and determined? This is because words are messages, and water responds to messages made of patterns of sounds, which consist of energy. We consist mostly of water. Water is impacted by sound patterns, which can be calming, stimulating, frantic, disturbing, invigorating, nurturing, or loving.

> "Words and magic were in the beginning one and the same thing, and even today words retain much of their magical power."
> – Sigmund Freud

Words placed in our memories can continue to bless or to curse us.

Just as poison makes people physically ill, which can impact the mind, so too might unkind words ail the mind, which can impact the body.

As a person experiences life, neural pathways are developed in the brain and other tissues in relation to what the person has experienced. In this way, poisonous words can create memory patterns of negativity and form an imprint of judgment over which all other thoughts travel.

> "Before you speak, ask yourself: Is it kind? It is necessary? Is it true? Does it improve on the silence?"
> – Shirdi Sai Baba

People curse each other and use negative words toward one another all the time. Many people have been told they are dumb, ugly, and otherwise flawed. These are the types of words that destroy self-esteem. These words may echo in a person's memory and begin to affect the way they think and act. They focus on the words and form an opinion of themselves that binds them or limits them. Remembering words spoken to us can bring about the same energy patterns that originally rippled through us when we first heard the words. In less than ideal circumstances, this may lead to limiting thoughts, self-hate, destruction of character, weariness, slothfulness, and failure. This is an example of how words create energy signatures in the minds of people who hear them.

> "Conversation is a meeting of minds with different memories and habits. When minds meet, they don't just exchange facts: they transform them, reshape them, draw different implications from them, engage in new trains of thought. Conversation doesn't just reshuffle the cards: it creates new cards."
> – Theodore Zeldin

> "Words are a lens to focus one's mind."
> – Ayn Rand

I'm not the type of person who goes to fortunetellers. I was once at a house party that, for its apparent entertainment value, featured a fortuneteller. While I sat and watched the guests fortunes being told, I played with the idea that perhaps fortunetellers don't so much as *fore*tell the future as *tell* it — explaining with such energy what may become that it paves the way for events to take place — beginning the energy wave with their thoughts and words in such a way that it plants the seeds of what may grow into an event.

> "For as he thinketh in his heart, so is he."
> – King Solomon

Very often people experience something that they say a person once told them would happen. This may be the expression of some sort of belief in words once spoken and heard. If people are told that they will one day accomplish or experience something, perhaps they might be more likely to play out the scenario of it happening in their thoughts. And as thoughts result in actions that bring about events, the whole process may be what is called a *self-fulfilled prophecy*.

> "If you keep saying things are going to be bad, you have a good chance of being a prophet."
> – Isaac Bashevis Singer

> "Assume a virtue if you have it not."
> – William Shakespeare

At any time, you can begin to instill uplifting thoughts into your mind, which will nurture positive actions and satisfactory life changes. You can do this with your thoughts, the words that you speak, the words that you read in the literature of your choosing, the goals you set and notes you write to yourself, and hopefully the nurturing words of those around you.

> "The best way to predict the future is to create it."
> – Alan Kay

Perhaps all our words are some form of prayer. Decide to use words that create the energy of and that prophecy a life that you desire.

As an exercise, make a list of the good, kind, and encouraging things people have said about and toward you. Also make a short list of the things you would like people to say to you. Consider that it may be helpful for you to read these lists regularly to help set a pattern of positive-thinking in your mind.

Create a section in your journal consisting of encouraging, nurturing, and healing words and statements. These may consist of inspirational quotations you have gathered and your own encouraging words. When you are feeling less valiant, open that section of your journal and read what you have written. Add to it by writing more positive words, statements, and intentions.

Reading and writing positive statements can be an especially powerful exercise when you are experiencing times of doubt or worry. The reading and writing will help cancel out negative thoughts you are experiencing, because the mind works in accordance with the influences suggested to it. Bringing positive thoughts into your mind will flow into your actions because the body acts in accordance with the thoughts the person is experiencing.

Writing positive affirmations will help you declare your intentions and shift your gears to remain on a healthful path. Once you declare them, stay busy by putting the positive thoughts into positive actions. By doing so you will form your declaration into a manifestation.

> "Be observant to the words you use in writing, typing, or talking. Negative words sabotage that which you really want in your life. It's like getting halfway across the bridge to happiness and cutting the ropes with negative, critical words."
> – Daniel Giovanni Morello

Continually arrange the words in your mind to create the terrain for healthful thought. Allow positive, encouraging, motivating, and loving words to become the constant flow of your mantra. Use this to collaborate your conscious mind to successfully cooperate with your subconscious mind in bringing about the change you wish to see in your life.

Use the words that you think and the words that you speak to accelerate your life toward happiness, vibrant health, and the fulfillment of your goals.

Transforming

I am one who believes it would be most helpful for people to take the initiative to stimulate their mind, their intellect, and their talent, and to learn and grow themselves into what would most likely be the best version of themselves.

> "Transforming yourself is a means of giving light to the whole world."
> – Ramana Maharshi

To start from somewhere, you must first be someplace. We are all someplace, but some of us don't know where we are.

Many people don't know their state in life. They have little idea what really happened in their past because they weren't paying attention, were kept in the dark by people around them, or were so far in denial that they skimmed right over it. They may also have hidden behind lack-luster activities as an escape mechanism.

> "When a man's self is hidden from everybody else, it seems also to become hidden even from himself, and it permits disease and death to gnaw into his substance without his clear knowledge."
> – Sidney Jourard

> "Normal is not something to aspire to, it's something to get away from."
> – Jodie Foster

> "I would much rather have regrets about not doing what people said, than regretting not doing what my heart led me to and wondering what life had been like if I'd just been myself."
> – Brittany Renée

Some people are caught up in living undercover, which is a pattern of role-playing to conform to what they think is the most acceptable form of behavior in alignment with the people around them. Living undercover can be damaging to the spirit, and cause a person's feelings and emotions to become rigid, stagnant, and stale. Even their facial expressions may become controlled by this earnestness to fit in with a particular persona that is truly fake, but that may be in tune with the repression of the true personality.

> "Most of the shadows of this life are caused by standing in one's own sunshine."
> – Ralph Waldo Emerson

Some people get into the habit of functioning as if they are being held hostage by situations or people in their life — including things and people from their distant past. They may almost lean on their feelings about these situations and relationships to support their attitude, which is a choice more than it is a curse.

> "There is no man, however wise, who has not at some period of his youth said things, or lived in a way the consciousness of which is so unpleasant to him in later life that he would gladly, if he could, expunge it from his memory."
> – Marcel Proust

Some continually agonize over the past as if it is an open wound being misted with rubbing alcohol. This is often done while placing blame and shame on others.

People also often don't know what is happening with their life, and they don't know what resources they have available to organize into something they can use to build a more satisfying, healthful life.

Some go through life seeking to get things done for them. They may be manipulative in getting what they can from each person around them. They may depend on and expect others to take care of them, or they wait to be directed on what to do, when to do it, and how to go about doing it. They may look for what is free in life, or for what they can attain for the least amount of work. By doing so they are both weakening themselves and draining those around them.

Some seem to be waiting around for someone else to provide the change they want to see in their life, and they may.

Some think buying a weekly lottery ticket will improve their life, and it may.

Others seem to think that it is up to their family to provide their change, and they may.

Others carry an illusion that the government is going to improve their situation. Unfortunately the government is more focused on crime, punishment, and corporate welfare than it is on activities that would improve the situation of humanity. The government largely functions as a host to corporations, caters to the demands of commerce and industry, and is more concerned about money and less concerned about people. The government is a business. Businesses don't have morals, they have managers, bookkeepers, lawyers, and servants.

When the government does focus on an individual, it is most often not in the most helpful way.

The U.S. spends more on jails and prisons than it does on education. Throughout the decade starting in 2000, in California the state government has been cutting funding to parks, cutting funding for children's programs, and cutting funding for schools, education services, and libraries while increasing funding for prison construction, for prison guards, and for increasing the number of police officers. This is in a state where, by 2007, about $6,000 was being spent on each school student while about $40,000 was being spent on each prisoner.

By 2009, the state of California alone had 158,000 prisoners, and that was in 33 prisons designed to hold a total of 84,000 inmates. Also in 2009, the University of California's Board of Regents voted to increase undergraduate education costs by 32 percent. Earlier in the same year, student enrollment in the U.C. system was cut by 6 percent. California Community Colleges also experienced a reduction in state funding by 8 percent. The state was number one in prison spending, and number 48 in education spending.

Unfortunately, what has been taking place in California is reflective of what has been going on in many other states, and in some other countries. At the beginning of 2008, the U.S. had 2.3 million people in prison and a total of 7.2 million Americans were either in prison, on probation, or on parole, and the U.S. was spending about $40 billion on the prison industry. For decades, the U.S. government has held more people in prison than any other country, and has built more prisons in the past five decades than in all the world's history. Instead of an educated generation, the U.S. has been producing a prison generation.

> "If we don't stand up for children, then we don't stand for much."
>
> – Marian Wright Edelman

With all the money spent on prisons in America, and all the cuts of funding in education, it seems there would be a realization that it is easier to educate a child and give a quality childhood than it is to try to fix someone who grew up disadvantaged, neglected, and/or abused. Unfortunately enlightenment seems hard to come by in the offices that direct government spending.

> "If it's possible to build prison camps powerful enough to destroy human personalities, perhaps it was also possible to create environments that can foster its rebirth."
>
> – Bruno Bettelheim

> "If the misery of the poor be caused not by the laws of nature, but by our institutions, great is our sin."
>
> – Charles Darwin

Just as your power is diminished by catering to the illusion that the government will improve your life, your power is also diminished by waiting for someone else to improve your life.

> "You are responsible for the world that you live in. It is not the government's responsibility. It is not your school's or your social club's or your church's or your neighbor's or your fellow citizen's. It is yours, utterly and singularly yours."
> – August Wilson

> "Nobody made a greater mistake than the person who did nothing, because they thought that they could only do a little."
> – Edmund Burke

> "Nothing strengthens the judgment and quickens the conscience like individual responsibility."
> – Elizabeth Stanton

> "It is not God's will merely that we should be happy, but that we should make ourselves happy."
> – Immanuel Kant

Thinking that someone else is responsible for your happiness weakens your vibrancy, creates laziness, is unrealistic, and may be considered foolish. Relying on others to do for us what we can do for ourselves is unhealthful, limits our learning, and can create a dysfunctional environment for all involved.

You cannot ride on the coattails of anyone and realistically expect your life to be the best that it can be.

> "If I wanted to become a tramp, I would seek information and advice from the most successful tramp I could find. If I wanted to become a failure, I would seek advice from people who never succeeded. If I wanted to succeed in all things, I would look around me for those who are succeeding, and do as they have done."
> – Joseph Marshall Wade

Many don't seem to realize that their life is a classroom. They also don't seem to care if they get a good grade, nor are they paying attention to the teacher or doing their homework.

"The only reason some people get lost in thought is because it's unfamiliar territory."
– Anonymous

"You have the power to choose your own happiness. People, situations, and events outside of yourself will affect you, but no one can give you happiness."
– Stephanie Dowrick

Your life is not about what it was. Your life is about what it currently is, and it is about what it can become. If you pay attention to it and use the lessons and opportunities presented to you every day it can become more satisfying than what it is.

Open your eyes to the possibilities within you. Change comes from within. It is up to you to bring out the substances of your self that will be most pleasing to you.

Your life can become completely different from what it currently is. You can transform yourself through diet, exercise, thoughts, words, emotions, activities, education, poise, daily choices, associations, and by adapting to the eloquence of your love. You can do this to such an extent that people who know you now may be unable to recognize you in one year.

"Let the beauty we love be what we do."
– Rumi

You can essentially mutate into a completely different version of yourself. Through infusing your body with the most nutritious fruits and vegetables available to you while staying away from low-grade foods, and by maintaining a quality daily exercise regimen, you can transform your health. Through working to improve the way you think through intellectual stimulation, you can transform your mind. By using your thoughts to set goals to change your actions, your life will change. Through improving the way you spend your time, energy, and other resources, you can transform your existence. These are the principles of transforming your life from the inside.

"To find yourself, think for yourself."
– Socrates

"Adventure is not outside, it is within."
– David Grayson

I reiterate, all transformation toward success and health in your life begins with your thoughts. Your outward appearance and the things you do are reflective of what is going on inside you. If you are going to appear healthier, you need to be more healthful on the inside. If you want your outside appearance to change, you are going to have to begin to change what you are putting into your body through not only your diet, but what you are feeding your mind, and how you are making your body move through daily exercise. All this has to do with thought.

> "When you are inspired by some great purpose, some extraordinary project, all your thoughts break their bonds; your mind transcends limitations, your consciousness expands in every direction, and you find yourself in a new, great and wonderful world. Dormant forces, faculties and talents become alive, and you discover yourself to be a greater person by far than you ever dreamed yourself to be."
> – Patanjali

> "Ideas won't work unless you do.
> – Author Unknown

> "Man stands in his own shadow and wonders why it's dark."
> – Zen theory

> "We must not, in trying to think about how we can make a big difference, ignore the small daily differences we can make which, over time, add up to big differences that we often cannot foresee."
> – Marian Wright Edelman

If you want to see change in yourself, change yourself. If you want the world to improve, improve your world. If you want to change the way people treat you, improve the way you treat people. If you want to transform yourself, begin the journey of that from within by transforming your thoughts.

Transforming your life is up to you, and nobody else. Get busy with it.

> "Circumstances may cause interruptions and delays, but never lose sight of your goal. Prepare yourself in every way you can by increasing your knowledge and adding to your experience, so that you can make the most of opportunity when it occurs."
> – Mario Andretti

"The man who makes everything that leads to happiness depend upon himself, and not upon other men, has adopted the very best plan for living happily."
– Plato

You Are Your Gatekeeper

Health is not something that will flow into us if we clog the gates with unhealthful foods, thoughts, and activities. It is something that will root and grow into our lives through healthful thoughts, actions, interactions, environment, and diet. Health also will more likely stay with us if we continually nurture a healthful environment within our minds, bodies, surroundings, and relationships.

To become healthful and to maintain health involves bringing health to us, from the inside out, and from the outside in. In this way health is continually transformational.

"It's no coincidence that four of the six letters in health are 'heal.'"
– Ed Northstrum

People can transform their being through many ways. This includes changing the body through quality, plant-based nutrition and daily physical activity. It also includes building thought processes that will beneficially change the way people deal with their situations. It involves building healthful interior and exterior atmospheres that provide the terrain where health can flourish.

"The quality of expectations determines the quality of our action."
– Andre Godin

When athletes succeed they know it is because of their own actions. Nobody can exercise for them. Nobody can restrict everything athletes eat, do, or think. They have to be disciplined enough to maintain their own dietary guidelines based on the nutrition they need to get their body to perform at the level of their goals. Similarly, we can succeed at life by training to succeed and working to attain the satisfaction we desire. To achieve vibrant health, train your being for life like an athlete trains for sport.

"By believing passionately in something that still does not exist, we create it. The nonexistent is whatever we have not sufficiently desired."
– Nikos Kazantzakis

Generally, once you are an adult, and no matter what your background, if you are physically able, you largely become responsible for the satisfaction you feel in life. If you do not work to attain success in health and in life, as the athlete trains to attain the win, you will not own the satisfaction you are capable of experiencing.

"There is absolutely nothing that separates the elite from the paupers except their expectations. If you wish to rise above the masses, then let the fire burn fiercely within you. Do this, and it shall be done!"
– J. Arthur Holcombe

Train yourself into attaining your goals by conducting your daily activities in a way that will bring you closer to the person you want to be.

Like an athlete, if you drop the ball, pick it up and continue aiming toward the goal.

"A real decision is measured by the fact that you've taken a new action. If there's no action, you haven't truly decided."
– Anthony Robbins

When you consider someone who decided on and successfully accomplished a physical goal, such as to run a marathon, you can see that they go through training that starts out slow and, over a matter of months or years, builds toward the goal of accomplishment. The training an athlete goes through is similar to experiencing success in any area of life.

"If you really want to get something done, start on it, keep at it, and it will eventually happen."
– Richard H. Goodwin

"Making the best of ourselves is the reason we were born, but it takes patience and perseverance."
– Sarah Ban Breathnach

The success of attaining a goal is bred by perseverance and dedication to experiencing accomplishment. Priorities must be drawn, goals must be set, and actions must be taken. All the reasons for doing everything throughout the days, weeks, months, and years it takes to accomplish the goal have to be done in association with the reason of wanting it badly enough.

> "Failure is, in a sense, the highway to success, inasmuch as every discovery of what is false leads us to seek earnestly after what is true."
> – John Keats

> "Motivation is what gets you started. Habit is what keeps you going.
> – Jim Ryun

Realize that it is often the little things you do that lead to accomplishment, and that continually thinking of and doing things to attain a goal builds patterns of behavior. As these patterns continue to evolve they create habits that become your common way of being.

> "If you think that something small cannot make a difference, try going to sleep with a mosquito in the room."
> – Anonymous

> "The greatest things ever done on Earth have been done little by little."
> – William Jennings Bryan

The level of your body's performance is highly dependent on the level of the life you are leading, which is dependent on the level of thoughts you are creating, and the level of foods you are consuming.

To accomplish a better, more healthful and satisfactory level of life, feed your body the highest-quality nutrients available to you.

To experience the best of health, strive for a diet largely consisting of live plant matter: fruits, berries, vegetables, sprouts, nuts, sea vegetables, and germinated seeds. Even better, use them fresh or otherwise in their unheated state, and not fried or tainted with processed sugars or salts, MSG, or synthetic preservatives, dyes, flavors, scents, or sweeteners. These vibrant foods from Nature will help you experience vibrant health that will increase your energy and drive. High-quality nutrients from a variety of plant substances are fuel for the accomplishment of your goals.

Starting today, make the changes you want by being a more present and effective gatekeeper of your life through the goals you set, the priorities you focus on, the foods you eat, the activities you engage in, the words you speak, the literature you read, the music you listen to, the thoughts you entertain, and the quality of your relationships.

> "Everything in this world is a manifestation of what you give the world. The laws of karma are in every scripture. They're in the Bible, and the Quoran, the Torah, they're in the yoga sutras. Every prophet tells you the same thing. It is really what you give the world that you get back from the world. Not that you have to trade, but give the world the positivity you want back. And you have to have faith that is what is going on. That is what is going on."
> – Russell Simmons

Infinite Intelligence

> "Look within. The secret is inside you."
> – Hui Neng

There are things you know that nobody ever taught you. They are things that are natural to you that you cannot deny exist. These are things that have to do with your essence. This is not a new discovery or teaching, but is something people have understood and taught for millennia. Many people have recognized the phenomenon of infinite intelligence. As examples, they speak of spiders that always construct their webs in a certain pattern, animals that eat exactly what is best for them, butterflies that follow the same migration route over thousands of miles, sea creatures that swim from ocean to ocean to get to their breeding bays; birds that build their nests in a particular style, and wildlife that feed their young exactly what they need. The beings of the wild know such things because they are tuned in to their infinite intelligence.

> "If you do not express your own original ideas, if you do not listen to your own being, you will have betrayed yourself."
> – Rollo May

Each person is connected to a spiritual side of life that accesses infinite wisdom. The cleaner and more pure the physical being through quality nutrition and exercise, through learning, and through use of talents and intellect, the better its nerve system will be able to tune into the high frequency of this infinite wisdom that works as instinct.

Those who maintain an unhealthful diet of fried and processed foods and are put into an unnatural environment filled with unhealthful air, toxic surroundings, violated land, and noise pollution, are presented with negativity, and their thought patterns are filled with negativity and doubt. In those conditions the individual will become less attuned to his or her natural instincts and the system becomes frustrated. This disturbance clogs the ability to tap into the high frequency needed to access basic and infinite intelligence, and subsequently not only limits potential, but also damages the expression of it.

> "Our own physical body possesses a wisdom which we who inhabit the body lack."
> – Henry Miller

You have inside you a being that is you and is attuned to what you desire. This being is who you are. It is your intelligence that can be utilized to resonate patterns of energy that direct your actions and words to formulate your life in the most beneficial way.

The true you consists of infinite intelligence. Infinite intelligence is what has brought the intricate structures of all living beings to form into what they are. It is what drives us to desire that which is beautiful, nurturing, and loving.

As with most people, it is likely that much of the infinite intelligence that would otherwise be available to you mostly goes untapped and gets muffled by leading a low-quality life while consuming low-quality foods, entertaining low-quality thoughts, participating in low-quality communication, engaging in low-quality activities, and anticipating less than ideal situations. By living a low-quality life you are not being the person you are capable of being. And you are not experiencing the joy, satisfaction, and love that would otherwise be available to you.

> "In the world to come they will not ask me, 'Why were you not Moses?' They will ask me, 'Why were you not Zusya?'"
> – Reb Zusya

When you purify your body through a plant-based diet; maintain your physical structure through daily exercise, such as yoga; develop your talents through practice of art or craft; expand your knowledge through study and intellectual stimulation; focus your mind by planning an agenda of achievement; clear your thought patterns through meditative thought; fuel your actions with positive-thinking; surround yourself with that which inspires you; and improve your communication with other people through respect, kindness, patience, forgiveness, and love, you are tuning your frequency to your instinct that is purely the work of infinite intelligence. By doing so you will be better able to recognize and utilize the potential and power you are.

Living in a way that is tuned to Nature through following a natural, plant-based diet while getting daily exercise awakens your body cells, your mind, and your whole system to the thing that had been dormant because of unwise living, unhealthful diet, low-quality thinking, unhealthful atmosphere, dysfunctional communication, and damaging relationships and concepts. Through living in tune with Nature your system begins to communicate with the frequency of infinite intelligence that can guide you toward health, happiness, achievement, beauty, and love.

> "There is an essence of the Divine in all living things. And each person is literally a microcosm of the universe."
> – Gloria Steinem

Various religious teachers have some understanding of a power that exists throughout the world and universe. They seem to have an idea of what acknowledging that power means, including aligning with it by way of thoughts, words, and actions. They teach that you can live your life better by paying attention to this power. Some have certain names for it. Some define it in a way that limits it to certain individuals or styles of living. Some say it is this thing, and others say it is that thing. But all seem to agree that it is there. Some call it a form of intelligence. Some call it an inner drive. Some call it spirit. Some call it soul.

> "Every time you don't follow your inner guidance, you feel a loss of energy, loss of power, a sense of spiritual deadness."
> – Shakti Gawain

Infinite intelligence exists in a realm that is both far beyond the façade of physical substances that are common to the worldly, but it is in a realm that is within all that exists. It is in all and through all. It is beyond the comprehension of the unnatural person, but saturates all the substances that everything consists of. It is tuned into the nurturing energy of love, which is the most powerful and pristine energy of all. It exists. It is there. It is the sacred power of Divinity that permeates all.

> "We don't realize that the gods are not out there somewhere. They live in us all. They are the energies of life itself.
> – Joseph Campbell

You can put infinite intelligence to work for you in your life. You know that it is there because you can see that it has formed you and those around you, and the plants, animals, birds, fish, insects, and all living things. You know that there are certain things you do that make you feel more comfortable and in alignment with this energy. Respect and reverence for your life, for the lives of others, and for the lives of animals, as well as living in a way that is in tune with Nature will help you to tune into the high frequency wavelength of infinite intelligence and keep it working for you in your life.

You are the manifestation of the energy of infinite intelligence. Live your days knowing that this is true.

Recognize and know unwaveringly that you are power, potential, and infinite, and that you can use your wisdom to create the life you wish to have.

> "Flesh and bone cannot contain the electrical energy that physically operates our body. To me, that is a physical, tangible, real sign of a soul, or that there is something unique in all of us that does not die."
>
> – Patrick Swayze

> "If the doors of perception were cleansed everything would appear to man as it is, infinite."
>
> – William Blake

Thinking

> "Every action has an ancestor of a thought."
>
> – Ralph Waldo Emerson

The slightest change in your thoughts can send you off on a path you may never have considered.

Very often people change their lives on the precept of one single thought that fuels the change, driving them to experience the life that most satisfies them.

> "The most beautiful experience we can have is the mysterious — the fundamental emotion which stands at the cradle of true art and true science."
>
> – Albert Einstein

Sometimes it is our curiosity that triggers us to recognize things that will greatly influence our lives. For instance, when Albert Einstein was five years old his father showed him a compass. The thought that this compass was working off an invisible power made such an impression on Einstein's mind that he attributed this thought to the setting of his life's journey. Five years later he was given a copy of Aaron Bernstein's multivolume *Popular Books on Natural Science*. These books fascinated young Einstein and further defined his path toward becoming one of the most recognized figures in history.

People say that Einstein's brain was different from the brains of most people. But after he died, his brain was examined and found to have no unusual features. His mind and his ability to utilize it is what made him so distinctive.

Perhaps we may not be able to use our minds in the same manner as Einstein did with his, but most people do have opportunities to access their intellect at a much deeper level than they have been accessing it.

Consider that just as the level of your physical health has much to do with the quality of your foods and how physically active you are, the level of life you are experiencing is reflective of the amount of your talent and intellect you are using, the quality of your thoughts, and otherwise the way you use your mind.

> "The problems we have today will not be solved by thinking the way we thought when we created them."
> – Albert Einstein

Thoughts fuel actions. Actions that improve your life are the results of thoughts. The animation of your body is the emotion of your thought energy. If you want to improve your life, improve your thoughts to fuel better actions that get you more satisfying results.

> "We are what we think. All that we are arises with our thoughts. With our thoughts we make our world."
> – Buddha

All sizes of human accomplishments are the results of thoughts. At first you may think that you want to go to a particular place or obtain a particular thing. The more you think about these, and the more you reason about them, the more likely you are to act on those thoughts and to go where you want to go and get what you want to get.

Luckily for us, thoughts can be guided.

Every one of your thoughts sends out a vibration. That vibration is guided by your spirit, and physically starts within your mind, which exists throughout your body.

By thinking specific thoughts you can bring about certain energies to your life.

Thoughts can be negative or positive in that they create energy charges that flow from within the body tissues and out into the surrounding atmosphere. Negative thoughts and positive thoughts are of two different frequencies.

Thoughts affect the fluid and mechanical structures of the body. They do this by changing the chemistry and electrical charge within the body, even to the point of changing the hormones and expressions, including where the blood flows. In this way, thoughts are like food in that they affect body chemistry.

Just as an unhealthful diet results in an unhealthful, acidic, toxic body, thoughts create chemical reactions that affect body tissues. Negative, acidic thoughts create more acidity in the body tissues, and this is seen as stress that can damage organs, suppress the immune system, and lead to injuries and disease. A most obvious example of this are the types of thoughts that create stress, which can trigger a number of physical reactions, such as anger, and physical ailments, such as high blood pressure and cardiovascular disease — which can be a combination of stressful thoughts, unhealthful environment, dysfunctional relationships, low-quality food, and lack of exercise.

> "I don't eat junk foods and I don't think junk thoughts."
> – Mildred "Peace Pilgrim" Norman

In combination with daily exercise, a healthful diet, and loving relationships, uplifting thoughts can transform the chemistry of your body in a good way. Simply changing your thoughts can change your blood pressure, the production of natural body chemicals, and the acidic level of your body.

> "Stress is not what happens to us. It's our response to what happens. And response is something we can choose."
> – Maureen Kiloran

Various types of thoughts are felt more strongly in certain parts of the body. Body chemicals formed in response to certain emotions are produced more prominently within specific body tissues. The emotion molecules travel through your body tissues, resulting in some sort of physical actions that then affect what is and who is around you, and then travel further into the surrounding pond of life. This is so just as a small leaf that falls onto calm water creates a trickle of waves that emanate out to the stretches of the pond.

> "Thoughts, like fleas, jump from man to man. But they don't bite everybody."
> – Stanislaw Lec

You can feel someone's thought energy. Just as you can feel how angry they are, you can also feel how serene a person is. "I could feel their vibes" may be considered a hippie term, but it gives an accurate description of the way a person's thoughts create an energy field that surrounds them and is absorbed into the surrounding people, animals, and objects.

> "I know of no more encouraging fact than the unquestioned ability of man to elevate his life by conscious endeavor."
> – Henry David Thoreau

> "Throughout all history, the great wise men and teachers, philosophers, and prophets have disagreed with one another on many different things. It is only on this one point that they are in complete and unanimous agreement. We become what we think about."
> – Earl Nightingale

If you want to transform your life, in addition to improving your diet, be particularly focused on your thoughts because, as the saying goes, your thoughts have your tomorrow inside.

Seeds produce after their own kind. A tomato seed sprouts into a tomato plant, not into a corn stalk. Thoughts are the seeds of your words and actions that produce results. To experience results that are more satisfying than the ones you have been getting, plant better-quality thoughts in your mind.

If you are not planting thoughts in your mind that you can nurture to get the results you want, then the only thoughts in your mind are those that just happened to land there, like weeds.

> "Whatever you persistently allow to occupy your thoughts will magnify in your life."
> – Frederick Douglass

Thoughts guide what you become and where you arrive. Similar to seeds, thoughts can be fed, nurtured, and grown into their potential. If you want your life to be uplifted, plant the seeds that would produce that harvest by thinking uplifting thoughts.

Your mind is always focused on something. You can choose to focus it on things that are beneficial to creating the life you want.

You are going to think, so you may as well think in a way that benefits you. You are going to exist, and you may as well work to exist in a way that is enjoyable to you.

If you focus on thoughts of accomplishing what you want, then you are more likely to attain your goals.

> "There is nothing you can say in answer to a compliment. I have been complimented myself a great many times, and they always embarrass me — I always feel that they have not said enough."
> – Mark Twain

> "You have it easily in your power to increase the sum total of this world's happiness now. How? By giving a few words of sincere appreciation to someone who is lonely or discouraged. Perhaps you will forget tomorrow the kind words you say today, but the recipient may cherish them over a lifetime."
> – Dale Carnegie

A mind that is fed constructive, complimentary, loving, uplifting, motivational, and helpful thoughts will most likely produce verbal and physical emotions that correspond with those positive thoughts.

Begin to think in a way that adjusts your energy to the frequency that you want to enjoy.

> "For as he thinketh in his heart, so is he."
> – Psalms 23:7

Just as a music conductor determines the way an orchestra plays a symphony, people can conduct the symphony of thoughts playing out in their minds.

Thoughts are power tools. The most successful people tune into a way of thinking that builds success. Similarly, a person who is a consistent failure is likely tuned into a way of thinking that results in failure. In this way those thoughts are creating a web that can capture what is desired, or what isn't. Some people call this a karmic affect. This is because your thoughts create your actions, and you can attract what your thoughts and actions create.

Nobody owns the license or copyright on the power of thought. It is free to everyone. However, many people only use a tiny bit of this power, while others learn to use thought power for what amounts to brilliance and magnificence.

> "Every day, think as you wake up, today I am fortunate to be alive, I have a precious human life, I am not going to waste it. I am going to use all my energies to develop myself, to expand my heart out to others; to achieve enlightenment for the benefit of all beings. I am going to have kind thoughts towards others, I am not going to get angry or think badly about others. I am going to benefit others as much as I can."
>
> – Dalai Lama

Unfortunately there are those who misuse their power and live lives that damage other forms of life and destroy Earth. They do not seem to understand that when you harm other life forms and Earth, you also harm yourself.

No matter what pattern of thinking you have allowed yourself to fall into, you can willfully change it.

You can resist damaging thought patterns. You can will away destructive emotions. You can consciously strengthen your abilities to think in a way that is more helpful to achieving happiness in your life, and in contributing to the lives of others. You can eliminate self-destructive tendencies and retool your thoughts and actions to build a foundation for good things in your life and within the society in which you live.

> "What we are today comes from our thoughts of yesterday, and our present thoughts build our life of tomorrow: Our life is the creation of our mind."
>
> – Buddha

The natural law that permeates all things is that of cause and effect. This law rules over the power of thought. It is evident in the lives of those who work to improve their condition. What you think about often comes about through your words and actions.

> "A single gentle rain makes the grass many shades greener. So our prospects brighten on the influx of better thoughts."
>
> – Henry David Thoreau

Stories originating from all parts of Earth carry a theme of people finding that the answers to their questions are sitting right in front of them. For a time they may have been blind to the messages that surrounded them. Their stubbornness in their refusal to open their mind and become enlightened made them unable to read the messages. They may have had resources of enlightenment surrounding them, but they did not access those. The tools may have existed, but they didn't do what it took to recognize and factor how to use them. Their possibilities and options were always there, but they did not notice them. But then a change of focus brought them to realize that they had the answers, the means, and the resources they needed to get what they needed. It was a change of thought that helped them.

> "We are all too much inclined to walk through life with our eyes shut. There are things all around us, and right at our very feet, that we have never seen; because we have never really looked."
> – Alexander Graham Bell

> "When the student is ready, the Master appears."
> – Buddhist proverb

Throughout world history the story has been recorded on cave walls, in ancient scripts, in novels and plays, and in modern films. It is the story that humans can overcome challenges. A common thread within these stories describes the change a person goes through within his or her mind enabling the person to overcome obstacles and achieve success in any situation. The message to be found is that it is up to the individual to conquer and prosper starting from where they are by using their intuition, skills, talents, and intellect.

> "Normally, we do not so much look at things as overlook them."
> – Alan Watts

Understand that learning and doing keeps your brain growing and active. Teach yourself about the things you need to learn to take the actions that will have you living the life you want to have. Continually engage in thoughts and activities that correspond with what you ideally see yourself thinking and doing.

> "The mind is not a vessel to be filled, but a fire to be kindled."
> – William Butler Yeats

When you begin to practice a task that requires a certain type of focus and movement, such as drawing, dancing, yoga, bike riding, or swimming, and you practice this task over and over during a period of weeks, months, and years, your brain rewires itself in relation to the parts of the brain that control the movements you are making. This is done in correspondence with your thoughts. That is a fascinating fact. This process reveals that what you think about and what you do with your physical body alters not only your muscles, but also the nerve cells inside your brain and throughout your body tissues.

> "A lot of what passes for depression these days is nothing more than a body saying that it needs work."
> – Geoffrey Norman

Because your neurons grow in accordance with what you are thinking, saying, and doing, it is important to continually think, say, and do the things necessary to participate in the life you want, and to start doing it as soon as possible.

Whatever it is that you want to do, learn about it and do it. Read books about it. Think about doing it. Plan on doing it. Write goals telling yourself that you are going to do it. And do it mentally and physically.

> "It's the repetition of affirmations that leads to belief. And once that belief becomes a deep conviction, things begin to happen."
> – Claude M. Bristol

Know that your thoughts are the sources driven by your spiritual force that will make you do what you want to do with your life.

Rather than thinking that your good fortunes are up to uncontrollable luck, think of luck as a matter of bringing about thought vibrations that are then manifested by the expression of good will in action. Control your actions to continually work for better fortunes to happen.

Cultivate your ideas into reality by using thoughts and actions to order substances and circumstances into your life that fulfill your needs and desires.

Let your thoughts liberate you from whatever it is in your life that has prevented you from succeeding. Think of things that will capture the good things about your life, as well as the possibility for good things to happen in the present and future.

Focus on thoughts of health brought on by invigorating exercise and vibrant foods.

Focus on thoughts of accomplishment and satisfaction from working on and completing projects.

Focus on thoughts of happiness resulting from intentional living that brings you to continually engage in goal-oriented actions that fulfill your wishes.

Focus on thoughts of loving, nurturing relationships cultivated by respect and beneficial communication.

Start now through your thoughts and actions to create your future happiness, love, and existence.

> "Finally, brethren, whatever is true, whatever is honorable, whatever is right, whatever is pure, whatever is lovely, whatever is of good repute, if there is any excellence and if anything is worthy of praise, let your mind dwell on these things."
>
> – Phillipians 4:8

Meditation: Deeper Thought

> "Imagination is more important than knowledge. For knowledge is limited to all we now know and understand, while imagination embraces the entire world, and all there ever will be to know and understand."
>
> – Albert Einstein

Diet, movement, thought, planning, and intentional, goal-oriented actions are all important in improving well-being, and especially in balance to experience vibrant health.

> "That which dominates our imaginations and our thoughts will determine our lives, and our character."
>
> – Ralph Waldo Emerson

A healthful mind is a major tool in balancing the physical structure. Nurturing the mind with worthwhile thoughts, intellectual stimulation, and social interaction is as important to maintaining health as are excellent nutrition and regular exercise.

Positive-thinking is so important to nurturing vibrant health that it could be considered an essential nutrient. This is because the activities of the mind are intermixed with and affect the tissues. Just as healthful foods, daily exercise, and a regular sleeping pattern balance body chem.-istry, healthful thoughts trigger the release of various hormones that influence the chemistry and function of all the tissues of the body.

"The world is full of people looking for spectacular happiness while they snub contentment."
– Doug Larson

Health and spiritual teachers throughout history have stressed the importance of the thought processes in conditioning health. In particular, they have taught about the health benefits of meditation.

Modern science has shown that meditation is healthful in that it reduces the production of cortisol, a natural hormone produced by the body when it is under stress and that degrades memory processes. Cortisol levels are also reduced by laughter.

"In the attitude of silence the soul finds the path in a clearer light, and what is elusive and deceptive resolves itself into crystal clearness."
– Mahatma Gandhi

"As irrigators lead water where they want, as archers make their arrows straight, as carpenters carve wood, the wise shape their minds."
– Buddha

By studying Tibetan monks who practice meditation for decades, Richard Davidson of the University of Wisconsin-Madison found that meditation influences the neural growth patterns of the brain. The temporal parietal junction region of the brain, which deals with processing empathetic feelings and expressions is one of the regions that meditation has been found to alter. Neurons of the insula region of the brain, which deals with emotional response, is also affected by meditation.

Meditation has also been found to build the cortex area of the brain, which is involved in higher functions, and typically thins as we age. Thus, meditation is an antiaging practice.

"Do you have patience to wait till your mud settles and the water is clear? Can you remain unmoving till the right action arises by itself?"
– Lao Tzu

When the word "meditation" is mentioned some people entertain images of people in zombie-like trances. Some are uncomfortable with the concept of meditation because it suggests a religious, or cultlike practice, which are both fallacies. Others may think of meditation as not in tune with what they consider to be mainstream. But maybe mainstream isn't as good as they may believe, and going outside of the mainstream could be greatly beneficial to them. Some think of meditation as an Eastern form of spirituality. But some form of meditation has been a common practice among people the world over. Ancient societies on all continents had their own form of meditation.

Still others may not like the concept of doing meditation because they simply may be uncomfortable with and unwilling to face up to their thoughts.

Some people have been in such unhealthful situations their entire lives that engaging in something healthful is foreign to them as it displaces the stress they are accustomed to feeling and the dysfunction they are accustomed to. Doing something truly healthful may make them uncomfortable, as if they are losing their footing and control because they are in an unfamiliar place — even if that unfamiliar place is better for them.

However, since meditation is simply deep thinking, it is doubtful that there is anyone who hasn't practiced it at some time when faced with a life-altering decision or situation. They didn't know that they were meditating.

> "Silence is the element in which great things fashion themselves together."
> – Thomas Carlyle

> "Let us be silent — so we may hear the whisper of the gods."
> – Ralph Waldo Emerson

Many people became familiar with the Eastern spiritual practice form of meditation when it was reported that the Beatles were studying transcendental meditation under the guidance of its founder, Maharishi Mahesh Yogi. The Beatles first studied with him in Wales. They traveled to Rishikesh, India, to continue their studies.

Maharishi was from India and held a degree in physics. After studying under various teachers, his spiritual regeneration movement began in 1957. With encouragement from his students, in 1958 he began traveling the world to spread the message that humanity can rid itself of discontent. Schools of Maharishi's teaching have been established in several countries. Some of the teachings include the study of the ancient Vedic text, the Bhagavad Gita, which Maharishi called "the scripture of yoga."

"Meditation is the discovery that the point of life is always arrived at in the immediate moment."
– Alan Watts

Meditating puts a person in a quiet state during which sensory input is reduced. This is similar to deep sleep, but with the consciousness remaining engaged. During this time, just as in sleep, the neurons of the brain can process new information and make the neural connections needed to remember and deal with recently learned thought and action processes. Those who regularly practice meditation, such as Buddhist monks, have been found to have strong gamma wave brain energy patterns that are associated with alertness, learning, and memory.

"Meditation is not just the means to an end. It is both the means and the end."
– Jiddu Krishnamurti

Going through your thoughts with which you are uncomfortable, understanding them, and arranging them in a helpful order is what can be done when meditating.

Meditation helps you let go of issues and grasp hold of others. It can be beneficial in dealing with the trials of life as well as learning how to associate with beneficial events and the constant present.

"It is as important to cultivate your silent power as it is your word power."
– William James

Using the mind to focus on self, or the essence of being during meditation, allows people to look at the engine of their mind, and service it. It allows people to take an inventory of their life, to consider on what their energies have been focused, to let go of the thoughts and feelings that are not helpful and that may need to be disposed of, and to assign focus to those things that need attention.

"I learned from them that inspiration does not come like a bolt, nor is it kinetic, energetic striving, but it comes into us slowly and quietly and all the time, though we must regularly and every day give it a little chance to start flowing, prime it with a little solitude and idleness."
– Brenda Ueland

"Meditation is the tongue of the soul and the language of our spirit."

– Jeremy Taylor

"See how nature — trees, flowers, grass — grows in silence; see the stars, the moon and the sun, how they move in silence. We need silence to be able to touch souls."

– Mother Teresa

Meditation may be practiced in combination with yoga, with introspective journaling, with artistic activities, with gardening, and with priority and goal review.

Getting into a daily morning practice of meditation, yoga, and goal review is an excellent way to start the day. Meditation helps focus the mind and tune the energy into the actions that need to be accomplished that day. This practice will help create progressive thoughts that trigger related actions.

"The struggle of the male to learn to listen to and respect his own intuitive, inner promptings is the greatest challenge of all. His conditioning has been so powerful that it has all but destroyed his ability to be self-aware."

– Herb Goldberg

Meditating, yoga, and journaling can be particularly helpful for someone during a day (or more) without food but only water, which is called "fasting." As you allow the body to take a rest from eating food while drinking only water, you allow it to focus its energies on elimination, detoxifying, and healing. Some people will go on a juice fast, which is when they spend a day or more avoiding solid food but will consume fresh vegetable and/or fruit juices, and water.

Another alternative to a pure water or a juice fast is to consume nothing but green smoothies and water for a week or more. Green smoothies consist of water blended with a fruit, such as apple, peach, banana, papaya, berries, or mango, and some green leaves, such as spinach, kale, Romaine lettuce, chard, collard, dandelion, parsley, cilantro, celery, chickweed, or other green leaf vegetables. Green smoothies contain more antioxidants than pure vegetable or fruit juices because many antioxidants are contained in the cell walls of the plants. Wheatgrass juice and fresh aloe gel are also excellent additions to green smoothies. Avoid putting starchy vegetables in green smoothies because the starch mixed with the fruit can cause bloating and gas. Also, it is good to avoid having the same green every single day. For more information, see Victoria Boutenko's book, *The Green Smoothie Revolution.*

When fasting and meditation are done on a day of rest from work, the mind has a chance to clear and refocus. Many people teach that fasting and meditation are helpful to practice at each change of season. Some people drink only water while abstaining from food for 24 hours on the day of the full moon.

Just as fasting allows the body to dispose of toxins and undigested foods, meditation can be used to clear toxic thoughts and to align with more helpful and healing thoughts in tune with the life the person desires.

> "We are frightened by our own solitude. Yet only in solitude can we learn to know ourselves, learn to handle our own eternity of aloneness. And love from one being to another is when two solitudes come nearer, to recognize and protect and comfort each other."
>
> – Han Suyin

Those who follow a fully plant-based diet and spend a day or two in meditation while fasting, practicing yoga, journaling, and visualizing their life as they would like it to be in tune with Nature, can reach into the power of their spirituality. This retreat session can be an amazing experience. When a fasting retreat is done regularly (such as once every season), it can help a person transform their being into one that is more healthful in all ways, and one that will become more focused on accomplishing their intentions.

> "I have learned to seek my happiness by limiting my desires, rather than in attempting to satisfy them."
>
> – John Stuart Mill

A person going through a personal retreat gains mental and spiritual strength. The benefits can continue after the fast by following a diet consisting of the best-quality plant-based foods available to them, and living intentionally with thoughts and actions corresponding with their goals.

> "Life does not consist mainly, or even largely, of facts and happenings. It consists mainly of the storm of thought that is forever flowing through one's head."
>
> – Mark Twain

To keep the mind healthful, think healthful thoughts; study literature relating to what you most desire to be doing; stay involved in healthful activities; work to maintain loving relationships; and give the brain the best nutrients through high-quality foods and intellectual stimulation.

The better health you obtain through high-quality nutrition, daily exercise, and intellectual stimulation in alignment with your goals, the more agile you will be in performing the tasks that will accomplish your intentions.

As you practice staying in a healthful, uplifting, positive state of mind, your brain will get accustomed to this and will work to support the posture you are working to hold. The body chemistry will also adjust to this, and the tissues will produce molecules of emotion in tune with the healthful state of the mind. This does not happen randomly, but is a result of your intentional thoughts and actions that create synapses in your neurons in tune with what you desire to be doing. This plays a major role in what you are able to achieve.

Exercise is important in all this because it helps the brain to function. When you exercise your body, you are exercising your brain and utilizing the nerve cells in all areas of the body. This increases the agility of both the body and mind. Through improving health with intentional thoughts and actions, you can better access formerly dormant areas of your brain.

A part of the brain that has been shown to function better through following a clean diet combined with intentional thoughts and actions is the pineal gland. It is located in the center of the brain and is known as the spiritual gland and the brains trigger, which is set off by inspiration. The health and function of the pineal gland especially can be greatly improved by a combination of vibrant foods, positive thoughts, intellectual stimulation, intentional and goal-oriented living, healthful relationships, quality exercise, and a regular sleep pattern.

> "I am convinced that there are universal currents of Divine thought vibrating the ether everywhere and that any who can feel these vibrations is inspired."
>
> – Richard Wagner

These concepts of taking care of the body to build a healthful mind are not new and are as old as the most ancient teachings. They permeate all societies and are part of the general concept of building a strong and healthful community no matter where it exists.

What the ancient people didn't have is the modern-day understanding of the substances within the foods they consumed. That is not to say they didn't know that certain substances impacted physical function and mental thought. They clearly did have an understanding of the medicinal qualities of plant substances. They used specific plants and mushrooms to influence changes in their physical and mental conditions.

> "The new formula of physics describes humans as paradoxical beings who have two complementary aspects: They can show properties of Newtonian objects and also infinite fields of consciousness."
>
> – Stanislav Grog

As you better understand these things, the more you will be able to use them in improving all areas of your life.

Start today to spend some time meditating on clarifying your intentions and on being present within the intentions, and then spend every day acting on the intentions.

> "Every single moment has a particular rhythm to it, and we have the capacity to expand or contract an individual moment as appropriate. One way to shift what's going on in our world is not to try to rush to do more, but to allow ourselves to go deeper into that moment of being present. Our ability to shift gears, to shift our rhythm to meet that moment and be present in it, is what allows us to experience the fullness of life."
>
> – Stephan Rechtschaffen

Visualization

Visualization techniques can play an important role in creating the life you want.

> "Never lose sight of the fact that all human felicity lies in man's imagination and that he cannot think to attain it unless he heeds all his caprices."
>
> – Donatien Alphonse "Marquis de Sade" François

> "All meaningful and lasting change starts first in your imagination and then works its way out."
>
> – Albert Einstein

"Thought is action in rehearsal."
– Sigmund Freud

Much of your life is initially created in your mind. The life within your thoughts manifests into reality through your actions.

Your thoughts control what your body will be doing, the tasks you will be performing, the communication you will be engaging in, and what you do to shape, color, and tone your environment. Because of this process, your life is more likely to resemble the ways in which you visualize your life.

"No matter how qualified or deserving you are, you will never reach a better life until you can imagine it for yourself and allow yourself to have it."
– Richard Bach

"Where there is no vision, the people parish."
– King Solomon, Proverbs 29:18

If you want your life to be a certain way, start thinking about it being that way and work your thoughts into actions that will create that life. Pay attention to the things that will inspire or influence your mind to bring this about.

"Dream lofty dreams, and as you dream, so shall you become. Your vision is the promise of what you shall one day be; your ideal is the prophecy of what you shall at last unveil."
– James Allen

It takes practice to get your mind to think about the things you want to happen. While in the past your life may have been slothful and unappealing, much of this likely had to do with the way you conducted your thoughts. To get out of that mindset, retrain your patterns of thought in a way that improves your time management, goal setting, communication, food choices, fitness, actions, surroundings, relationships, satisfaction, and the expression of your talents, skills, intellect, and other graces.

"Vision is perhaps our greatest strength. It has kept us alive to the power and continuity of thought through the centuries, it makes us peer into the future and lends shape to the unknown."
– Li Ka Shing

Visualize yourself experiencing vibrant health; eating a natural, plant-based diet that is largely raw; enjoying nurturing and loving relationships; expressing kind and uplifting words and thoughts to those around you who reflect these back to you; utilizing your talents in ways beneficial to your happiness; exercising your intellect to create peace, and becoming attuned to all that is good.

> "The first step towards getting somewhere is to decide that you are not going to stay where you are."
> – John Pierpont Morgan

Imagine your life being simple, clean, uncluttered, and free of the things that are unhealthful, unhelpful, unkind, damaging, wasteful, and unsustainable. And keep visualizing yourself consistently and persistently improving your life and the condition of Nature that supports your life.

> "Your vision will become clear only when you look into your heart. Who looks outside, dreams. Who looks inside, awakens."
> – Carl Gustav Jung

Make it a habit to visualize what you want to come about. Let it fuel actions that bring about desired changes

Permeate your thoughts with those that are in alignment with realizing your goals.

Bring an emotional attitude into play that will help you progress toward the life you want. In alignment with this, carry the physical posture of the version of yourself that you want to be.

Mental imagery can help you improve your physical, mental, and spiritual being. But a major key to obtaining the life you want is that you absolutely must physically work to attain the things you want, and not simply fantasize about them.

> "In order to change an existing paradigm you do not struggle to try and change the problematic model. You create a new model and make the old one obsolete."
> – Richard Buckminster Fuller

Use the power of your mind and body to work diligently to continually transform your vision into reality.

Keep visualizing yourself as a success no matter what happens and work toward that visualization through positive actions. Use your intuition to guide you through any difficulties while focusing on attaining your goals. Continually select thoughts and actions that intentionally bring a positive out of every change.

> "Go confidently in the direction of your dreams! Live the life you've imagined. As you simplify your life, the laws of the universe will be simpler."
> – Henry David Thoreau

As I mention elsewhere, when you begin to practice a task that requires a certain type of focus and movement, such as drawing, dancing, yoga, biking, or swimming, and you practice this task over and over during a period of weeks, months, and years, your brain rewires itself in relation to the parts of the brain that control the movements you are making. This shows that what you think about and what you do with your physical body alters not only your muscles, but also the form and function of the neurons both inside your brain and throughout your body tissues.

> "If you are seeking creative ideas, go out walking. Angels whisper to a man when he goes for a walk."
> – Raymond Inmon

Choose to use the power of your visualization to fuel and nurture your life.

Uplift yourself through inspirational thoughts. Let the common theme of your thoughts be what empowers you. If it is a poem, think it. If it is a song, let it sing inside you. If it is an image, visualize it.

> "The soul is dyed the color of its thoughts. Think only on those things that are in line with your principles and can bear the full light of day. The content of your character is your choice. Day by day, what you think, and what you do is who you become. Your integrity is your destiny. It is the light that guides your way."
> – Heraclitus

> "Paint the walls of your mind with many beautiful pictures."
> – William Lyons Phelps

Visualizing into Your Future

> "Most people are not really free. They are confined by the niche in the world that they carve out for themselves. They limit themselves to fewer possibilities by the narrowness of their vision."
> – Vidiadhar Surajprasad Naipaul

Read this chapter fully. Then, close your eyes and participate in it.

> "I shut my eyes in order to see."
> – Paul Gaugin

As an exercise, close your eyes and picture your life the way you want it to be. Keeping your eyes closed, hold that image of your desired life and explore what it looks like. Recognize what it is that you see. Work it into a simple and sustainable image.

> "What a man thinks of himself, that is what determines, or rather, indicates his fate."
> – Henry David Thoreau

Visualize your life decluttered, organized, environmentally sustainable, fed with high-quality foods, intellectually stimulated, professionally successful, infused with health and love, and in all ways satisfactory to you.

Pay particular attention to what you see in this vision of your life in a satisfied and sustainable form. What will you be doing in the satisfactory life? What will you be eating? How will you exercise? What will you be working on? Where will you be? With whom will you be? What do the surroundings look like? What are you going to be doing to transform this image into reality?

Open your eyes.

Write down and/or draw what you saw in your visualization. Include details.

Make a list of goals that you can read and adjust every morning to start your day with purpose and intention focused on creating your life the way you want your life to be.

Welcome to your future.

Begin now to create it.

> "Every day is a journey, and the journey itself is home."
> – Matsuo Basho

"Take the first step in faith. You don't have to see the whole staircase. Just take the first step."
– Marin Luther King, Jr.

Be Your Life Architect

"We are what we repeatedly do. Excellence then is not an act, but a habit."
– Aristotle

"Life is raw material. We are artisans. We can sculpt our existence into something beautiful, or debase it into ugliness. It's in our hands."
– Cathy Better

Just as a stone worker can create a building out of a pile of sand and rocks, you can create a life for yourself out of whatever materials it now consists of.

Being a proactive architect of your life involves instructing yourself towards success. By this I mean that you would benefit by being specific with your instruction and action as if putting a recipe together. By continually thinking thoughts that fuel actions that create change in your life, you are constructing a new life for yourself. Just as the repetition of a wheel advances a vehicle to a new location, through your repetition of positive thoughts and intentional, goal-oriented actions your life will get to a different place.

Constructing something is about working with patterns.

When considering a human-built structure it is easy to recognize geometric patterns within its design. The structure was also constructed by a pattern of work that put the materials together that were also formed by a geometrically produced pattern of growth and/or compaction of substances.

"Nature is an endless combination and repetition of a very few laws."
– Ralph Waldo Emerson

There are patterns in your body, in your fingers, eyes, and through all the structures of your being, including the cells, and within the substances that make up the cells. These structures are formulated by an inner energy that has directed the formation of the structures in relation to a pattern. The things you eat have patterns within them and were formulated by growth patterns that continually form within the laws of Nature. The pattern of digestion breaks down the substances you eat into materials that are then used by the body in a pattern that creates the patterns of your tissues.

There are also patterns in thoughts.

> "Thought is the sculptor who can create the person you want to be."
> – Henry David Thoreau

> "Teaching music is not my main purpose. I want to make good citizens. If children hear fine music from the day of their birth and learn to play it, they develop sensitivity, discipline and endurance. They get a beautiful heart."
> – Shinichi Suzuki

After twenty years of research, in 1993 University of California Irvine physicist Gordon Shaw published a study in which he concluded that listening to classical music could temporarily increase a person's IQ. Over the course of decades, Shaw studied the brain's ability to recognize symmetries and patterns in sounds. He found that people apply this process in solving math problems, in playing music, and in performing tasks, such as playing chess. In his research, Shaw concluded that the brain's patterns resemble classical musical compositions. In reverse, he hypothesized that the brain could also be influenced by classical music. In his research, he worked with cellist and psychologist Frances Rauscher to put three-year-olds through a six-month test with half of them receiving voice lessons and the others receiving instruction in piano. After six months, those who had the piano lessons displayed improvement in spatial-temporal reasoning. With another test, Shaw put college students through tests that showed their IQs improved by nine points after listening to classical music. The study involved having the students go through various stages of tests that included silence, relaxation tapes, and listening to Wolfgang Amadeus Mozart's Sonata for Two Pianos in D Major. Shaw's research showed an increase in the IQ of the college students who listened to the Mozart sonata. This announcement, now known as "the Mozart effect," brought Florida state-funded childcare centers to play music by Ludwig van Beethoven, and the state of Georgia to distribute classical music recordings to new mothers. Using Shaw's research as a marketing tool, companies began selling classical music recordings specifically meant for parents to play to their babies and toddlers. Shaw went on to write a book, *Keeping Mozart in Mind*, and developed a piano keyboard process specifically designed to improve math skills. In subsequent studies, Shaw used magnetic resonance imaging to show that Mozart's music stimulated the brain's cortex more than music by Beethoven, which left Shaw puzzled.

> "If I were not a physicist, I would probably be a musician. I often think in music. I live my daydreams in music. I see my life in terms of music."
> – Albert Einstein

One of my favorite descriptions of how humans relate to the patterns of music is in the opening of Randall Grass' book, *Great Spirits: Portraits of Life-Changing World Music Artists*. In it, Grass writes, "Music has a way of ineffably penetrating our hearts and minds and souls. Perhaps, then, it should not be surprising that the most recent theory concocted to explain the universe is string theory, which posits that the smallest, irreducible element at the core of any piece of matter is a single, vibrating string. In other words, according to this theory, music is the essence of the universe: the cosmos is one massive symphony of vibrations and waves pulsating at myriad frequencies, tempos, and rhythms." Grass, who is a musician and master in world music, theorizes that, "The capacity of humans to relate to music may be simply an innate means for people to comprehend and connect with the cosmos at the most profound level."

> "Rhythm and harmony are essential to the whole of life."
> – Plato

> "To understand is to perceive patterns."
> – Isaiah Berlin

Just as the notes of music put in a certain pattern can be either chaotic or pleasant, so too are the patterns of your thoughts, which play out in your actions. Thoughts help form the network of neurons within you, the actions your tissues make, and the arrangement of the things around you. As you do, hear, feel, say, and see things, the memories of those are stored as patterns in connections between neurons that are formed according to what you are involved in. It is the repetition and patterns formed within the neurons of your brain and body combined with the way certain experiences, memories, behaviors, and chemistry turn on and off specific genes, and the patterns of those genes, that collectively create what you call "my life."

"Mathematics possesses not only truth, but also supreme beauty."
– Bertrand Russell

There are patterns in leaves, in seeds, in cells, and in all the structures of all living things. The surface structures of animals and plants have patterns. More patterns are in the structures of the tissues, and other patterns are in the microscopic structures of the cells, in the intercellular structures, in the nucleus, chromatin, DNA, molecules, and in the subatomic electrons and protons, and the intricacies of smallness. There are patterns in the trillions of activities that take place within living cells during every second. The patterns are created by energy, which is the power of Nature, which is of Divinity, which is in us, throughout us, and surrounds us.

There too are patterns in your essence. And there is power there. These powers are your talents, abilities, instinct, and intellect guided by the elegant power of your spirit. You can, with your power, use these to formulate your life and build it into what it could be. You have the strength within you to make this happen. You know it is there; it drives you to be attracted to and to be pleased by particular sounds, colors, shades, textures, smells, shapes, and feelings — which all consist of patterns. Left to randomness these attributes can be like the pieces of a puzzle in a pile. Organized and managed, they can create the picture of what your life can become if you would engage your powers to make it that way.

Understand and accept that your life can be a beautiful and satisfying combination of patterns.

Begin to think in a way that adjusts your energy to the patterns of frequency you wish to enjoy. Align yourself with patterns of good. Work to awaken the patterns of powerful energy that rests within. Build patterns in everything you think and do that are in alignment with the results you desire.

"A successful man is one who can lay a firm foundation with the bricks that others throw at him."
– David Brinkley

Every building, machine, product, business, and document is the product of an idea, which is a thought.

The first structure that exists before something is built is the structure made of thoughts formulated inside the architect's mind. Similarly, your mind is the architect of your future life. Use your mind as the tool to carve your life into what you want it to be.

Just as an architect first thinks up plans, then draws them out before bringing them into reality by creating a structure, you too can work your thoughts into reality by writing down your goals, and then working to create them into reality. Writing down your goals is one of the most basic steps in bringing them into reality.

Consider that the cells of your body have a game plan, or a blueprint that they follow. It is called the DNA and the pattern within it determines the design and function of the cells.

Each person is like a vine that is constantly growing. The vine can be guided to grow in a certain way, or it can be left to grow in whatever way it happens to grow. Like a gardener coaxing a vine to grow through the pattern of a trellis, each person can guide the ways in which their life develops and what pattern it follows.

Actions result in learning, which is knowledge that can be used to bring about more actions to create what you desire.

Your knowledge-driven actions are sewing a fabric into the life around you. What you do becomes part of your surroundings just as a thread becomes part of the fabric it is sewn into.

As you continually work to attain your goals you will learn what you need to know to achieve them. As you work toward what you want, the path toward the life you want will keep unfolding before you in a pattern relating to how you lead your life, which is in accordance with the pattern of your thoughts.

> "We are weaving character every day, and the way to weave the best character is to be kind and to be useful. Think right, act right; it is what we think and do that makes us who we are."
> – Elbert Hubbard

What you do each moment of each day creates a furrow. The seeds planted in that furrow consist of whatever you are nurturing through your thoughts, emotions, words, and actions. Those thoughts and actions that are helpful and beautiful will continue to flower as you nurture them; the opposite thoughts and actions will result in negatives, and will need to be weeded out. Thus the longer you live, much of the reality surrounding you becomes part of your own making.

> "We know what a person thinks not when he tells us what he thinks, but by his actions."
> – Isaac Bashevis Singer

There is a Biblical law that states, "As you sew, so shall ye reap" (Galatians 6:7). That law is not something that is limited to those who believe in the Bible. It is a fundamental law that exists throughout life. Your actions will most often bring about results in accordance with the actions, which are the blossoms of your thoughts.

> "No matter how small and unimportant what we are doing may seem, if we do it well, it may soon become the step that will lead us to better things."
> – Channing Pollock

Where you are right now is where you can begin using the knowledge you have to get you to where you want to be. The actions you take from where you are will create your future.

> "Any place that we love becomes our world."
> – Oscar Wilde

As artists use their imagination to create works of art, use your imagination to make your life into your art. Let that be your pattern.

> "'What are you?' someone asks. 'I am the story of my self,' comes the answer."
> – M. Scott Momady

Resonational Inheritance

> "Memories of our lives, of our works, and our deeds will continue in others."
> – Rosa Parks

The resonation of others has an impact on our physical, mental, and every other aspect of our being. The more closely you live in relation to someone the more of an influence you have on each others' thoughts, actions, and lives.

Those who spend a lot of time together, such as married couples, often not only start thinking the same, they also begin to resemble each other, tend to express the same mannerisms and vocal patterns, and often adapt to doing things in the same way.

Medical anthropologists at the University of Würzburg in Germany have discovered that when babies as young as three days old cry, they already imitate the melody patterns of their mother's language. The study, which was in the November 5, 2009 edition of the journal *Current Biology*, concluded that babies learn the melody patterns of the mother's language while still in the womb. Babies of French-speaking mothers were found to cry in a different melody than babies of German-speaking mothers. By three months, babies can mimic the vowel sounds in their parents' language.

> "What you leave behind is not what is engraved in stone monuments, but what is woven into the lives of others."
> – Pericles

Children often not only speak in tonal qualities similar to their parents, they also often develop the same wants, appetites, emotional behaviors, concerns, and breathing patterns. This is because they are often exposed to the same patterns of thoughts, actions, words, sounds, and nutrients.

Vibrational patterns can last generations. The subtleties involved with how your parents lived likely had to do with the life choices of their parents, grandparents, and other ancestors.

Science has discovered the presence of what are called "mirror neurons." This term is used to describe neurons within our brains and body tissues that respond to the way those around us are conducting themselves.

A simple example of how mirror neurons work is to watch people who are in the audience of a sporting event. The spectators are often physically responding to the actions of the sporting team members. Neurons within us that control our voluntary and involuntary movements, such as moving away from danger, or going toward something we want, have been shown to react to watching someone going toward something desirable, or moving away from something that is not desirable. This is why we squinch our faces when we are watching a character in a film who tastes something that is highly undesirable. It is also why we nearly jump from our seats when we see a character in a film suddenly experience extreme danger or pain.

To understand how mirror neurons work and how the brain wires itself in relation to what the person experiences is to understand that we can become wired in relation to what we see other people doing, saying, and experiencing. The simple act of continually being around someone helps to formulate our neural growth. In this way, we can inherit some of the neural growth patterns of the people we spend a lot of time around. Some of the neural growth patterns in us relate to what other people have been exposed to, and in how they respond and react to daily situations.

> "Long after a deed is done, the trace or momentum of the intention left behind it remains as a seed, conditioning our future happiness or unhappiness."
> – Gil Fronsdal

The vibrational octaves of your ancestors are likely to keep flowing through your body in thought processes, in habits, in choices of food and lifestyle, and in how you communicate. These ancestral memories are expressed through your mannerisms, the tone of your voice, the words you use, and in other subtle ways.

The voice is often a good example of how patterns that developed in your ancestry continue through you. Vocal tone is one vibration that often continues from generation to generation. Even a person who is adopted into a family will take on the resonance, inflection, and other voice qualities of the adopted family. The vibrations that travel through the parents and out through their voice boxes will most likely tune the children's voices into the same vibration. This phenomenon represents that of energy influencing neural growth and tissue development.

Children also absorb the energy vibrations of other areas of their parents' lives, including unhealthful thought processes (which are also vibrations) that are expressed through the person's words, actions, and attitudes, which are all tonal qualities.

> "The past is never dead. It's not even past. All of us labor in webs spun long before we were born, webs of heredity and environment, of desire and consequence, of history and eternity. Haunted by wrong turns and roads not taken, we pursue images perceived as new but whose providence dates to the dim dramas of childhood, which are themselves but ripples of consequence echoing down the generations. The quotidian demands of life distract from this resonance of images and events, but some of us feel it always."
> – William Faulkner

We are all tuning forks taking on the vibrations of what we are exposed to. By continually being around others, you are playing a role in tuning them. Be aware that you can send the vibrations of your life into the lives of the people who surround you, such as your family, friends, lovers, fellow students, neighbors, and co-workers.

The inciting incidents of your life also leave you with traits that are the evidence of your experiences. These traits are also vibrational tones expressed through body language, facial movements, attitudes, words, and lifestyle.

Unfortunately you can carry on the negative and generally unhelpful energies that may have been carried by your ancestors and those you've spent time around.

The good news is that you can readjust your being, retune your energy, and conduct yourself in more healthful ways that will build more helpful neural growth patterns.

> "Don't seek to merely get rid of the negative things in your life. Instead, transform their energy into something of real positive value."
> – Ralph Marston

Some of us have been lucky in that our ancestors and relationships have been relatively healthful. That does not mean that we can't begin to make unwise choices that bring us into unhealthful patterns. Nor, if we came from an unfortunate background, does it mean that we need to continue participating in unhealthful patterns that may be resonating from our ancestry and associations.

We can recondition our conditions. Every day and every moment we can choose to saturate our lives with healthful behavior that is in harmony with a higher level of consciousness.

> "There is more hunger for love and appreciation in this world than for bread."
> – Mother Teresa

Some of us were born into families that carry a history of generations of brutal, drunken, poverty-stricken, depressed, angry, abused, uneducated, malnourished, unloving ancestors whose fractured lives were rife with addictions, homelessness, failure, petty crime, infighting, slander, dishonesty, unwise confrontations, and all forms of ruin. Often these sorts of family issues can be traced back several generations, and the pattern is the same — tragic or defeated lives that could have been otherwise if people had used their power to change their state.

It can often be heard that we should honor our ancestors and the sacrifices they made. For some of us, this is noble and helps bring honor to our lives because we had ancestors who really strived to become wonderful people who did good things.

For some of us the strongest impressions we have of our ancestors are of the unfortunate decisions they had made. Under such conditions, being told that we should honor them may take a leap of faith, and may be a step into the unwise den of denial. Instead of feeling obligated to pay tribute to lives rife with ruinous behavior, we can at least live more healthfully for ourselves, for those around us, and simply perpetuate whatever beauty we can generate. By doing so we would be going forward out of blame and surpass the unhelpful activity of judging those who may no longer exist and whose mental conditions, life situations, and decisions we may never be able to understand.

Many families carry on unhealthful patterns developed over decades, and even centuries. Unwise family histories seem to thrive in the lives of some people to such an extreme that they are unable to function in society. It is as if they are intellectually paralyzed by the unfortunate choices of past generations, and as if they are the end of the tuning fork, which squeals with the heightened vibrations of whatever tonal qualities were experienced in the root of the tuning fork. Unfortunately for many people the unhealthful ways of their ancestors resonate so strongly in their lives that tragedy ensues.

Vibrational inheritance can be blazingly apparent in the frenzied lives of politicians. We can see this manifested in certain families that have had generations of political corruption infusing their business and personal lives. Their lives seem to be a crescendo of all the energy of greed, lies, hypocrisy, and corruption generated by their ancestors. It is a disconnection from and opposite to the healthful vibrancy of Nature wherein they become an enemy of Nature. Many of the wealthiest, money-hoarding people of the planet resonate with this damaging energy. It is displayed in the lives of those who own and/or run companies that do great harm to the environment, such as the factory farming, petroleum, coal, nuclear energy, bomb-making, weaponry, and prison industries.

> "There is no king who has not had a slave among his ancestors, and no slave who has not had a king among his."
> – Helen Keller

Without placing blame, review your ancestry, life history, and family heritage. Explore what you find. Consider that the choices your ancestors made are impacting your life.

It is very likely that the behavior of your ancestors is subtly — and perhaps loudly — playing out the way you are living your life.

> "Each difficult moment has the potential to open my eyes and open my heart."
> – Myla Kabat-Zinn

If your life is not working for you, recognize that you can become actively engaged in changing the vibrational patterns resonating through you so that your energy is in tune with your potential of experiencing satisfaction, health, and love.

Behind your genetic makeup is the mechanism that is your spirit, or essence — your spiritual genetics. This mechanism formed your being, and it remains as a tool you can use to reformulate your life. It functions better when you live more healthfully. It can be clarified through wise life choices to work in tune with intellectual stimulation, a healthful diet, a daily exercise regimen, and intentional, goal-oriented actions to create an amazing life.

By living healthfully, you can retune your body cells and your spirit from a history of unhealthful ancestors. I suggest to the people who are interested in doing this to tune into the vibrations of Nature through eating a vegan diet that consists chiefly of fresh, organically grown fruits and vegetables, and ideally some that are home grown; being close to and protecting plants and animals; filling their mind with life-confirming and encouraging literature and music; developing talents, craft, and skill; working to have healthful, nurturing relationships; and filling their days with intentional, goal-oriented activities.

Following a diet consisting of high-quality and mostly uncooked vegan foods while getting into the habit of daily morning yoga, priority review, and then intentionally engaging in activities throughout every day that are associated with goals are some of the most powerful steps you can take to break unhealthful intergenerational vibrations.

Living healthfully accesses the cryptic backup copy of your being to correct the damaging patterns that had been running through you. As you live more healthfully, your neurons will rewire to be in tune with the healthful lifestyle you lead.

> "The greatest discovery of any generation is that human beings can alter their lives by altering the attitudes of their minds."
> – Albert Schweitzer

Honor your life by moving onto a better path than the one that may have been created for you.

Be your own journey and remember that you may be helping to create the journey of those who walk beside you, and also who arrive after you.

> "The quality and fullness of our lives is not measured in length, but in the love and examples we leave those we have left behind."
> – Cindy Crawford

"Our greatest responsibility is to be good ancestors."
– Jonas Salk

Knowledge Is Power

"Do not seek to follow in the footsteps of the wise. Seek what they sought."
– Matsuo Basho

"You can't always be happy, but you can almost always be profoundly aware and curious, and reap the psychological and physical benefits. Thankfully, curiosity is not a fixed characteristic. It's a strength we can develop and wield on the path to a more fulfilling life."
– Todd Kashdan

To increase the likelihood of becoming the best version of yourself, become proactive in stimulating your mind, intellect, instinct, talents, skills, craft, and other graces to learn, act, and grow into what you desire to be.

"Education is for improving the lives of others and for leaving your community and world better than you found it."
– Marian Wright Edelman

"Whoever acquires knowledge but does not practice it, is as one who plows but does not sow."
– Saadi

Many people lead lives far beneath what they are capable of living. Many never read a book, rarely experience local cultural events, and don't get involved in or even know much about the region where they live. All this is representative of how they may never exercise their power within any of the areas of their life outside their most basic needs, and even in these they may be slothful.

It may seem easy to disconnect from parts of life that have great impact on our lives, but doing so may lead to results we do not wish to experience. It will likely also negatively impact the lives of others.

It may seem easy to ignore things that we think don't matter, but which may matter more than anything else. What may seem easy may amount to neglect that makes life, and the lives of others, more difficult.

People often recognize too late that they had in fact neglected part of their life that might have offered much benefit if they had given it more attention. Often they realize that what they did focus on was what didn't matter, or was less important than things that should have been getting attention.

We live in an age in which information is constantly being spewed out of the media at a rate at which no one person can keep up to speed. From books to newspapers, magazines, newsletters, and journals, to audio- and videotapes, to theatrical and documentary films, to radio and TV shows to the Internet, and to live entertainment and educational seminars and classes, information today seems to be present everywhere.

Information overload has become an issue with those who spend their days paying attention to the mass media. While there is an enormous amount of information being presented by these outlets, much of it is useless nonsense that results in wasted time and mind clutter. But the information is often presented in a way that makes it appear as if it is especially important to you.

It has been found that those who watch the most amount of TV are often the least informed on issues that greatly impact their lives. Concurrently, people who watch a lot of TV are most informed about celebrity culture and corporate brands. People who watch the most TV are also more likely to be overweight and experience health problems related to obesity, low-quality foods, and lack of physical activity. This is reflective of the junk mindset and junk diet created by corporate mass media.

> "The degree of one's emotions varies inversely with one's knowledge of the facts — the less you know the hotter you get."
> – Bertrand Russell

The strongest message you should be getting from the mass media is that paying attention to the mass media is a waste of your time, energy, and resources, and fills your mind with useless trivia while encouraging you to go into debt while eating the lowest-quality foods.

Just as there are people who can zap your energy, time, resources, and spirit, there are substances in commercial culture that can rob you of the same.

Just as it is beneficial to wisely choose the persons with whom you would like to spend time, and with whom you would allow to influence you, it is also wise to select what sort of information you choose to listen to.

Whether you are aware of it or not, you are constantly being influenced, you are always learning, you are always absorbing molecules and energy patterns, your mind is continually factoring your surroundings, and you are always making decisions based on the information you are exposed to — and your nerve cells are reacting to and forming in relation to all this. The good thing is that you have some control over this, can choose what information you will pay more attention to, and can decide which information to use for your benefit.

> "He that to what he sees, adds observation, and to what he reads, reflection, is in the right road to knowledge."
> – Caleb Colton

Information is like food. Just as you can choose the most healthful foods that will build your physical structure, you can select which information you want and use it to help construct thoughts and nerve patterns that will formulate your life. Fortunately, there is an amazing assortment of information you can use to learn what will improve your life.

Learning is a part of health. It is just as important to feed your mind quality educational thoughts as it is to feed your body vibrant nutrients. Just as your body can thrive when fed high-quality nutrients, so too can your mind thrive if you will give it what it needs to perform the tasks necessary to nurture your life in the direction you want it to go.

> "When I look back, I am so impressed again with the life-giving power of literature. If I were a young person today, trying to gain a sense of myself in the world, I would do that again by reading, just as I did when I was young."
> – Maya Angelou

There are many stories of people who overcame amazing physical and mental feats and who later mention that they got through the situation by focusing their mind on something specific. In the same way, you can choose to focus on what you need for guiding your self toward accomplishing a goal.

If you are leading an unsatisfying life, or are feeling stuck in your situation, begin to focus your thoughts on what you want. You will go toward what you continually focus on.

"When people go to work, they shouldn't have to leave their hearts at home."
– Betty Bender

Work to place your self in a situation that is in alignment with what you want. By studying what you desire to know about, focusing on what you desire to have, thinking of what you desire to think about, working toward what you desire to obtain, and doing things that you desire to be doing, you will be a part of that which you desire.

"Education is not the filling of a pail, but the lighting of a fire."
– William Butler Yeats

I find it unfortunate that many people today do not read books. I have a couple of friends who say they never have read a book in their entire lives. Almost every week I hear about bookstores and libraries closing. Even schools are considering saving money by doing away with books and school libraries. I really don't know how people can receive a well-rounded education without reading a variety of books written throughout and about history. This issue brings up memories of a film I saw when I was young in which the main character finds himself in a future where books are ancient relics that are turning to dust, and nobody seems to care.

"We read to know we are not alone."
– C. S. Lewis

Awaken your brain with reading. Literature is food for the mind. People who regularly engage in reading are found to have healthier brains with a wider variety of neural activity.

"Always read something that will make you look good if you die in the middle of it."
– P. J. O'Rourke

There is wisdom in literature; thus, reading is a way to learn from those who have been before you. Use literature to gain knowledge to better utilize your power. Read about things having to do with what you want to do. Read about people who have succeeded in what you want to succeed in. Read what will nurture your thoughts to stay focused on your goals. Read things that will inspire you to become the version of yourself you want to be. Read and plan and act and work and nurture yourself into the life you desire.

"I suggest that the only books that influence us are those for which we are ready, and which have gone a little farther down our particular path than we have yet got ourselves."
– E. M. Forster

As your thoughts and actions become more attuned with the life you want to lead you will be harvesting the fruits of your labors. You will associate yourself with thoughts, actions, and people who are more aligned to what you want. The mix of thought and action is the power of association that can be a positive force in all areas of your life.

Just as any person who is involved in a culture, and who associates with others in that culture, then becomes part of that culture, everything you do becomes a part of you.

"Sometimes we understand grace only in retrospect. If someone were to ask me what grace is, I would probably respond, 'It's all grace.'"
– Bo Lozoff

By thinking about your talents, planning your life in association with your talents, and passionately working with your talents, and associating yourself with those who are healthful and in tune with their talents, you will find yourself involved in a culture of health and the expression of your intellect and passions. In this way, by following a healthful diet and lifestyle, you will be helping to create a new paradigm of life-force throughout the planet.

"It is in self-limitation that a master first shows himself."
– Johann Wolfgang von Goethe

"In today's environment, hoarding knowledge ultimately erodes your power. If you know something very important, the way to get power is by actually sharing it."
– Joseph Badaracco

"To be a man of knowledge one needs to be light and fluid."
– Yaqui mystic

"The wisest mind has something yet to learn."
– George Santayana

Grow Up and Surpass Your Past

"In the past, oppressed peoples often resorted to violence in their struggle to be free. But visionaries such as Mahatma Gandhi and the Rev. Martin Luther King Jr. have shown us that successful changes can be brought about nonviolently. I believe that, at the basic human level, most of us wish to be peaceful. Deep down, we desire constructive, fruitful growth and dislike destruction.

Many people today agree that we need to reduce violence in our society. If we are truly serious about this, we must deal with the roots of violence, particularly those that exist within each of us. We need to embrace 'inner disarmament,' reducing our own emotions of suspicion, hatred, and hostility toward our brothers and sisters."

– Dalai Lama

"Every adversity, every failure, every heartache carries with it the seed of an equal or greater benefit."

– Napolean Hill

Some people don't get on with healing their life and moving on to create an amazing life for themselves because they are too busy pointing fingers, placing blame, projecting guilt, and otherwise rehashing everything that they consider wrong about their past relationships.

"Healing yourself is connected with healing others."

– Yoko Ono

"Hurt not others with that which pains yourself."

– Udanavarga 5:18

Some people allow themselves to be held back because they are permitting their thoughts to be filled with regrets, shame, guilt, and sadness.

It is time to do away with regrets, shame, guilt, and sadness, and to no longer allow them to confuse and distort your image, thoughts, relationships, talents, intellect, worth, or life. Make the decision right here, right now, at this very point in your life, that you will not allow your past to halt your progression into a more healthful and satisfying life.

"That which we do not confront in ourselves we will meet as fate."

– Carl Gustav Jung

"If you are irritated by every rub, how will you be polished?"
– Rumi

Some of us have adapted to being overly sensitive to what we perceive as the mistreatment, unwelcoming tonal qualities, and askance glances of others. By taking the reactions, words, and behaviors of others personally, you assume that others are reacting because of you. But they are actually reacting because of what is going on in their mind based on their own history. You can't control what their history was, and you can't control their mind. What you can do is think and act in ways that are responsible and beneficial to your own progression, and you can do it without reducing yourself to destructive and aggressive behavior.

"Bad things do happen; how I respond to them defines my character and the quality of my life. I can choose to sit in perpetual sadness, immobilized by the gravity of my loss, or I can choose to rise from the pain and treasure the most precious gift I have — life itself."
– Walter Anderson

"Never regret. If it's good, it's wonderful. If it's bad, it's experience."
– Victoria Holt

It is always time to put your childhood and former self into a healthful perspective, to live with intention of accomplishing your goals, and to learn from your experiences and use them to get on with improving your life. And it is always time to remember that not everyone will like you, will welcome you, or will treat you with the best manners. The loving, or unloving, behavior of others is not your responsibility. And that includes the people in your past, which you cannot change.

"The turning point in the process of growing up is when you discover the core strength within you that survives all hurt."
– Max Lerner

"Rudeness is a weak man's imitation of strength."
– Eric Hoffer

When someone says something rude to you it is about what is going on in their mind, and not what is going on in yours. Allowing yourself to feel bad because of what they say is agreeing to their viewpoint, their concept, and their belief. It is absolutely okay to disagree with someone who has a negative view of you. It is also realistic to understand that not everyone will like or accept you, and that you can progress in your life without bothering to address everyone who does not favor you. Avoid stopping at every bump in the road. Do not stall, move forward.

> "The most beautiful people we have known are those who have known defeat, known suffering, known struggle, known loss, and have found their way out of the depths. These persons have an appreciation, a sensitivity, and an understanding of life that fills them with compassion, gentleness, and a deep loving concern. Beautiful people do not just happen."
> – Elizabeth Kubler Ross

Stop allowing yourself to be negatively impacted or distracted by what you perceive to be the bad treatment of others toward your person. Keep your calm and refuse to role-play into the unfortunate choices and negativity of others. Part of growing up is holding the wisdom to conduct yourself in a healthful manner no matter what others may have chosen or are choosing to do.

> "Children are the living messages we send to a time we will not see."
> – John W. Whitehead

Your parents were the physical gateway through which your spirit manifested itself into physical form. That was the main purpose of your parents. Of course it would be good for parents to also protect and nurture their children, but many don't. Instead of being parents in the traditional style, which is most helpful in bringing children into a situation where they can grow to live independently and healthfully with people they cherish, the unfortunate parents instill traditions of failure and ruin.

> "You and I possess within ourselves, at every moment of our lives, under all circumstances, the power to transform the quality of our lives."
> – Werner Erhard

Rather than dwelling on the fact that certain relatives, or others, were not exactly perfect examples of loving nurturers, consider making yourself into the person you hoped they would be. You can endlessly twirl around thoughts in your mind about why certain people were various levels of badness to you, but this likely will bring about no good, and will also likely keep you lost in the past. You can't improve your life by focusing on the wasted energies and damaging memories of your past. But you can work beauty into your life by using the lessons of your past, and the energy and resources of the present to continually build a better life.

> "Wisdom denotes the pursuit of the best ends by the best means."
> – Francis Hutchenson

Recognize that you may be living in the debris of a ruined life. Realize it, and then get on with nurturing your life. Many of us have had to do this — to live our way toward our answer, to surpass our past and to rise out of it, orphaning ourselves from our past, and starting anew in fresh surroundings with goals that we continually and intentionally engage in fulfilling through everyday actions.

> "Eventually everyone sits down to a banquet of consequences."
> – Robert Louis Stevenson

> "They always say time changes things, but you actually have to change them yourself."
> – Andy Warhol

Some of the debris of a ruined life may comprise your thought patterns, how you communicate, and the way you go about things.

Unfortunately, many people have so much experience with living in households that were confrontational, possessive, verbally abusive, scandalous, and otherwise disrespectful and unkind that they are in the habit of always being in the hyperdefensive mode. They have been conditioned to be confrontational, accusatory, and to assume that people are eager to reveal their so-called flaws, to ridicule them, to take advantage of them, to dismiss their safety, to devalue their intellect, or otherwise to do them harm. Their common way of communicating tinges on the unhealthful experiences long since past, and they continually respond to situations in ways that carry on the damage, which creates more.

Some of your thoughts and behaviors are what you developed to cope with situations in which you once existed. Now is the time to release thoughts and behaviors that may have drifted into the unhealthful, that may not be best for your current situation, and that may be continuing to damage or revictimize you.

"No problem can be solved from the same level of consciousness that created it."
– Albert Einstein

Some of us are so stuck in the past that we continually think about how our childhood was wasted and tragic. And we tragically waste large chunks of our adulthood thinking about how our childhood was tragically wasted. And we spend our time telling everyone who will listen about how much our childhood was wasted and tragic. And we may be living as if our life is left petrified in the state of what happened to us, which is a tragic waste of life.

"If you have time to whine and complain about something, then you have the time to do something about it."
– Anthony J. D'Angelo

Some of us who are products of unhealthful households get stuck in the past, choosing to believe that we are unworthy and allowing ourselves to get buried by the problems we experienced. We choose to feed the critical voice within us, allowing the negative comments said to us to become so loud that the critical voice becomes our dominating thought pattern. In this way we are feeding the negative, choosing to dwell in despair, and are assaulting ourselves through internalized shame and self-defeating behavior.

Some of us have gotten stuck in worrying about what others think of us, and continually adjust ourselves to what we perceive to be the critical views of others.

"You probably wouldn't worry about what people think of you if you could know how seldom they do."
– Olin Miller

Some of us use various pills, forms of alcohol, and other substances to medicate away the psychological pain of our past, numbing our ability to learn to deal healthfully with life's issues. This continual escapism may lead to addictions that can destroy. If someone confronts us out of concern for our well-being, we may cleverly rationalize that their perceptions are unfounded, and that we are perfectly fine.

In the modern-day, television, computer games, and other technological instruments can become addictive, are used as escapism, and can lead to ruin through wasted time, resources, and energy. Many people are spending so much time with their electronic toys that their relationships and lives are falling apart around them while their eyes are focused on the technogadget screens.

> "There are two ways of exerting one's strength: one is pushing down, the other is pulling up."
> – Booker T. Washington

Some of us have treated people wrongly, have thought ourselves better than others, have been haughty, snobby, dismissive, impatient, unmannerly, unkind, and self-righteous. The cynical crown we put on our royal heads may sparkle with grand jewels of delusion that place us under a continual burden of spiritual debt. We may have placed it there as a defensive measure as we were afraid of allowing others to see that we are no more than they, and we may have been afraid that we were less.

> "I had gone through life thinking I was better than everyone else and at the same time, being afraid of everyone. I was afraid to be me."
> – Dennis Wholey

> "The keenest sorrow is to recognize ourselves as the sole cause of all our adversities."
> – Sophocles

> "When nobody around you seems to measure up, it's time to check your yardstick."
> – Bill Lemley

This isn't to say that there are not people of whom it would be most helpful to steer clear, or that lowering our standards is raising them. But it is meant to say that opening the mind to the possibilities of what may be helpful could lead us to discover things that may benefit us, and these may be things that we have ignored, and to which we may have been closed. It is also to say that reconsidering our situation may allow us to grow past our past, to reconfigure what matters and what is helpful, and to proceed with a renewed awareness while focusing on and working toward our goals.

> "One must not hold one's self so divine as to be unwilling occasionally to make improvements in one's creations."
> – Ludwig van Beethoven

"As youth fades and time brings changes, we may change many of our present opinions. O let us refrain from setting ourselves up as judge of the highest matters."

– Plato

Some of us carry on in one big foggy pit of life because we have not allowed ourselves to realize that we may have been a large part of what became our problems. We may be lying in the shards of a shattered life, and the shards keep scraping our soul, and when we feel the hurt we take it out on other people, perpetuating the damage. We may not have treated people in the best way, may have judged them too harshly, caused harm to others, and chose actions and words that damaged our relationships. We may have treated others badly because we believe that they have treated us badly. Even if people have treated us badly, doing the same to them is like banging one's head against a wall of the pit in which we are dwelling. If that describes you, pull yourself out of that stubborn hole. Forgive yourself, forgive others, forgive each other, and get on with life — and do it with more kindness and greater aim toward realizing what you are and are not, while not expecting others to be what you think they should be. And forget about trying to change your experiences with others into something that they cannot be. The past cannot be reformulated, but it can be refactored and put in its place.

Remember one thing about the past: it's over.

Instead of expecting the past to be something it wasn't, focus on making the future into something that it can be.

"When I was a boy of fourteen, my father was so ignorant I could hardly stand to have the old man around. But when I got to be twenty-one, I was astonished at how much he had learned in seven years."

– Mark Twain

Once you have placed the past in its place, you may be amazed at how it can uplift you. If you are someone who once hated and despised certain people and their choices, you may be amazed at how much you don't hate them when you get on with moving forward into a better life. If you really want to heal and change your life for the better, what will work is getting busy with it.

"Shun idleness. It is a rust that attaches itself to the most brilliant of metals."

– François-Marie "Voltaire" Arouet

Continually heal, work to build confidence, choose to nurture good things in all areas of your life; follow a nutritious, plant-based diet; work through the residues of your past, use your talents, develop your skill, create your craft, feed your intellect, accept the power of love, and move on into a more healthful life.

> "Yesterday has nothing to do with who you are, only who you thought you were."
> – Neale Donald Walsch

All of us who lived in unhealthful household situations would be better off not allowing abuse, neglect, and bad choices to define us. It would be beneficial to make certain never to let the mistreatment by anyone define us. Instead of continuing to allow ourselves to be damaged, respond smartly to unwise treatment and choices.

> "That's what happens when you're angry at people. You make them part of your life."
> – Garrison Keillor

> "Perhaps all the dragons in our lives are princesses who are only waiting to see us act, just once, with beauty and courage. Perhaps everything that frightens us is, in its deepest essence, something helpless that wants our love."
> – Rainer Maria Rilke

Stop being spiteful, angry, and otherwise discouraging toward yourself and others. Do not scrape open old wounds and harm the child that has already felt the pain there.

Realize that by being hurt, you are more likely to hurt others. Hurt people hurt people. Extinguish the fire of memories burning you, let a list of goals and the practice of engaging in an intentional life be your salve, and begin the healing process before you spread your hurt into the lives of others.

> "A problem is a chance for you to do your best."
> – Duke Ellington

Refuse to be one of those victimized people who limits yourself to the mental traps formed in your mind when you were dealing with your aggressors. Break through the walls of conditional acceptance, the limiting thought patterns, the self-pity, the destructive forms of communication, and the post-traumatic behavior. Refuse to dwell in the victim mentality and the ghetto thought patterns. Instead, live your life welcoming the blessings that come when you live a life ruled by your spirit graces while expressing your Divinity, living your true intellect, and flourishing in your talents.

> "Loneliness is the way by which destiny endeavors to lead man to himself."
> – Hermann Hesse

In breaking away from the past you may find yourself feeling alone. The feelings of loneliness and sadness can be a sort of mourning for any sort of good that you did, or hoped to experience. Instead of working to create a better way, in loneliness you may find yourself traveling down old paths, associating with old feelings, consuming low-quality foods, and communicating with people who did you harm, who may not have truly changed their ways, and who may very likely continue to treat you badly.

> "Lying to ourselves is more deeply ingrained than lying to others."
> – Fyodor Dostoyevsky

You can make the unhealthful choice of feeding your loneliness with nostalgia and by romanticizing the past into a fabrication of something it wasn't. In that state you may be revising your memories of bad situations by telling yourself that they weren't so bad. By doing so you can drift into formerly unhealthful relationships and thought patterns that put you into the same old rut.

Stop allowing yourself to go through the same damaging consequences over and over.

> "To see your drama clearly is to be liberated from it."
> – Ken Keyes

Identify when you are going into a mindset of negative feelings that distort your abilities and that bring you to a conclusion that leaves you in sadness and despair. If you are constantly allowing your mind to drift into the past, it is likely that you are fumbling there. Rather than focusing on the past that you didn't like, bring yourself into the present, work on your goals, live intentionally, and create a future that you will truly enjoy.

> "I skate to where the puck is going to be, not where it has been."
> – Wayne Gretzky

Begin to think and behave in ways that are in alignment with health, satisfaction, and a life of intentionally improving your situation.

> "You can't have a better tomorrow if you are thinking about yesterday all the time."
> – Charles F. Kettering

> "Your past is not who you are, it's who you were."
> – James Ray

Bring yourself into the present, and create your future.

Choose to recognize and connect with your talents, skills, craft, intellect, and beneficial qualities.

Command yourself to break out of negative-thought patterns.

Force yourself into habits that are positive, life-affirming, and that build upon your beauty.

> "You've got to get up every morning with determination if you're going to go to bed with satisfaction."
> – George Horace Lorimer

Stop living in the past.

Keep busy in the present creating the life you want by living intentionally with defined purpose toward your future.

If you need ideas on how you want to change your life, go to the library and use the resources of knowledge stored in the books. Find what interests you, heals you, and brings you into a better life. Get busy planning, organizing, and making your life change. Other people have done it, including people who have experienced tremendously horrible situations. You can do it.

Focus on a short list of goals and priorities by writing them on paper in colored ink to bring them into your consciousness. Then write them a second time, and a third. And read them every single morning.

Decide to create a solid and continual internal voice that heals, nurtures, motivates, loves, and moves you into a more healthful life.

> "In the middle of difficulty lies opportunity."
> – Albert Einstein

What if you allowed yourself to live your life guided by love?

Healing from Trauma

"Character is formed in the stormy billows of the world."
– Johann Wolfgang von Goethe

"We are kept from the experience of spirit because our inner world is cluttered with past traumas. As we begin to clear away this clutter, the energy of divine light and love begins to glow through our beings."
– Tomas Keating

As you clean up your life you may find yourself dealing with suppressed issues. These may involve things you have not thought of in a while, such as feelings, relationships, emotional trauma, experiences you perceive of as failures, and unpleasant memories.

Many people have found suppressed issues to be part of the cleansing that goes on when cleaning up the diet. It seems that just as the body tissues detox as a person follows a much better diet, the emotions can go through somewhat of a detox stage as a person works to live a more healthful, goal-oriented life. This may be related to years spent emotionally eating, using food to shove feelings down, and once the emotion-driven food feast ends, an emotional purge begins.

"Turn your wounds into wisdom."
– Oprah Winfrey

"Failure should be our teacher, not our undertaker. Failure is delay, not defeat. It is a temporary detour, not a dead end. Failure is something we can avoid only by saying nothing, doing nothing, and being nothing."
– Denis Waitley

What you have faced in the past, however unpleasant it may have been, could be a most useful tool in getting what you want in the future. The trials and problems as well as the happiness and successes you have experienced can be utilized as your personal lessons to propel you into being a wiser, more skillful, and effective person.

"What lies behind us and what lies before us are tiny matters compared to what lies within us. And when we bring what is within out into the world, miracles happen."
– Ralph Waldo Emerson

While memories may bring up a lot of unpleasant emotions, try not to get caught up in the emotion of a memory.

Do not allow the past to hold you back or make you stumble. Do not be afraid or troubled by what you have already been through. Instead, take control by working with the lessons of the events of your life to your advantage.

"Be not the slave of your own past — plunge into the sublime seas, dive deep, and swim far, so you shall come back with self-respect, with new power, with an advanced experience, that shall explain and overlook the old."
– Ralph Waldo Emerson

Take the remnants of your past and weave a better life. Welcome it, deal with it, learn what you can from it, don't dwell on it, but do let go of it, and move on while looking forward to a better way of life and a more healthful future.

"Every man's memory is his private literature."
– Aldous Huxley

"Cancer is my secret because none of my rivals have been that close to death and it makes you look at the world in a different light, and that is a huge advantage."
– Lance Armstrong

Reinterpret your past as something that can help you rather than something that harmed you. If it did harm you, then that is what happened. But that doesn't mean that you have to keep dwelling on it in a negative way that continues the flow of hurt. It also doesn't mean that you should keep using it as a crutch to keep wobbling around on the same path where you have already stumbled, fallen, and felt pain.

"Sometimes we stare so long at a door that is closing that we see too late the one that is open."
– Alexander Graham Bell

"All healing is first a healing of the heart."
– Carl Townsend

Refuse to get caught in past regrets and the reverberating energy of unfortunate incidents. If you are swimming in a river of resentment, it's time to get out of the water and dry off!

"If the world seems cold to you, kindle fires to warm it."
– Lucy Larcom

What may be helpful is to metaphorically compost the leftovers of your past into a nurturing soil. Root into it, grow from it, and rise above it. Shade it with the beauty consisting of the branches, leaves, and blossoms of a more healthful and satisfying existence.

"Often we allow ourselves to be upset by small things we should despise and forget. We lose many irreplaceable hours brooding over grievances that, in a year's time, will be forgotten by us and by everybody. Now, let us devote our life to worthwhile actions and feelings, to great thoughts, real affections, and enduring undertakings."
– Andre Maurois

"With all its sham, drudgery, and broken dreams, it is still a beautiful life."
– Max Ehrmann

"We consume our tomorrows fretting about our yesterdays."
– Persius

Stop brooding over your past, as that is an absolute waste of time, energy, and resources. Do what it takes to stop being upset with yourself and your history. Move on toward better things through goal setting, life reorientation, healthful food, daily morning exercise, and continually and intentionally connecting with and using your talents and intellect.

Formulate the now. Look and grow toward a better future from where you are, not from where you have been.

"The future depends on what we do in the present."
– Mahatma Gandhi

If you begin to feel the waves of any bad memories flow through your being, choose to focus on goal-oriented thoughts that are more helpful and that will move you into more confident and uplifting thoughts. Instantly become involved in a healthful activity based on what you do want, and not on what you do not want.

> "Although the world is full of suffering, it is also full of overcoming it."
> – Helen Keller

Consider others who have succeeded and gotten past tremendously horrible life situations. Know that you too can bring yourself out of whatever rut you have been in.

Understand this: It is up to you to form the thoughts, factor the solutions, and take the actions that make the changes that will improve your life.

> "The most authentic thing about us is our capacity to create, to overcome, to endure, to transform, to love, and to be greater than our suffering."
> – Ben Okri

Work to eliminate those things from your life that are not in alignment with the life you want. This includes eliminating unhealthful and unhelpful patterns of thinking, patterns of eating, patterns of acting, patterns of communicating, and patterns of activities. By constantly focusing your life away from what you don't want, and onto what you do want, you will naturally be drawn to things that you do want. Freeing your life of those things that you don't want allows you to make room for, to better accept, and to welcome that which you do want.

If you are in a situation of damaged and damaging relationships, plan and take action to improve or to end them. Recognize that damaging relationships often involve one person projecting shame, guilt, discouragement, or disgust on another with the goal of controlling that person. This is weak, guilt-ridden, dysfunctional, and pathetic behavior.

If you are in an abusive situation, get out of it. Don't play the game in which you will always lose, and where there are no winners.

Do not allow yourself to be controlled by the negativity and ugly behavior of others, and stop hoping for their behavior to change. Getting into a pattern of waiting for other people to change before your life can improve is being co-dependent, diminishes your power, and obliterates your chances of living a healthful life.

Stop hoping for someone to change when it is up to that person to change. Adults who are not leading the life you think they should be leading are responsible for their own thoughts and actions. You can't control their mind, but you can take a large role in conducting the thoughts of your own.

Instead of participating in a relationship where you are being a people-pleaser, and where you may be stuck in a co-dependent relationship wherein you allow your emotions and quality of life to be controlled and dominated by the mood swings of others, get on with your life by using your intellect, talents, and power to improve yourself.

Stop hoping that things were different, which is wasted hope. Stop being controlled by end results, which are of energy already spent. Work to create things that have more satisfying end results. Place hope in the now, and in the future.

> "False hope is unnecessary pain."
> – Rod Steiger

Many people who perceive that they have been wronged then proceed to entertain thoughts of revenge. This is a tremendous waste of time and energy, and it perpetuates any damage that may have been done to them.

> "To be angry is to revenge the faults of others on ourselves."
> – Alexander Pope

> "An eye for eye only ends up making the whole world blind."
> – Mahatma Gandhi

Do not take revenge on people from your past. Instead, take responsibility to be more responsible by spending your time creating your future.

> "The best form of revenge is success."
> – Vanessa Williams

If you were living in an unhealthful household as a child, it is not your fault. Do not feel guilt or shame about it. Do not feel that you are responsible for not changing the situation. Realize that you were a child. As a child you likely couldn't even think of the words and/or didn't have the words in your vocabulary to describe the trauma and abuse you experienced. Even if there were someone around who could have helped if you were able to reach out to them, it is no fault of yours that you were unable to manage the situation better. You were a child and you factored and lived as a child. Now you are an adult and you can manage your life better and be proactive in creating a healthful life for yourself.

> "The shadow is the greatest teacher for how to come to the light."
> – Ram Dass

I wouldn't advise that you become a great display of someone who has been through a lousy situation. Some people get so caught up in analyzing their life, and in talking about it that they become a tedious bore to be around. Improving your life out of your past is not about burdening everyone around you by constantly talking about your difficulties. Cast your life into the light of enlightenment, and don't let it be in the shadow of any sort of dark past.

> "Complaining is not only hideously boring, but worse — it only increases the pain."
> – Peter Megargee Brown

Many people who have been through tremendous difficulties have learned very well that it is best to move on into a smarter, focused, and intentional life in which they live in the present, not in the past.

The key to all this is to progress into healing and to grow into a vibrantly healthful version of yourself in which you are following a well-rounded plant-based diet, setting goals and attaining them through intentional actions, and living your intellect smartly and confidently.

The sooner you go about creating a better life for yourself with more healthful thinking patterns, the better off you will be.

Continually thinking of things that created stress in your childhood is not good for your brain, and can leave you dwelling in the energy of regret and dissatisfaction, which will add to the damage that was done.

Daily stress creates stress chemicals that can kill brain cells, interferes with brain growth, and subtly restricts the flow of blood to the brain. Children who are continually exposed to bad situations may have experienced the type of stress that interferes with brain growth. Long-term stress can play a part in heart disease, diabetes, back pain, disorders of the digestive system, muscle injuries, weight gain or loss, and other health problems.

Being continually exposed to situations in childhood that caused danger, violence, and frantic emotions can result in an overabundance of neurons forming in the locus coeruleus area of the brain stem. This is so because regularly being caught in situations of danger required the fight-or-flight hormones, norepinephrine and adrenaline, to be released by the brain. This is conducive to the post-traumatic stress disorder (PTSD) common in people who have been exposed to dangerous, violent, and/or otherwise extremely upsetting situations.

In January 2010, it was reported that researchers at the University of Minnesota and the Minneapolis VA Medical Center studied brain scans conducted on veterans of the Iraq and Afghanistan wars and detected distinct patterns of activity within the brains of those suffering from PTSD. The researchers used an MEG (magnetoencephalography) brain scanner which captures electrical signals taking place every millisecond. By studying the scans of the electrical patterns within the soldier's brains, the researchers identified specific biomarkers as being common in 90 percent of the war veterans in the study diagnosed as suffering from PTSD.

Unfortunately, PTSD symptoms are seen in a variety of people who have been exposed to dangerous and extremely upsetting situations, including children who have been abused. Luckily, the brain has some capacity to heal and reform itself as the formerly abused child learns how to cope and becomes more attuned to a healthful way of living.

Thinking plays a major role in healing and maintaining a high level of health. There truly are toxic emotions that cause the body to create damaging body chemistry. In the 1950s, George Solomon coined the term *psychoimmunology* after he theorized that personality and the emotions can play a part in people's health, and in what diseases and pain they may experience.

Luckily, we can learn to conduct our minds in a more healthful manner. Healthful thinking impacts the electrical circuitry of the body and helps to form healthful cells. As people heal and learn to conduct their being in a more healthful manner, the tissues throughout the body become attuned to creating more healthful molecules of emotion, known as peptides and ligands, which are messenger molecules.

Science has proved how thoughts play a part in creating specific chemicals in the body, and how healthful thoughts absolutely do result in a more healthful body chemistry.

The body creates chemicals in relation to whatever a person is thinking. These chemicals are created throughout the body simultaneously, not just in the brain, but in the other organs, and even within the blood system. This reveals that the mind exists not only in the brain, but throughout the body.

The cells in every part of the body feature receptor sites for the neuropeptide and ligand chemicals, which are the physical structures created by thought. When we conduct our thoughts in a certain way in combination with a healthful diet and exercise program, our body cells create more receptor sites that receive the peptides and ligands aligned with health, and the body creates more neuropeptides and ligands in alignment with how healthfully we are living. This process is why we feel emotions throughout our entire bodies, and not just in our brain, but also in our fingers and toes, our legs and arms, our back, chest, and tummy, and in our shoulders, neck, and cheeks.

Because certain parts of the body contain more receptor sites for certain neurochemicals, we feel some emotions stronger in certain areas of our body, such as stress in the stomach because there are more stress chemical receptors there, and the desire for sex in the sex organs because there are more receptors on the cells in those body parts to receive the chemicals that are in alignment with those emotions (however, sex hormones, which are different, are not peptide-based, but are steroids, and interact within the nucleus of the cells). We also store memories throughout the body, and not just in the brain, which is why certain memories are also felt throughout the body. Feeling is a whole-body experience because body chemistry and thinking comprise a whole body experience.

The process of the membranes of our cells creating more receptor sites to receive the self-produced chemicals that make us feel good, including how the cell membranes can be consciously changed, is one of the miracles of healing. It can be greatly assisted by a healthful, plant-based diet; intellectual stimulation; daily exercise; goal-oriented living, and nurturing relationships.

> "Biochemicals are the physiological substrates of emotion, the molecular underpinnings of what we experience as feelings, sensations, thoughts, drives, perhaps even spirit or soul."
> – Candace B. Pert

The cellular processes continually happening in relation to thinking and activity, and how thoughts and actions alter both cell growth patterns and the production of chemicals within the body and brain reveal that people are always involved with creating their common level of health.

In response to thoughts and actions, human cells create mind-altering molecules called endogenous opioids, including neuropeptides and cannabinoids. The most commonly known are the endorphin opiate peptides associated with the euphoric *runner's high*. Cannabinoids cross the blood-brain barrier, are produced by the neurochemical endocannabinoid system, and may be more responsible for that elation. Exercise triggers the production of the chemicals, the body cell membranes to form endorphin receptors, and the brain and body cell membranes to form cannabinoid receptors (the same receptors that receive the cannabinoids found in cannabis, thus the *high* a person gets if they smoke or ingest marijuana. Exercise is the better choice for obtaining the natural high, and clearly is more beneficial).

Even acts of kindness produce pleasurable chemicals in the body, including endogenous opioids and also hormones such as oxytocin, which triggers the blood cells to release nitric oxide, causing the dialation of the vessels, reducing blood pressure, stress, and the presense of free radicals, and leading to a more relaxed mood and less acidic body chemistry. So again, an action, kindness, which is the result of thought processes, triggers a cellular response: the production, release, and reception of feel-good hormones and chemicals that improve health.

You can become accustomed to experiencing thoughts and actions that trigger the production of pleasurable chemicals just as much as you can become accustomed to experiencing those that lead to the manufacture of body chemicals that make you feel lousy. It is your choice.

There is communication between the conscious and unconscious functions of the body. Neuroscientists have proved that the chemicals of emotion produced within the body are tied in with breathing, blood flow, salivation, gastrointestinal activity, body temperature, cellular replication, hormonal production, electrical fields, and even in what is eliminated by the body. This reveals that we consciously play a role in our total health experience.

> "If you think your body and mind are two, that is wrong; if you think that they are one, that is also wrong. Our body and mind are both two and one."
>
> – Shunryu Suzuki

Even the immune system, including the bone marrow, spleen, lymph, and certain blood cells, is conducted with the exchange of various types of peptides between the immune cells and the endocrine system and nerve system, including the brain. In other words, in addition to genetics, environment, diet, relations, and exercise, your immune system is impacted by your thinking patterns because your thoughts help trigger your cells to release some of the chemical cues that guide immune responses. This means that your mind is part of your immune system.

Through high-quality thinking, diet, exercise, action, and communication choices, you can consciously create your own vitality and reformulate your body chemistry to be in alignment with all things healthy.

> "Vitality shows not only in the ability to persist but in the ability to start over."
>
> – F. Scott Fitzgerald

This understanding of how we change not only the body chemistry, but also the formation of our cell membranes through what we think should be easy enough to motivate people to also understand that it would be most helpful for them to stop doing the things that damage them, and to constantly be involved in living healthfully. It is through thinking healthfully combined with healthful communication, actions, diet, and exercise that our cellular structures will heal from unhealthful experiences.

> "Focus more on your desire than on your doubt, and the dream will take care of itself. You may be surprised at how easily this

happens. Your doubts are not as powerful as your desires, unless you make them so."
– Marcia Wieder

You will become the person you wish to become by conducting yourself more commonly in the way you wish to be. The trinity of thought, action, and communication is how you create your paradigm.

Two exercises that can help you think more healthfully include yoga and meditation. In her book, *The Molecules of Emotion*, Candace B. Pert, whose life work is the study of peptides, writes, "When stress prevents the molecules of emotion from flowing freely where needed, the largely autonomic processes that are regulated by peptide flow, such as breathing, blood flow, immunity, digestion, and elimination collapse down to a few simple feedback loops and upset the normal healing response. Meditation, by allowing long-buried thoughts and feelings to surface, is a way of getting the peptides flowing again, returning the body, and the emotions, to health."

The patterns of your thoughts and the type of health you are experiencing are an integration of your entire life. The state of your mind reflects the state of your immune system, which reflects the state of your fitness level, which reflects the state of your diet, which reflects the state of your happiness and satisfaction with being able to express your intellect, talents, and love.

"There is healing available to us and it can come through our imagination if we honor ourselves and our situation and if we keep open to the potency of the universe, which is also the potency within us."
– Henry Seltzer

All of this information is in alignment with what I am speaking of throughout the book. It is that you can heal your life, and that if you really desire to experience vibrant health, you can. It is why I specifically approach a whole-life solution to healing. And it is why I include a fully plant-based diet and an active exercise program, such as by practicing yoga every morning, as part of true health maintenance. And it is why I believe it would be most helpful that daily goal review, daily intellectual stimulation through study, and the daily practice of talent be included in healing.

If you were in a horrible situation while you were growing up, it is even more important for you to choose highly nutritious foods, to eliminate all low-quality foods, to get daily exercise, to stimulate your mind with quality literature, to develop your intellect, to practice your talents, to improve your quality of communication, and to live intentionally to create the life you want, and in which you flourish in health.

Be aware that those who were raised in violent and abusive homes may have some form of post-traumatic stress disorder. One brain chemical found more prominently in those who have experienced traumatic, violent, and/or neglectful childhoods is cortical releasing factor (CRF). Those who go on to live more healthful lives, including children who are removed from violent and neglectful homes, are found to experience a reduction of CRF to the point of a healthful level. This is especially the case if they go on to experience healthful, nurturing relationships and constructive, uplifting, goal-oriented lives. I believe that more important than all relationships is the relationship of self, and nurturing the self to blossom into health, which will open you up to others who are living more healthfully.

> "Healing is not a matter of technique or mechanism; it is a work of spirit."
> – Rachel Naomi Remen

Now is the time to heal from unfortunate experiences, to get out of the rut that was dug for you, to use your strength to rise above the past, and to purge your demons — without delay. This is something I strongly believe in. Many people have been there and know what it is like to be in a horrific childhood situation. If you are one of them, know that you can rise out of it, that your life can be fabulous, and that the only person who can change it is you.

> "Thought is the creative power, or the impelling force which causes the creative power to act; thinking in a certain way will bring riches to you, but you must not rely upon thought alone, paying no attention to personal action. That is the rock upon which many otherwise scientific metaphysical thinkers meet shipwreck — the failure to connect thought with personal action."
> – Wallace D. Wattles

You are the rescuing spirit you have been waiting for. Allow your restorative spiritual genetics to kick into gear. Begin now to live each day intentionally progressing to a more healthful and satisfying life by working to get it.

> "This is the way of peace: Overcome evil with good, falsehood with truth, and hatred with love."
> – Mildred "Peace Pilgrim" Norman

Don't get caught in the bottomless whirlpool of thoughts centered on the fact that you were robbed of a nurturing childhood. Live your life as if your days are golden, and not stolen.

If you feel that you have more for which to be sorry than grateful, work every day to create the situation in which you do feel grateful.

> "Biology is the least of what makes someone a mother."
> – Oprah Winfrey

> "Perhaps our greatest gift is helping people choose truly loving family, what we here in Hawaii call 'ohana — literally the circle of those who breathe together."
> – Richard Koob

If you spent time living in a home where lying, stealing, slander, deception, verbal abuse, mockery, and other unhealthful behaviors were common, it is likely that you have incorporated some of these unhealthful qualities into your adult behavior. If so, you need to learn to rid yourself of these habitual tendencies that can damage you and your relationships. Make a personal, written declaration that you will heal yourself from these damaging tendencies. Work to be a more trustworthy, sincere, kind, respectable, committed individual who lives with a high degree of integrity. Refrain from assaulting, insulting, mocking, undermining, or slandering others, and refrain from lying. Work to treat others as you desire to be treated.

> "I have never for one instant seen clearly within myself. How then would you have me judge the deeds of others?"
> – Maurice Maeterlinck

> "It is a bit embarrassing to have been concerned with the human problem all one's life and find at the end that one has no more to offer by way of advice than 'Try to be a little kinder.'"
> – Aldous Huxley

Stop allowing the poison energy of others to poison your life. By focusing on the poison energy of others, you are the person who is spreading the poison. Get out of that practice. One way to do so is to focus on your life and on your choices, on your goals, and on your future, and not on your past, or on the choices of others.

If you find yourself treating others badly, walk away from it. Reorganize your thoughts based on kindness and love rather than frustration, anxiety, spitefulness, ridicule, mockery, meanness, hate, or anger.

> "Healing may not be so much about getting better, as about letting go of everything that isn't you — all of the expectations, all of the beliefs — and becoming who you are."
> – Rachel Naomi Remen

In an unhealthful situation, not only will people hide their talents, but will also assume a fake personage that is a complete role-play of what they think is the most acceptable way to conduct themselves. They do this to avoid any harsh comments.

If you lived in a terrible situation, consider that a part of you may have been abandoned. Not by someone else. But abandoned by you. And it may have been done as a coping mechanism. As you grow out of the unhealthful situation and the mindset that were the results of consequences and your coping mechanism, it may help if you were to figure out if that abandoned part of you is something that you should get back.

Give yourself permission to grasp the parts of your intellect and talents that will help you to heal, to experience joy, to express the person you are, and to nurture love and beauty in your life.

> "The people who get on in this world are the people who get up and look for the circumstances they want, and, if they can't find them, make them."
> – George Bernard Shaw

Dignifying your life is accomplished by living intentionally, by giving meaning to your actions, by conducting yourself in a focused manner, and by fulfilling defined goals. Doing so will be a way to respect your time, energy, and resources, and those of others. And it will help your life flourish.

> "The love we desire is already within us."
> – Anonymous

The infinite power of the universe is what you are a part of.

Be aware of and enlightened to the fact that you have the energy to conduct yourself in ways that heal and transform your life into a healthful being.

Love your self.

Forgiveness

> "Forgiveness is the fragrance the violet sheds on the heel that has crushed it."
> – Mark Twain

> "Never does the human soul appear so strong as when it forgoes revenge, and dares forgive an injury."
> – Edwin Hubbel Chapin

If you are trying to move forward from a fractured life and into a more healthful existence, what may be beneficial to your progress is an understanding of forgiveness.

> "The weak can never forgive. Forgiveness is the attribute of the strong."
> – Mahatman Gandhi

One exercise in forgiveness that some people have found useful in releasing toxic thoughts and venting their anger toward someone in their past is to write the offender an undelivered letter expressing the anger, and to conclude it by telling the offender they are forgiven. Key to this exercise is that the letter not be sent to the offender. Instead, it should be torn to pieces, or otherwise destroyed and disposed of immediately after it is written. The exercise is to explore your feelings rather than to suppress them. In this way you are able to express anything you want to say to the person without concern for harming anyone's feelings. It is important to destroy the letter, to not send it, and to get on with your life by immediately becoming involved with a specific activity aligned with a priority or goal. One reason this exercise is healthful is that it can do away with pent-up anger. Because emotions and thoughts influence the immune system, releasing toxic emotions can improve the immune system and allow the person to function more healthfully. In that way, the exercise of letter writing and immediate letter destruction can be part of the process of forgiving and moving on to better things.

> "Self-importance is our greatest enemy. Think about it — what weakens us is feeling offended by the deeds and misdeeds of our fellowmen. Our self-importance requires that we spend most of our lives offended by someone."
> – Carlos Castaneda

Another exercise in forgiveness involves recognizing the problems your perpetrators or offenders experienced. Realize that they also may have had difficulties in their life, including problems that led to their unfortunate behavior. Perhaps they were abused, neglected, or otherwise in a terrible situation when they were young. Maybe they had physical and psychological ailments that caused them problems, that may not have been diagnosed, and that were not healed. They may have been subjected to any number of problems and life difficulties that constricted their life, constructed their disaster, set them on a pattern of destruction, and played into their unwise decisions. Maybe they had it so bad that they lacked an understanding of what they did, or did not have the resources, capacity, or ability to deal with it.

> "Yet, taught by time, my heart has learned to glow for other's good, and melt at other's woe."
> – Homer

> "With a little time, and a little more insight, we begin to see both ourselves and our enemies in humbler profiles. We are not really as innocent as we felt when we were first hurt. And we do not usually have a gigantic monster to forgive; we have a weak, needy, and somewhat stupid human being. When you see your enemy and yourself in the weakness and silliness of the humanity you share, you will make the miracle of forgiving a little easier."
> – Lewis B. Smedes

> "It is unwise to be too sure of one's own wisdom. It is healthy to be reminded that the strongest might weaken and the wisest might err."
> – Mahatma Gandhi

Recognize that those who did you wrong may never admit it, may deny it, may not be concerned about it, may not recognize it, and may continue doing unwise things to others. But realize that your healing does not depend on your perpetrators acknowledging anything. They are not your brain, mind, abilities, talents, craft, intellect, body, life, elegance, or spirit. They cannot guide your thoughts, set your goals, choose your actions, conduct your relationships, lead your life, or heal your wounds.

> "Forgiveness, another word for letting go, is learned drip by drip, day by day, not as an act of altruism but as a necessary cleaning of the past, a purification of our souls so we can live and function effectively in the now. The soul does not grow into its potential

fullness when it harbors past hurt and turns it over and over. That is the way to grow bitterness, not soul."

– Matthew Fox

Focusing on unfortunate decisions and painful events depresses, frustrates, angers, and generally upsets and stumbles a person. It places people in that bottomless pit of being a victim of consequence, circumstance, and despair, and it robs them of their energy, power, talent, intellect, joy, and health.

"Darkness cannot drive out darkness; only light can do that. Hate cannot drive out hate; only love can do that."

– Martin Luther King, Jr.

Focusing your anger on what someone did to you, or on a mistake you made, swirls negative energy through your body. This process triggers your cells to release stress hormones. Continually engaging in this process creates a pattern that is poison to your life. Changing how you think about the deceit, action, or mistake can change the energy of it within you.

Be compassionate to your self, and have compassion for others. Realize that you make mistakes, and others will also. Don't be a stick-in-the-mud unwilling to move, to change your opinion, and to get on with better things, including healing relationships.

"The man who never alters his opinion is like standing water, and breeds reptiles of the mind."

– William Blake

Begin to think and act in ways that heal, and move your life forward so that you lead your life undefined by the damaging relationships, choices, and actions of others, and any unfortunate events of your past.

Perhaps there is no perfect forgiveness, especially if severe abuse occurred or extremely unfortunate decisions were made. But there are ways to live more presently so that you can stop dwelling in the harm and stagnating in the negative energy of victimization, and then start getting on with your life so that you are not your wounds, but are your talents, intellect, and love.

The goal of understanding forgiveness is to aim for a brighter future that is not constantly dimmed by unwanted memories.

> "Forgiveness is almost a selfish act because of its immense benefits to the one who forgives."
> – Lawana Blackwell

Forgiveness is an essential nutrient for the soul. Ancient people considered it a virtue that renewed spiritual health. Forgiveness benefits the forgiver perhaps more than the forgiven. It releases constraints, diminishes pain, relieves depression, disperses chronic anger, invigorates cellular structures, frees blockages, melts fears, heals wounds, disperses crippling tempers, ends harshly defensive behavior, fractures hostility, ends grief, enhances happiness, sweetens bitterness, opens possibilities, and renews potential.

> "A man who studieth revenge keeps his own wounds green."
> – Francis Bacon

Forgiving and getting rid of the burden of anger allows you to align with more helpful expressions of energy.

> "Forgiveness is another word for letting go."
> – Matthew Fox

Forgiveness does not always mean reconciling with those who subjected you to their dishonesty, slander, anger, violence, or other damaging behaviors. It also does not mean unwisely allowing damaging relationships and situations to remain present in your life while pretending they are not.

> "Forgiveness is letting go of all hope of a better past."
> – Annie Lamont

> "Forgiveness is freeing up and putting to better use the energy once consumed by holding grudges, harboring resentments, and nursing unhealed wounds. It is rediscovering the strengths we always had and relocating our limitless capacity to understand and accept other people and ourselves."
> – Sidney and Suzanne Simon

Forgiveness has to do with moving on toward your future, and creating a better life, rather than dwelling in your past and/or continuing to passively exist in denial while engulfed in an unhealthful situation.

"Children begin by loving their parents; as they grow older they judge them; sometimes they forgive them."
– Oscar Wilde

What forgiveness sometimes does is stop you from placing blame on the wrong people. These are people you may have treated unfairly because someone else treated you badly, which means that you are perpetuating the damaging energy you were served. Therefore, through forgiveness and behaving in a kinder and fair manner, you stop propagating harm.

Forgiveness acknowledges that people aren't perfect, including you.

Forgiveness may have to do with forgiving yourself, which can be an invigorating, liberating, and motivating act that rids a person of regret, self-hate, misery, anguish, and self-inflicted wounds. The wounds you may be inflicting on yourself out of anger and regret includes harming yourself with low-quality foods, thought processes, interactions, activities, or lack of activity, which is wallowing in slothfulness.

Free yourself of the concepts of blame. The process of releasing blame is to free yourself of pointing your finger toward and focusing your mind on that which you believe is what caused your problems.

Blame is about putting the responsibility on others, focusing on the past, and dwelling in regret, dissatisfaction, anger, and victimization.

"If you judge people, you have no time to love them."
– Mother Teresa

If you have been involved in repeatedly reminding people of what they may have done, perhaps you may want to consider the strong possibility that you are carrying on the damage, and continuing to inflict the same wounds caused by the problem. The skewers you are putting through people to continually roast them over the flames of shame and guilt are likely skewing your life as you carry the burden of holding and focusing on them. By continuing to scratch open old wounds, you are likely causing more harm to your relationships and self-worth, which means that you are choosing to exist in the energy of victimization.

When you think you are making someone else look bad, you are actually making yourself look bad.

"You can stand tall without standing on someone. You can be a victor without having victims."
– Harriet Woods

To counteract the practice of blame, work to intentionally live your life focused on what you need and want to do, and not on what has been done and what you don't want to re-experience.

Intentional, goal-oriented living is the opposite of blame and is about focusing on what can be done for today and the future through actions that improve things.

Let go of blame. Doing so will relieve stress, strengthen your immune system, relax your arteries, increase your blood flow, and help lay the groundwork for vibrant health.

> "You want to place blame on people, but I don't think it's fair. You're dealt the cards that you're dealt. You can let that be your downfall or a springboard to become something better. For me, I just thought, 'What a waste of time to be angry at my parents. What a waste of time to feel sorry for myself.' The best thing I can do is learn all the things I've learned from them, good and bad, have my own family someday, and just keep on going. So many things are thrown at us as human beings, but you can't let any of them get you down, or you're just going to be defeated."
> – Drew Barrymore

Just because you may have been raised around people who didn't express patience, kindness, nurturing love, and encouraging words doesn't mean that you also have to conduct yourself in the same unhelpful manner. You can continually choose to make wiser choices in your relationships than those choices others around you have made.

> "Kindness is a language which the deaf can hear and the blind can see."
> – Mark Twain

> "People are lonely who build walls instead of bridges."
> – Mark Buber

Get away from the bad forms of communicating and the continual assumptions of disgust that you may have learned from living in an unhealthful household. Assumptions and lack of communication within families are like the mold and fungus that destroy in darkness.

Stop the destruction of your self. Learn to communicate healthfully, conduct your self with dignity, and recognize that your future can be better than your past.

Rid your self of negative thoughts and feelings. By thinking positively with an eagerness for a more healthful life you will be creating positive energy flows within your mind and being, which will create a beneficial body chemistry that will resonate out into your life and the lives of those around you.

> "Respond intelligently even to unintelligent treatment."
> – Lao-Tse

Many people who have experienced horrible things get stuck in the memory of the incidents and linger there for the rest of their lives, thus allowing their experience with negative events to define them. Many also continue to attract the same kind of drama, same types of damaging people, and same variety of problems into their lives while never seeming to learn their role of creating or in not changing the events.

You can be the creator of circumstance, or the victim of it. It all has to do with what you choose to do with your mind. We are all subjected to circumstance. You can choose what you do with the circumstance to which you have been exposed. You can make better choices than worse choices. You can engage in thought patterns that result in more healthful ways of communicating and conducting your life.

> "Every suffering is a seed, because suffering impels us to seek wisdom."
> – Bodhidharma

While many of us have been subjected to negative, unpleasant, and damaging situations, we do not have to dwell on those situations, or in the energy that surrounds those memories. We can break free of the things that have stopped us from succeeding in life. This includes releasing the energy surrounding negative personal relationships; cruel comments and actions; unfortunate choices; laziness and slothful behavior; and low-quality and damaging food choices.

We absolutely can be proactive in healing the festering wounds of our life and reform our lifescape.

> "To forgive is to set a prisoner free and discover the prisoner was you."
> – Unknown

To move on from a past that haunts you, it may be beneficial to seek the help of a therapist, to attend group therapy, and to read books that help you understand ways of working through your issues.

The thing that will most likely change your life for the better is a specific plan to improve your life mixed with daily thoughts and continual actions that bring this plan into fruition.

> "There is overwhelming evidence that the higher the level of self-esteem, the more likely one will treat others with respect, kindness, and generosity. People who do not experience self-love have little or no capacity to love others."
> – Nathanial Branden

You can stop thinking bad thoughts about those in your life. Instead, acknowledge the positive. You can stop rummaging around in the damage that was done to you and that you also may have created with cruel words and unwise actions. You can be wiser with your time, energy, and resources. You can consume a more balanced diet of the most highly nutritious foods available to you while avoiding foods that are damaging and unhealthful. You can take better care of your body and mind through exercise and education. You can communicate better, choose gracious manners, and nurture healthful relationships. Doing these things is liberating, empowering, healing, nurturing, and loving.

> "Friendship with oneself is all-important, because without it one cannot be friends with anyone else in the world."
> – Eleanor Roosevelt

> "Many years later, I had a chance to ask him. I said, 'Come on, you were a great man, you invited your jailers to your inauguration, you put your pressures on the government. But tell me the truth. Weren't you really angry all over again?' And he said, 'Yes, I was angry. And I was a little afraid. After all I've not been free in so long. But,' he said, 'when I felt that anger well up inside of me I realized that if I hated them after I got outside that gate then they would still have me.' And he smiled and said, 'I wanted to be free so I let it go.' It was an astonishing moment in my life. It changed me."
> – Bill Clinton (on Nelson Mandela)

> "Man's goodness is the flame that can never be extinguished."
> – Nelson Mandela

> "Only the brave know how to forgive; it is the most refined and generous pitch of virtue human nature can arrive at."
> – Laurence Sterne

Spiritual Beliefs

> "My position concerning God is that of an agnostic. I am convinced that a vivid consciousness of the primary importance of moral principles for the betterment and ennoblement of life does not need the idea of a law-giver, especially a law-giver who works on the basis of reward and punishment."
> – Albert Einstein

As far as this idea of a God person who many people view as this glorified being, I have a strong belief that there are beings in the form of spirit energy somehow involved in what this world is. I will forgo attempting to define this energy, and only leave it open to whatever it is the reader's understanding is, or is not. I mean to refer only to a spiritual energy of sorts that is far beyond our present comprehension, but that is easily within our impression.

As I see it, what we call spiritual beliefs and practices — along the lines of living healthfully and taking care of the body and environment — are in tune with the natural masterful pattern that is evident in the way things formulate and function, such as in cellular structures, electrical fields, molecules, atoms, particles, and so forth. Through living more in tune with Nature, especially through a plant-based diet free from junk food, we are living more in tune with the powers of the spiritual energy that rules Nature, and we are inviting this amazing power into our lives.

> "You are not a human being in search of a spiritual experience. You are a spiritual being immersed in a human experience."
> – Pierre Teilhard de Chardin

People ask me if I believe in religion, but they have their own classification of what they mean by religion. My understating of what religion is and what they mean by religion could be two very different things, and likely is.

> "I'm not into isms and asms. There isn't a Catholic moon and a Baptist sun. I know that universal God is universal. I feel that the same God-force that is the mother and father of the pope is also the mother and father of the loneliest man on the planet."
> – Dick Gregory

Someone once asked me if I believe in creationism, evolution, or intelligent design. My answer is "Yes, we are here."

I avoid engaging in what often turns into some form of a debate or gentle argument about these religious topics. Often the discussions have to do with people wanting others to agree with their concept, as if they need to be validated in their opinion of what it all means. We are here, which stands as enough evidence for me. I can leave the details of how it all happened up to something we may possibly understand at the next stage in the juncture. While discussions may be helpful in sharing understandings, and to formulate opinions, any sort of argument about it all seems to be a nonsensical waste of time and energy.

I often hear people say that certain religions are "weird." And it is often said in a tone that implies the speaker's religion is not weird. Is one religion less weird than the other, or more antiquated, important, cartoonish, awkward, bizarre, cultish, or less believable? Is one person less of a person, or less important because they believe in one way, and not the other? Are they foolish, normal, or more important if they believe their gods resemble them, or a dog, a cow, a tree, a belly dancer, a supermodel, the mysteries of Nature, or nothing at all?

Conversations and debates about religion could go on forever with no two people agreeing on the same principles or concepts. It isn't important to me which religion someone espouses. What matters more to me is that people live to do what is the best they know how in the best way they respect each other, wildlife, and the environment.

This is what I know: We are made up of a variety of substances, and there is an energy holding these substances together in a form that we define as us. There are things we can do to help us function better, and other things that can cause us to function negatively. Everything beyond that knowledge is what people tend to argue about, which is what I am not interested in doing. I'm working to live in a way that gets me to function better, and preferably more in tune with Nature, which I think is best for all, including for wildlife and Nature. Otherwise, I wouldn't be doing it. And sometimes, like probably everyone, I am not the best at it.

> "The cosmos is a vast living body, of which we are still parts. The Sun is a great heart whose tremors run through our smallest veins. The moon is a great nerve-center from which we quiver forever. Who knows the power that Saturn has over us, or Venus? But it is a vital power, rippling exquisitely through us all the time."
>
> – D. H. Lawrence

People ask me if I believe in astrology. I am not a person who seeks out information about my astrological impressions. My exposure to astrology has been from reading a little about it and randomly meeting people who are somewhat knowledgeable about astrology. Sometimes these people say things that interest me. Sometimes they don't. Sometimes they are interesting to listen to simply because of their theatrical delivery. Some have attempted to explain it all to me, or their understanding of it, but I don't dwell on it. However, I do believe that, as the moon and stars affect the tide that is the water of the sea, so too are we, who largely consist of water, affected by the intricacies of the heavens.

> "The truths — those surprising, amazing, unforeseen truths — which our descendants will discover, are even now all around us, staring us in the eyes, and yet we do not see them."
> – Paramhansa Yogananda

I believe that what we do always plays into natural laws existing in patterns, and even within what people refer to as *sacred fractal geometry*. We are either doing what is in tune with patterns that build health, or we are doing what is in tune with the opposite. In that way we are in tune or out of tune with what will benefit us. In that way our decisions impact us so that when we make choices that don't coincide with what is best we often get what is in sync with our bad choices. Somewhere within that is my concept of right and wrong, or what some may call their religion.

No matter what religion a person is, it seems to me that the main thing is to know oneself, and to understand something deeply about your soul in a way that you will be committed to leading a life that aims for the best you can be while using your talents, intellect, and other graces. And to do so in peace with others while living a life that respects Earth and protects animals. Everything else seems secondary and trivial.

> "He who knows others is wise; he who knows himself is enlightened."
> – Lao Tzu

I believe that Nature is the manifestation of the beauty of divine spirit energy. I believe that we are spirit energies and that we can help manifest the beauty of Nature in cooperation with a more glorious and glorified being with which we may one day interact on a spiritual level — and that we are continually interacting with on some level — which is always spiritual in one way or another. I believe that when we live closer to Nature, respect wildlife, and follow a plant-based diet, we are more likely to build a stronger relationship with our loving spiritual side. I believe that enlightenment has to do with respecting Earth and protecting animals.

> "A knowledge of the existence of something we cannot penetrate, of the manifestations of the profoundest reason and the most radiant beauty, which are only accessible to our reason in their most elementary forms — it is this knowledge and this emotion that constitute the truly religious attitude; in this sense, and in this alone, I am a deeply religious man."
>
> – Albert Einstein

Too often it appears "religions" focus on shame and guilt, limit potential, and drive people to lose the beauty of their individuality — all while working money out of people's pockets to support self-serving ministers and unsustainable church infrastructures. And a lot of it is done with the undercurrent of telling people they should live as told, or risk experiencing some sort of vague and unpleasant eternal something-or-other.

> "When I do good, I feel good; when I do bad, I feel bad, and that is my religion."
>
> – Abraham Lincoln

A preacher once asked me, "Son, don't you fear God?" I asked him, "Why would I fear God?" He said something about how, if I feared God, I would live more righteously. I told him that I think people can live righteously without being fearful.

I don't want to be motivated by shame, guilt, or fear. I also don't feel that it is helpful to use those conditions as a way to get people to act.

Not that I am anything close to being a perfect example of them, or any righteous virtue, but I think it is better to be motivated by beauty and love.

I feel no connection to churches that project shame, guilt, and fear as motivational factors for leading a good and honest life. I also have no interest in ministers telling me what is going to happen to me after I die. I think it would be better to motivate people to focus on and live in the present while creating a beautiful life.

To me it seems you will have a better chance of becoming a world-renowned artist by attending truck-driving school than you will of becoming closer to God by associating with the churches that are in business. I also do not consider these money-grabbing churches to be associated with the teachings of their so-called idealized Divinity of choice, or whatever distorted image of it they have conceptualized.

Some of these churches may as well be worshipping cartoon characters. If their members considered how their idealized person actually lived, they would likely find someone who lived naturally, and far distant from how the so-called church leaders are living with their greed, self-righteousness, projections of shame, expensive clothing, and theatrical rituals.

> "Peace I leave with you, my peace I give unto you: not as the world giveth, give I unto you. Let not your heart be troubled, neither let it be afraid."
> – Jesus Christ

When I am asked if I am a Christian and I answer "yes," people apply their own definition of this to my answer. But their definition of Christian is likely very far removed from what I mean when I say that I am a Christian. It is likely that I am more in tune with what they consider to be a vegetarian Buddhist than I am of being their version of a Christian. Not that I am, or am not, a Buddhist.

To paraphrase Gandhi: I like Jesus, but I don't like these Christians; they don't remind me of Jesus. Too often they seem to have overlooked Jesus' teachings on love, and they do so while appearing to strive toward being examples of what he taught about greed and those who covet.

Many churches appear to be organized to feed off people who have given up, or who never have taken hold of their power. The money-making endeavors of these churches blend in perfectly well with the companies that exploit every possible religious holiday by manufacturing and selling various products in connection with the those holidays. Most of what religion has become seems to be a big marketing sham to get money from the so-called pilgrims in every which way possible. To me, Christmas and other mass-marketed holidays have as much to do with God and spirituality as bricks and boulders have to do with soft.

> "A clergyman earns his living by assuring idiots that he can save them from an imaginary hell."
> – Henry Louis Mencken

Many churches glorify not in what is best for the people, but in what can make the church bigger and grander. There is no way to explain their brash techniques other than to recognize that their main goal is to get money from people. Their leaders, both male and female, dress in elaborate clothing to represent their man-given titles and engage in man-invented mystical and theatrical rituals. None of their activities have anything to do with Divinity, but have more to do with traditions driven by megalomania. The leaders self-glorify and validate their vanity by gaining the favor of men and women. They speak as if they know every nuance of the thoughts of Divinity, and mostly lead unsustainable lives out of tune with Nature. They project shame and guilt when it would be greatly more beneficial to build and nurture intellect, talents, and gifts of the spirit while advocating a sustainable, plant-based diet free from junk food.

> "Being a Baptist won't keep you from sinning, but it'll sure as hell keep you from enjoying it."
> – James Dean

Many churches condemn people for being outside the robotic and extremely limiting standards that the churches have defined as the only acceptable form of behavior. It seems to me that those who most adamantly promote such teachings are dealing with their own self-hate, repression, neglect, and denial.

> "Whoever undertakes to set himself up as judge of truth and knowledge is shipwrecked by the laughter of the gods."
> – Albert Einstein

Isn't it interesting that some of those most fervent in preaching against certain moral issues are found to be leading secretive double lives completely out of tune with what they so strongly preached against?

To understand what some people are struggling with in the shadows of their minds, sometimes all you have to do is listen to what they confess to hate.

> "Stories serve the purpose of consolidating whatever gains people or their leaders have made or imagine they have made in their existing journey through the world."
> – Chinua Achebe

I am not one who believes in proclaiming hellfire on those who don't live according to organized church definitions of godly behavior. Churches base their distorted understanding and interpretation on a few words written in a book largely consisting of poetry, lyrics, parables, metaphors, and romanticized and fancified tales based on ancient myth mixed with some traces of reality — and written in such antiquated style that nobody seems to agree with what is actually being said. I view many of the scriptural stories as lessons giving examples of situations, and some as mistranslations, or purposeful rewordings by clever minds operating under various agendas.

> "The greatness of a nation and its moral progress can be judged by the way its animals are treated."
> – Mahatma Gandhi

It seems to me that the humble people described in many of the various scriptural texts wouldn't relate very well to a vast majority of those who claim to be living in tune with scriptural teachings, and whose daily food intake involves many of the most life-damaging foods ever created. Many people who also confess to leading their lives according to scriptural teachings also seem to overlook the number of characters in the texts that are murderers, prostitutes, slave owners, rapists, and that otherwise engage in all sorts of ruinous behavior.

Many churches are clearly teaching people to reject others and are encouraging remote attitudes, cold-heartedness, and the denial of the obvious, leading to pain in the hearts of the two-spirited. Many churches teach people to be afraid of themselves and shameful of their natural desires for great sex. It is sex that would otherwise be spiritual and loving if it were expressed respectfully between two adult people in a committed, nurturing relationship. But many of the church teachings nurture denial, dysfunction, and self-hate. Narrow-minded church teachings have brought about such restraint in some people that this restraint leads to double and high-risk hidden lives that harm what would otherwise be those living safe monogamous lives, accepting who they are while living in communities that would otherwise be tolerant, welcoming, and appreciative of diversity.

> "Our Western institutional religious tradition has essentially repressed and distorted the sexual instinct and thereby created a variety of personal and social pathologies. In so doing it has also effectively removed sexuality from its spiritual foundation."
> – Gunther Weil

In his book, *The Hidden Spirituality of Men*, Matthew Fox writes, "So often religion seems more bent on controlling sex than on mining it for its spiritual power," and that, "In the West, we prefer linking sex to shame rather than to the sacred."

Rather than being inspirational, much of what I see in some churches are lessons in greed, narrow-mindedness, unkindness, and even hate. Their actions speak much louder than their words. What they are doing is creating problems, teaching people to reject anything other than what the preacher says, and getting people to shut down what may be the best parts of themselves.

> "What it comes down to is the churches are not operating like instruments of love. They're hate machines. They're ignorance factories."
> – Sean Penn

I believe that whether or not we belong to a religion, we can receive our own inspiration.

> "If we cannot see how what we are doing or not doing is contributing to things being the way that they are, then logically we have no basis at all, zero leverage, for changing the way things are — except from the outside, by persuasion or force."
> – Adam Kahane

> "Where questions of religion are concerned, people are guilty of every possible sort of dishonesty and intellectual misdemeanor."
> – Sigmund Freud

Many people who consider themselves religious and who belong to organized religions often espouse political views that are pro-war; live selfishly in opulent homes, or aim to; support politicians who vote to spend more money on prisons than on schools; support officials that allocate more money for the military and corporate welfare (which can be the same thing) than on protecting the environment and wildlife; and appear to live with the attitude expressed through their diet and lifestyle that Earth and animals are here for us to exploit, violate, plunder, and destroy.

While the last paragraph unfortunately describes a lot of people, there are other people who are living lives disconnected from organized religions and who find spiritual inspiration in a variety of things and in a number of ways not necessarily associated with what some people consider to be a religion.

> "Every day people are straying away from church and going back to God."
> – Lenny Bruce

Some people find inspiration to be a better person by creating music, poetry, and other forms of art. Others find inspiration to be a better person by spending quality time with family members, friends, neighbors, and lovers. Others find it in making and/or growing food and sharing it with others, including the less fortunate. Some find it in working with the disabled, working with those who are troubled, or working with rescued animals.

> "Connection with gardens, even small ones, even potted plants, can become windows to the inner life. The simple act of stopping and looking at the beauty around us can be prayer."
> – Patricia R. Barret

Some find inspiration to be a better person in the wilds of Nature, in surfing, in spending time hiking in forests, in kayaking in rivers, by planting and maintaining culinary gardens, in nurturing wild edible native plants, and in working to clean, restore, and protect wildlands and wildlife habitat. I understand how people can relate more to these types of activities than to sitting in a building listening to a preacher. Working to build strong human bonds and to protect Nature can be much more beneficial to both the planet and the person than sitting in church.

> "Anything else you're interested in is not going to happen if you can't breathe the air and drink the water. Don't sit this one out. Do something. You are by accident of fate alive at an absolutely critical moment in the history of our planet."
> – Carl Sagan

Imagine how many millions of acres of pristine wildlands have been bulldozed to build churches and church parking lots, and how much damage has been done to Earth to provide all the materials to build all those churches. Imagine how much electricity and fossil fuels are used to light, heat, and otherwise run and manage the church facilities, and how much damage is continually being done to Earth to access these resources and turn them into products.

> "Show by your lives that religion does not mean words, or names, or sects, but that it means spiritual realization."
> – Sri Ramakrishna

> "Don't be content in your life just to do no wrong. Be prepared every day to try and do some good."
> – Nicolas Winton

"Everybody needs beauty as well as bread, places to play in and pray in, where nature may heal and give strength to body and soul."
– John Muir

"I am I plus my surroundings and if I do not preserve the latter, I do not preserve myself."
– Jose Ortega Y Gasset

Imagine how much better the world would be if instead of sitting in Church for hours every week, the congregants went out and did environmental service; if instead of donating money to churches they donated money to groups restoring and protecting forests, rivers, and wildlife habitat, such as the Natural Resources Defense Council, Earth Island Institute, Earth First, Sea Shepherd, and the Green World Campaign; and if instead of church buildings and parking lots covering millions of acres of land, there were millions of acres of wildlife habitat protected and held as havens of Nature and natural sanctuaries for worship.

"I believe in Spinoza's God, who reveals Himself in the lawful harmony of the world, not in a God who concerns Himself with the fate and the doings of mankind."
– Albert Einstein

"A morning-glory at my window satisfies me more than the metaphysics of books."
– Walt Whitman

A friend once asked me what provides me with my inspiration. I answered that some people look in books to try to find the mysteries and magic things of life. I see the miracles and mysteries in the plants, animals, soil, rivers, ocean, and sky.

Later, my friend sent me the following quotation:

"In music, in the sea, in a flower, in a leaf, in an act of kindness. I see what people call God in all these things."
– Pablo Casals

It would be nice if churches, which are tax-free and major land owners on every continent, would stop building parking lots and buildings, which are destroying the planet; discontinue investing money in commercial sprawl, which is destroying the planet; and in investing in the stocks of companies that are destroying the planet. Instead, it would be good if they became more involved in aggressively protecting the sanctuary of Nature that is this wonderful planet created by the God they profess to worship.

> "Our intellect has achieved the most tremendous things, but in the meantime our spiritual dwelling has fallen into disrepair."
> – Carl Gustav Jung

I find it interesting that churches function under for-profit business plans with investment portfolios while claiming to be nonprofit. I find it pretty much unfortunate that churches are working out of huge, high-maintenance structures accompanied by parking lots for cars that are all very clearly destroying the creation of Divinity, robbing the land of beauty, creating toxic air, and ruining many hundreds of thousands of acres of land that should have been left as wildlife habitat on every region of the planet.

People may say that churches are needed to provide social support. It is true that churches provide some obvious social benefits, including structure for people who are struggling, and some provide shelter for those who are destitute. Studies have concluded that gathering with people in a nurturing environment is healthful on many levels. It is known that isolation from human contact can cause depression and increase the chances of dementia in old age. In this way, churches provide something that many people would not otherwise get: a social structure where they are exposed to a variety of people with various interests. However, churches are not the only solution for providing social stimulation. Continuing education, participation in volunteer work, being involved in environmental causes, going to a yoga class, and belonging to arts, gardening, music, and community organizations also provide social involvement that stimulates the neural pathways of the brain.

> "Dogs give unconditional love. For me they are the role model for being alive."
> – Gilda Radner

Interestingly, science has shown that interacting with animals provides some of the brain stimulation a person can get from interacting with people. This stands as another reason why we need to take care of the animals and protect wildlife and the environment.

> "The human race is challenged more than ever before to demonstrate our mastery, not over nature but of ourselves."
> – Rachel Carson

Churches throughout history have played a role in the arts, including music, painting, sculpture, architecture, and craftsmanship. But much of this has been to enrich the churches disproportionate to the benefits to the worshippers. Many churches own art, land, jewels, gold, and other belongings gathered from people in various ways, and often deceptively, sometimes violently, or otherwise unrighteously.

If I were to attend a church regularly, I would have to concern myself with how the church is benefiting the people and the environment.

We are living in amazing times. While so much needs to be done to transform society to protect the planet, it seems the main focus of many governments is on war; on providing welfare for the most environmentally damaging industries and corporations; on making the rich more wealthy; on catering to commercialism; on passing laws that cage more of the poor in tremendous prisons while government administrators slash funding for childcare, the arts, libraries, and education; and in building structures that both cause terrific damage to the planet and provide venues for Earth-damaging activities.

> "In wildness is the preservation of the world."
> – Henry David Thoreau

> "The world is charged with the grandeur of God."
> – Gerard Manley Hopkins

I believe that we have a sacred responsibility to take care of Earth and the delicate web of Nature. I believe that if we are to gather and unite for a purpose it should be to tune each other into more environmentally sustainable beings actively involved in protecting and restoring wildlife habitat. That is the mastery that I believe would be most helpful for all of us to be working on and striving for.

> "Religious people must do more than offer prayers if the world is to become a better place to live."
> – Dalai Lama

For those who say that churches must exist, and who are involved in creating churches, to them I say: Consider meeting in the cathedral of Nature that is a forest, or under a large canopy of sorts to protect the people from the elements. Or in any of the many structures that already exist, rather than by building new structures. Consider building no new parking lots or structures that destroy meadows, woodlands, wetlands, hillsides, or any other wildlife habitat, or otherwise fallow land. Existing structures could be converted to be more sustainable, such as by landscaping roof tops with native plants; unpaving some of the land; restructuring with sustainable materials, such as bamboo and biodegradable substances; and using maintenance products that are more environmentally safe. Consider nonelectrical instrumentation (electricity is most often produced using fossil fuels). Consider the encouragement of good and the nurturing of talents and abilities in tune with sustainable living. Consider people gathering and encouraging one another in festive social gatherings in Nature with healthful vegan cuisine freely given, and none of the spiritually robbing substance of alcohol.

> "Community means strength that joins our strength to do the work that needs to be done. Arms to hold us when we falter. A circle of healing. A circle of friends. Someplace where we can be free."
>
> – Starhawk

> "If more of us valued food and cheer and song above hoarded gold, it would be a merrier world."
>
> – J. R. R. Tolkien

Some people say it wouldn't work, that I'm being an idealist, and they may make other discouraging remarks about this, but I have already been to such gatherings, and they are becoming more common.

> "It is no use walking anywhere to preach unless our walking is our preaching."
>
> – St. Francis of Assisi

One diverse group of people I hung out with for a weekend called themselves the "Church of Love and Sunshine." They said they guided themselves by indigenous American principles where everyone of all colors, ages, genders, and sexualities are welcome to gather in peace free from alcohol, and with the purpose of protecting and restoring Nature. No money was to be exchanged, and nothing was to be sold, but only traded or freely given. We went into the hills for a fire-free campout with singing and conversation while lots of fresh fruit was handed out. The next day, everyone gathered trash and some trees were planted. After the work was done, a feast of vegan food was served. This was followed by dancing to the sounds of percussion, wind, and stringed instruments. Some of the participants were massage therapists who gave massages to other gatherers. Late in the afternoon, we hauled out all the trash we had collected, and left the land better than when we had enter-ed it. If church gatherings consisted of more of those activities, the world would be a better place.

> "In the life of the Indian there is only one inevitable duty — the duty of prayer — the daily recognition of the Unseen and Eternal. He sees no need for setting apart one day in seven as a holy day, since to him all days are God's."
>
> – Ohiyesa, Santee Dakota

To everyone's benefit, there are many people in all religions who are becoming involved in environmental issues by working on protecting wildlife, on restoring forests, on living more sustainably, and on following a diet that is more respectful of the treasures of Nature. There are vegan groups in many religions, and others are forming.

On January 1, 2010, which marks the annual World Peace Day, members of the Catholic Church were told by Pope Benedict that, "Respect for creation is of immense consequence, not least because creation is the beginning and the foundation of all God's works, and its presservation has now become essential for the pacific coexistence of mankind." He added, "It is imperative that mankind renew and strengthen that covenant between human beings and the environment, which should mirror the creative love of God, from whom we come and toward whom we are journeying." It would be excellent if people took action in tune with that advice. Following a plant-based diet free of synthetic chemicals would be a good place to start, as food is the number one way in which we interact with Earth.

There are also some of the money-collecting churches that are (finally!) doing a good job of accepting a broad variety of personalities, including those who have been rejected by other churches based on sexuality. Instead of projecting shame, punishment, fear, and guilt, and teaching about sin and apostasy, these churches are encouraging and nurturing people with the intention of bringing out their talents, intellect, and individual beauty. Instead of pointing to two adults and forbidding them to be together, they say, let them be and let them love. Some offer social activity or otherwise fellowship programs that include dance, art, music, song, poetry, literature, environmental responsibility, yoga, and plant-based nutrition.

If you are a churchgoer, consider organizing an environmental group among your fellow worshipers, and especially one that is involved in restoring and protecting local wildlife habitat.

> "I don't believe that the solutions in society will come from the left or the right or the north or the south. They will come from

islands within those organizations, islands of people with integrity who want to do something."

– Karl-Henrik Robert

"I do not believe in a personal God and I have never denied this but have expressed it clearly. If something is in me which can be called religious then it is the unbounded admiration for the structure of the world so far as our science can reveal it."

– Albert Einstein

If you are going to church to find inspiration to live your life, but all you are doing is sitting around trying to get inspired, how much inspiration are you truly getting? If you are not being inspired to use your talent, intellect, skill, and other graces to become busy creating a better world, then what are you being inspired to do?

"You are not just a meaningless fragment in an alien universe, briefly suspended between life and death, allowed a few short-lived pleasures followed by pain and ultimate annihilation. Underneath your outer form, you are connected with something so vast, so immeasurable and sacred, that it cannot be spoken of."

– Eckhart Tolle

"Quantum physics tells us that the space between the molecules is not nothing, but rather is energy. And that energy is the same in all things. Everything, everyone, contains this same energy — God! But it is when we focus on something with our consciousness that we actually merge with it, become one with it somehow, or rather become more conscious of this common energy of which we are all part — that our energies join and the boundaries diminish. Therefore, if I focus on my uniqueness, I become more myself. If I focus on someone else, I become more like them. And if I focus on the God in me, I become more like the God in me!"

– Jinjee Talifero

"The eye with which I see God is the same eye with which God sees me."

– Meister Eckhart

Know that your thoughts are the sources driven by your spiritual force that will bring you to do what you want to do with your life.

Be an inspiration unto yourself, and take action to manifest the inspiration through your words, actions, foods, and lifestyle to awaken the beauty within and around you.

> "We do not destroy religion by destroying superstition."
> – Marcus Tullius Cicero

> "I have learned so much from God that I no longer call myself a Christian, a Hindu, a Muslim, a Buddhist, a Jew. The truth has shared so much of itself with me that I can no longer call myself a man, a woman, an angel, or even pure soul. Love has befriended Hafiz so completely, it has turned to ash and freed me of every concept and image my mind has ever known."
> – Hafiz

> "Always remember that you belong to no one, and no one belongs to you. Reflect that some day you will suddenly have to leave everything in this world — so make the acquaintanceship of God now."
> – Paramhansa Yogananda

> "You don't have to be religious to have a soul; everybody has one. You don't have to be religious to perfect your soul; I have found saintliness in avowed atheists."
> – Harold Kushner

> "Spirituality is about joy, fun, creating, and playing. It is absolutely not rigid, full of rules, or judgmental. It is about freedom, love, and laughter."
> – Karen Bishop

> "My religion is kindness."
> – Dalai Lama

> "Humanity and divinity will be identical when we recognize divinity in humanity."
> – Ernest Holmes

> "Everything is holy! Everybody is holy! Everywhere is holy! Everyday is eternity! Everyman's an angel!"
> – Allen Ginsberg

"Our task is to say holy yes to the real things of our life."
– Natalie Goldberg

"The way is not in the sky. The way is in the heart."
– Buddha

"The kingdom of God is within you."
– Luke 17:21

Love

"Love is the greatest refreshment in life."
– Pablo Picasso

Similar to the other aspects of a person, the soul can experience illness that impacts the physical structure. An ailing soul manifests its ailment in low-quality thoughts, words, and behaviors, and in the consumption of junk food. A sign that the souls of people are suffering is that they are doing harm to others, to themselves, and to Nature.

I believe that the health of the soul is the most important of all. The soul is the root of the person, and the connection to Divinity. One healing agent Divinity provides is that of love.

"The story of a love is not important — what is important is that one is capable of love. It is perhaps the only glimpse we are permitted of eternity."
– Helen Hayes

A sign that people are healthful is that they know to carry the energy of love in their words, actions, and lifestyle. I know that I feel more healthful when I do this, and less healthful when I waiver.

"Neither a lofty degree of intelligence nor imagination nor both together go to the making of genius. Love, love, love, that is the soul of genius."
– Wolfgang Amadeus Mozart

The importance of loving everyone is a concept I would like to believe in. However, I have not been so successful at this. Some people seem to be doing their best to shatter the possibility of the concept from becoming reality.

In addition to being a healing agent, love is an essential nutrient. It needs to be both synthesized within us and obtained from outside sources. This nutrient helps us to experience Divinity.

> "Love is a force that connects us to every strand of the universe, an unconditional state that characterizes human nature, a form of knowledge that is always there for us if only we can open ourselves to it."
> – Emily Hilburn Sell

Studies conclude that if you don't receive nurturing, loving interaction when you are young, your brain does not develop the receptors that respond to kindness and to related pleasurable feelings and emotions. This is one of the tragedies of child neglect and abuse.

I theorize that because the society in which we grow up also helps our brain to develop, the children growing up under the stressful conditions of war-torn and poverty-stricken countries are also not being given the opportunity to develop healthful brains. This is one level of the horror of war, and the damage caused by ill-advised, stubborn, power-hungry, greedy politicians and governments.

> "Whether one believes in a religion or not, and whether one believes in rebirth or not, there isn't anyone who doesn't appreciate kindness and compassion."
> – Dalai Lama

No matter how we have lived or what we have experienced, I believe that we can choose to live in a way that heals us. Luckily the brain continues to form and rewire itself throughout our life, thus living healthfully at any stage of life allows us to become the healthful beings we were meant to be — and that we strive to be. To heal our brains from unfortunate experiences, we need the healing energy of love present in our daily lives. Even better if this love is combined with the best-quality foods available to us, intellectual stimulation, daily exercise, the use of talents and intellect, and intentionally goal-oriented living.

> "As the body needs food to survive and grow, the soul needs love. Love instills a strength and vitality that even mother's milk cannot provide. All of us live and long for real love. We are born

and die searching for such love. Children, love each other and unite in pure love."

– Mata Amritanandamayl "Amma" Devi

Love is the most positive, life-affirming energy a person can feel. It permeates all, is the strongest power of all, and is the only superpower. Because it can be generated from within, love is available to us at all times.

"There is no remedy for love, but to love more."

– Henry David Thoreau

Love is the song inside you that gently and compassionately encourages you to tune into your spirit and express your intellect through healthful, intentional living.

"What else is the world interested in? What else do we all want, each one of us, except to love and be loved, in our families, in our work, in all our relationships?"

– Dorothy Day

Love is the nutrient of and gift from the spirit. When love is present, people communicate, learn, heal, play, think, feel, and sleep better. Loving thoughts are uplifting, kind, patient, healing, bring solutions, and result in good works.

"When we love, we release our thought energy and transpose it to the recipient of our love. Our primary responsibility is to love."

– Marcel Vogel

The problems of the human world are strongly related to the fact that humans refuse to love one another and to act lovingly toward the other sentient beings with whom we share this amazing planet.

Many people have suffered tragedies, experienced failure, been subjected to the harsh treatment of damaged people, and have gotten caught in the energy of failure. All of these have brought them to dwell in that bottomless pit of disappointment, anger, depression, sadness, and psychological and spiritual pain. These can become their normal and most common feelings. They may get to the point where they don't know anything closely resembling joy and feel they are continually descending. Anything outside this pain can make them feel uncomfortable. They can be so focused on and attached to this draining energy of suffering that they become lost in it and dwell in the martyr energy. They can get to the point where they lack an understanding that they have energy resonating inside them that can help them change their situation. This energy is the healing and ascending energy of love.

Love is necessary for a life to be healthful. Love uplifts and brightens. It helps those who are sad to become happy. It helps those who are ailing to heal.

Sigmund Freud philosophized that happiness is obtained through work and love. The nurturing energy of love brings people to prosper by uplifting them and getting them to use their intellect, talents, and abilities.

> "We love because it is the only true adventure."
> – Nikki Giovanni

To bring love into your life, you must first love your self. Love for self includes taking care of and respecting your physical being as well as other life forms, such as the animals of the land, sky, and water. Love for self includes believing that your essence is worthy of love. Knowing that you are worthy of love will drive you to improve your life in every way.

> "To love oneself is the beginning of a lifelong romance."
> – Oscar Wilde

When you carry love and work to rule your self by love, you are working to be a holder of the consciousness of Divinity.

Emotions that are in alignment with love include kindness, forgiveness, patience, encouragement of good, and respect for the safety, talents, skills, intellect, and health of others.

> "Too often we underestimate the power of touch, a smile, a kind word, a listening ear, an honest compliment, or the smallest act of caring, all of which have the potential to turn a life around."
> – Leo Buscaglia

Loving someone does not mean doing everything for them that they are capable of doing for themselves. Instead, love in a relationship means respect while nurturing a life together.

Things attract complementary things. All good things are in alignment with the energy of good, which is of the energy of love. Nothing good can happen without love. If you want good in your life, you must align yourself with the energy of love.

"Everything in the future will improve if you are making a spiritual effort now."
– Paramhansa Yogananda

With the energy of love, you can perceive yourself, others, and everything around you in an entirely different way.

Where Jesus is quoted in the Bible as saying that we should not allow our hearts to be troubled or to be afraid, I believe he is directly addressing the topic of toxic thought patterns. Allowing yourself to feel troubled and afraid is damaging to you, creates stress, and harms your body tissues. Being troubled and afraid is the opposite of love.

By allowing yourself to be ruled by love, to act out of love, to project love, and to promote love, you are participating in the strongest energy of all. It is the energy of bliss, of euphoria, of nirvana, of the power of Nature, of heaven, and the resonance of Divinity.

"Once you begin to acknowledge random acts of kindness — both the ones you have received and the ones you have given — you can no longer believe that what you do does not matter."
– Dawna Markova

Aim to love everyone. Sometimes you may find this concept difficult to practice, especially because of the way certain people conduct themselves. But you will be better off doing it than not.

"The essence of nonviolence is love. Out of love and the willingness to act selflessly, strategies, tactics, and techniques for a nonviolent struggle arise naturally. Nonviolence is not a dogma; it is a process."
– Thich Nhat Hanh

"Nonviolence means avoiding not only external physical violence but also internal violence of spirit. You not only refuse to shoot a man, but you refuse to hate him."
– Martin Luther King, Jr.

Just because others select words, actions, and expressions that are opposite of love does not mean that you have to participate in the same behavior.

You can always take the opportunity to be a holder and server of love.

Love is not afraid and is the essence of all that is good and worthwhile.

Things that are not worthwhile are violence and war.

Refuse violence. Refuse to participate in war. Dispose of weaponry.

"Love lights more fires than hate extinguishes."
– Ella Wheeler Wilcox

People often act violently out of fear. Work against this by guiding yourself more by love than by fear.

Choose to take the higher road. Whatever you do, don't forget to do it with love. Love for yourself, and love for those around you, including the animals.

Follow and be led by love.

"Do not think that love, in order to be genuine, has to be extraordinary. What we need is to love without getting tired."
– Mother Teresa

Love is in alignment with magnetizing your life to attract success, health, and happiness, and to be in loving relationships.

Demonstrate your love for yourself by nurturing and using your talents and intellect, getting daily exercise, following a plant-based diet, stimulating your mind with high-quality and inspiring material and activities, and in living intentionally to fulfill your goals.

"Teach only love for that is what you are."
– Marianne Williamson

Always remember that the most powerful energy is that of love.

Uncover the beauty and infinite supply of the spirit of love in your life.

Transition into love and evolve through love.

"The moment you have in your heart this extraordinary thing called love and feel the depth, the delight, the ecstasy of it, you will discover that for you the world is transformed."
– Jiddu Krishnamurti

"Like the in breath and the out breath. You gather the light and then you give it out. That's just the way it works."
– Nancy Rivard

"Dare to reach out your hand into the darkness, to pull another hand into the light."
– Norman B. Rice

"Love is a fruit in season at all times, and within reach of every hand."
– Mother Teresa

In their recipe book *I Am Grateful*, Terces Engelhart and Orchid of San Francisco's Café Gratitude present this perpetual question: What would love do?

"The purpose of life is to express love in all its manifestations."
– Count Lev Nikolayevich Tolstoy

Magnetizing Your Life

"It's not what you are that holds you back, it's what you think you are not."
– Denis Waitley

"The only place where your dream becomes impossible is in your own thinking."
– Robert H. Schuller

The mind is an incredible tool that constantly observes situations, and factors answers for what it needs and wants. It works better when the person is an active participant in thinking the words that make up the questions, then seeking the answers, creating solutions, and acting on the agreements.

"Many things are lost for want of asking."
– English proverb

There is a law of Nature that works in all life forms. Some call it *the law of attraction.* It can be seen in all living things, the substances, and in energy. It functions simply and can be explained by comparing it to the way a nail is drawn to a magnet. The law of attraction is the natural rule that certain things are attracted to other specific things.

> "All things appear and disappear because of the concurrence of causes and conditions. Nothing ever exists entirely alone; everything is in relation to everything else."
> – Buddha

There are certain popular positive living books that seem to focus on the law of attraction as a formulator of success while mentioning little to nothing about the actions that would be most helpful for people to participate in to help get the law of attraction to work. In that way, many positive living books cut their readers short and fail them. It is good to have faith that good things should happen, but a person would experience more benefits by taking the actions that correspond with the law. Faith without works is dead.

> "Vision isn't enough unless combined with venture. It's not enough to stare up the steps unless we also step up the stairs."
> – Vance Havner

> "Do not sit down and try to attract the thing you want to you; but begin to move toward the thing you want, and you will find it coming to meet you. Action and reaction are equal; and the person who steadily and purposefully moves forward with one thing in view, becomes a center toward which the thing he seeks is drawn with irresistible power."
> – Wallace D. Wattles

There are also certain success books that seem to place an abundance of value on expensive material possessions, and all too often give the ideal example of success as someone who lives a life of luxury. However, I do not think that living an opulent lifestyle should be the ideal. In fact, I think an unsustainable lifestyle is an example of failure, especially if a person has the resources to live in a way that would be much more respectful of the environment and wildlife.

> "Abundance comes not from stuff. In fact, stuff is an indication of non-abundance. Abundance is in the sacred; it's in the connection of love. We will find abundance through hard times when we find each other."
> – Rebecca Adamson

I place value on the lifestyles that are more in tune with Nature, and that are filled with the things that help support both human, wildlife, and environmental health, which are the same.

What you need to exist healthfully may be completely different from what you have agreed to as being your ideal, which may be based on what commercial culture has groomed you to believe.

> "There are many things in life that will catch your eye, but only a few will catch your heart. Pursue those."
> – Michael Nolan

Things are naturally attracted to those that help them to exist. One way the law of attraction is displayed is in the movement of leaves turning toward Sun. Another way it is displayed is in how the roots of a plant are drawn to damp soil, and deeper into the nutritious, mineralized soil. You can plant a seed in a jar that has one side packed with rich soil, and the other side packed with sand. The roots of the plant will naturally become more abundant in the soil-filled side of the jar.

> "Our limitations and success will be based, most often, on our own expectations for ourselves. What the mind dwells upon, the body acts upon."
> – Denis Waitely

The law of attraction also works with people. The difference is that people can play a part in where their roots of attention and energy reach. It is your choice to associate with energies, situations, people, sounds, and substances that will help you grow in a positive way, or with those that will lead to boredom, stifled potential, or self-destruction. This aspect of your person is active whether or not you are aware of it.

> "There is no defeat except from within, no really insurmountable barrier save our own inherent weakness of purpose."
> – Elbert Hubbard

> "This life is yours. Take the power to choose what you want to do and do it well. Take the power to love what you want in life and love it honestly. Take the power to walk in the forest and be a part of nature. Take the power to control your own life. No one else can do it for you. Take the power to make your life happy."
> – Susan Polis Schutz

We all probably know people who bury themselves in excuses. People have an amazing capacity for making excuses for everything and anything. A lot of excuses for not succeeding have to do with not wanting something badly enough, which is the motive for not surpassing things that are creating a wall blocking us from allowing us to experience satisfaction and joy.

While I was writing this I happened to be speaking with a friend who was concerned that she wasn't getting enough sleep. She said she had been suffering from insomnia for a few months and had tried everything to get to sleep at night. When I met with her she said she needed some coffee. I asked her why she would be drinking coffee if she were concerned about sleeping better. She said coffee or green tea, which both contain caffeine, are the only things that will keep her awake during the day. She said she had been really good about staying away from caffeine until a few months prior, which is when she started having trouble sleeping. The solution seemed so obvious that there wasn't much I could say.

Many of our problems can be solved with simple solutions, and often the solutions are found within our reasoning that creates the excuses that stumble us.

> "Be faithful in small things because it is in them that your strength lies."
> – Mother Teresa

If you want certain things, people, and events to be present in your life, they are much more likely to become present if you align your thoughts and actions to attract them and bring them in.

You can feel better about yourself. You can experience more vibrant health. You can think better-quality thoughts and respond better to that which is presented to you. You can utilize your time and resources more wisely. All of this is what you can do with the goal of improving and building things into the way you want them to be for your life.

> "Your ultimate goal in life is to become your best self. Your immediate goal is to get on the path that will lead you there."
> – David Viscott

Vibrant health, success, and satisfaction are more likely to be present when you work to be in sync with them, become fluent in them, and bring gratification into your being.

If certain substances don't exist, whatever is attracted to those substances does not show up. A bee is not attracted to a plant until the plant presents what a bee wants: a vibrant flower containing pollen and nectar.

To bring in what you want in your life, present the right substances and work to pull in those things that you desire.

Everything you think, say, and do works for or against you in a way that is its equal. You can either manipulate things to work for you one way, or you can manipulate things to work for you another way. Or you can choose to settle for whatever happens. It is up to you.

> "Visualize this thing you want. See it, feel it, believe in it. Make your mental blueprint and begin."
> – Robert Collier

If you want certain things in your life, then it would be beneficial to focus on those things. Visualize them in your life. Plan and work for them to become present in your life. Magnetize yourself to them, and them to you. But the key to making the things you want to be present in your life is that you must work for them through actions.

If you want health, happiness, and success, seek these things. They are more likely than less likely to happen in a way that is relative to the efforts you put toward experiencing them. Plan and work to make them happen.

> "One ship drives east and the other drives west by the self same winds that blow. It's the set of the sails and not the gales that determines the way they go."
> – Ella Wheeler Wilcox

Similar to plant roots that grow toward the most fertile areas of soil, your life will be guided into the energies and substances that you want to absorb — as long as you set the power of your mind to work in that direction and continually act on those thoughts through intentional actions.

> "Don't let life discourage you; everyone who got where he is had to begin where he was."
> – R. L. Evans

Steer your life away from that which holds you back. Aim all your thoughts and actions toward that which brings you health, happiness, and success. Arrange your surroundings into that which nurtures health. Clean and organize your belongings in a way that allows you to function at a higher level. Get rid of clutter.

Free yourself of thoughts that hold you down. Work to dispose of that which is negative — including the negative influences of other people, and the residue of energy left over from low-quality living.

Take every element of your life and place it where it works for you. Make it function. Form it into what is best for you. This includes your diet.

> "The ability to simplify means to eliminate the unnecessary so that the necessary may speak."
> – Hans Hofmann

To attract a most radiant and abundant life filled with satisfied goals and people who love and respect you as you love and respect them, work to attract that situation.

The originating force in your actions is what you are thinking. Begin now to think yourself healthful and satisfied.

> "Life is not easy for any of us. But what of that? We must have perseverance and above all confidence in ourselves. We must believe that we are gifted for something and that this thing must be attained."
> – Marie Curie

Constantly develop and prepare yourself to receive the situation you want. Do it through healthful plant-based food choices of the highest-quality available to you; through physical preparation of exercise and a confident stance; through dress; through mental awareness, knowledge, focus, visualization, and rationalization; and through using your intellect, talents, abilities, and graces to set the stage for magnetizing your life to draw in the life you desire.

You cannot continue to eat a degenerating diet and expect to generate health. In the same way, you cannot think negative thoughts and expect positive actions out of your being.

Just as a seed that generates power from within to grow by using both the energy of Nature and the nutrients taken from its environment, you can generate your power to grow your life into the form you want it to be.

The nutrients, knowledge, energy, objects, and people you need to become the person you want to be are all available to you at some level.

> "Most people search high and wide for the keys to success. If they only knew, the key to their dreams lies within."
> – George Washington Carver

Pieces of the puzzle you need to build the life you need are also contained within you.

The level of your power frequency influences everything you say and do, everything you have, and everything you create. It is the frequency that rules Nature — from the tiniest creatures at the bottom of the sea to those on the highest mountains. It is a force that you can use to transform your life into what you want it to be.

Perhaps the things you need to experience the life you desire have been presenting themselves to you throughout your life, but you were not attuned to the right frequency to recognize these things, or were not aware of how they can work to educate, or otherwise provide for you.

> "If you want to be respected by others the great thing is to respect yourself. Only by that, only by self respect will you compel others to respect you."
> – Fyodor Dostoyevsky

Perhaps your abilities to recognize your resources were dulled by unhealthful foods, thoughts, relationships, and activities. Once you have adjusted your frequency through respecting your life by taking care of yourself, your abilities to recognize the things you need will clarify.

Align and conduct your energy, thoughts, words, and actions to deflect what you don't want while attracting what you do want. As you do this, your transition into the life you desire will accelerate. When this happens, your focus and being will surpass the law of attraction, and you will have transitioned into what I call *the law of manifestation.*

> "One can never consent to creep when one feels the compulsion to soar."
> – Helen Keller

People

> "Consider the following. We humans are social beings. We come into the world as the result of others' actions. We survive here in dependence on others. Whether we like it or not, there is hardly a moment of our lives when we do not benefit from others' activities. For this reason it is hardly surprising that most of our happiness arises in the context of our relationships with others."
> – Dalai Lama

The people around you are power sources emitting energy through thoughts, words, and actions that can alter your energy. Our brains react to seeing and hearing, reading the words of, listening to the music of, observing the creations of, and otherwise interacting with other people. The study of mirror neurons has revealed that the people around you play a part in how some of the neurons in your brain form, connect, and function, which plays a role in what you think, say, and do, and what sorts of natural chemicals your body is producing in relationship to these activities.

Just as there are foods that are more nourishing and foods that are less nourishing, there are people who are nurturing and those who are at various levels of being the opposite.

> "It takes a variety of people to challenge us, encourage us, promote us, and most of all, help us to achieve a broader dimension of ourselves."
>
> – Glenn Van Ekeren

Some people are wonderful to be around because they propel themselves toward creating an amazing life for themselves. They are well connected to their beneficial attributes and their presence can invigorate, enlighten, uplift, and nurture others.

Some people are their own worst enemy. This may be so because they don't live up to their own power while allowing themselves to be influenced by the negative energy of others. They may fail to face the truth, and instead choose to live in denial so deep that their life becomes one of laziness and self-deception. They may fall so far below their potential for doing good that they drift into darkness, and they carry others down with them.

> "Power is strength and the ability to see yourself through your own eyes and not through the eyes of another. It is being able to place a circle of power at your own feet and not take power from someone else's circle."
>
> – Agnes Whistling Elk

Explore the role you play in each of your relationships. Are your relationships healthful and nurturing? Do you feed off others, or do others feed off you? Do you play a role as an enabler who allows — and even encourages — others to participate in damaging behavior? Are you an underminer who continually slanders, belittles, and says negative things of others? Or are you inspired and inspiring? Do you feel loved and are you loving?

If you don't like what you find in the assessment of the people in your life, without projecting blame, shame, or accusations, take action to change things. This may include working to im-prove your relationships, or simply not staying in touch with certain people.

> "The best measure of a human being is in how we treat the people who love us, and the people that we love."
> – Lynda Carter

Sometimes the best parts of people get lost in relationships as they may abandon their true selves to maintain a certain level of a relationship that may not be worth the price they are paying.

If all you are doing is role-playing in your relationships, then you might benefit by considering on what your relationships are based — other than a fake personage you have developed as a sort of character in a theatrical presentation. It would likely be beneficial to you to stop role-playing in your relationships in ways that stifle your spirit, bury your talents, or otherwise hold you back from experiencing a better life.

Role-playing is normal. It occurs within families, in relationships, among friends, at work, in social interactions on all levels of society, and among all people. It happens when a person conforms to a particular set of real or imagined values and/or expectations to adjust to the role they are assuming to communicate with the person or persons they are with. It has to do with why people conduct their mannerisms in consideration of the people in their presence. Much of it is allowing only one side of their personality to be exposed in a way that works for them, or for what they perceive is being expected of them by the people they are with.

Sometimes role-playing patterns of behavior can be less than helpful as they can stunt a person's social, emotional, creative, spiritual, and other areas of development. In an abusive or neglectful relationship, role-playing can be most harmful as the person conforms to the down-trodden underling as they become the victim of whatever abuse or neglect is occurring.

The way you carry yourself, the actions you take, the words you choose to use, and the attitude you express toward others in your body language has a great influence on those around you, on how they think of you, and in what gets accomplished.

At work many people have to role-play to associate on a "professsional level," which means a veil of vagueness is cast over some of their real emotions, and over their private life. There is a healthful level of role-playing at work that is best for the tasks being done, and to maintain a professional relationship. However, this can carry over to other areas of life to the point that people are always living undercover and trying to portray themselves in a certain way they have somehow agreed to as acceptable, even when it may not necessarily be helpful, or healthful.

> "The beginning of love is to let those we love be perfectly themselves, and not to twist them to fit our own image. Otherwise we love only the reflection of ourselves we find in them."
> – Thomas Merton

Many people get so caught up in trying to present a certain image that the most unique and admirable aspects of their character become hidden. This can lead to people becoming lost in trying to build the façade of what they consider to be the most acceptable way to present themselves. In this situation they may spend their money shopping for things they don't need with the goal of impressing people they don't know. When they finally do try to associate with people, they may work to reach some level of intoxication before they feel comfortable expressing themselves.

> "Our deepest fear is not that we are inadequate. Our deepest fear is that we are powerful beyond measure. It is our light not our darkness that most frightens us. We ask ourselves, who am I to be brilliant, gorgeous, talented and fabulous? Actually, who are you not to be?
>
> You are a child of God. Your playing small does not serve the world. There's nothing enlightened about shrinking so that other people won't feel insecure around you.
>
> We were born to make manifest the glory of God that is within us. It's not just in some of us; it's in everyone. And as we let our own light shine, we unconsciously give other people permission to do the same. As we are liberated from our own fear, our presence automatically liberates others."
> – Marianne Williamson

You may know of people who have many talents, skills, and high levels of intellect, and who do nothing with these attributes. They likely are involved in self-destructive behavior, or mindless activities, such as spending lots of time staring at the television or Internet, or hanging out with other people whose lives are wasteful or are tragedies. Perhaps you see some of your traits in them. Maybe they are some of the people who are closest to you.

"To live is so startling it leaves little time for anything else."
– Emily Dickinson

If your life is highly unsatisfactory to you, it is likely that you are surrounding yourself with similar people. This has likely become your normal, but it is not your natural, and it never can be.

If that last paragraph describes you and your most prominent relationships, you are due for a major life overhaul.

"To free us from the expectations of others, to give us back to ourselves — there lies the great, singular power of self-respect."
– Joan Didion

Some of the people who have been zapping your energy will be able to deal with your actions to take control of your life. They may recognize their low-quality behavior, improve their ways, and choose to conduct themselves with respect to your life in a way that greatly benefits both of you. Others may get upset and respond like spoiled children as you work to stop allowing them to continue the unhealthful relationship. Still others may feel overwhelmed by the change they see in you and become a nuisance and a problem to you. This can be taken as a red flag indicating that you need to disassociate yourself from them.

"By acknowledging your own fears and insecurities and corruptions, you start to have a much more gentle and profound sense of where they come from in other people."
– Andrew Harvey

Some people walk around spreading toxic thoughts by criticizing those around them. Sometimes it appears they are expecting others to be doing things in ways that they themselves aren't doing. It seems they think of themselves as the ones making the better choices when they may be making the lowest-quality choices, including those devaluing the lives of those around them.

It is interesting how certain people conduct themselves in relation to how they expect others around them to respond. They may be so accustomed to using other people as crutches that they feel lost when their subordinate role-player is not available. They may have based much of their identity and daily agenda on continuing their unhealthful treatment of others.

> "I have been through some terrible things in my life, some of which actually happened."
> – Mark Twain

Some people continually choose to participate in and/or create the most dramatic events they can possibly involve themselves in as a way of feeling validated. It seems that they feel more important if they are successful in eliciting dramatic responses in other people. What they may not realize is that the things they think matter are pure nonsense.

Some people feed off one-night stands that turn into one-night scandals. Then they spew the story to anyone who will listen while embellishing the story with flavor and spice. The better their delivery, which often involves trying to make the other characters appear as fools, and the more of a rise they get from the listener who agrees with them, the more they feel satisfied and validated by their pathetic behavior.

Some people always seek to be viewed as making the best decisions, often on the shoulders of others while working to surround themselves with people who will agree with them.

> "Self righteousness is a loud din raised to drown the voice of guilt within us."
> – Eric Hoffer

This all goes along with the age-old question: How is it that people think they can point out what they perceive to see as the flaws in others if they have not worked to correct their own?

> "Behavior is a mirror in which every one displays his own image."
> – Johann Wolfgang von Goethe

What many humans seem to do best is to display their issues and flaws. Often you can listen to a person who is criticizing another and understand that they are unknowingly displaying their own issue. This scenario may be why the issue is foremost in their mind. They are engaging in transference as they are seeing their own traits in others, and they may be completely unaware of it. The issues they are noticing in others may be something they themselves have struggled with, or had their life affected by. It may be some aspect of their being that they may be uncomfortable about, and especially something with which they would never want to be associated. It is true that when someone points a finger at another person, there are three fingers pointing back at them.

> "The judgment of others does not change who I am. Quite the opposite is true. It reveals who they are. Those who deem me unworthy at a glance and pass me by, have my blessing to keep walking, for they have a long way to go. They have not reached the point where they are able to see and appreciate me for who I am."
> – Terri McPherson

There are also other reasons people may belittle those around them. This aspect of undermining has to do with control. If they can keep others down, they can continue to walk all over them. They may want to take into consideration that their low-level treatment may have to do with a lower level of self-esteem.

> "As long as you keep a person down, some part of you has to be down there to hold him down, so it means you cannot soar as you otherwise might."
> – Marion Anderson

Some people leach off the energy of the people around them by using them, taking whatever they can get, and drawing others into their problems and drama. They are takers and basically function as energy parasites, and are dependent on others to continue their unhealthful behavior.

People who live off the energy of others may be so accustomed to doing so that they lead their lives through other people. They may appear strong and in control, but they are likely weak and unable to carry themselves on their own energy. It is the enabler relationship that allows them to continue. When they have no one from whom to leach, they flail about in life and may become desperate, grasping for someone to dominate.

Don't allow parasitic people to rely on you to continue their unhealthful ways.

> "The wrongdoer is more unfortunate than the man wronged."
> – Democritus

Be aware of your influence on other people. Just as a dog becomes fine-tuned to, relies on, and responds to the emotions of its caretaker, the people around you are responding to your emotions — and vice versa. Just as resting musical instruments, such as drums and guitars, may vibrate by the sound waves hitting them from another instrument in the room that is being played, the vibrations, or emotions, of a person affect the vibrations of the other people with whom they come into contact.

> "You can understand and relate to most people better if you look at them — no matter how old or impressive they may be — as if they are children. For most of us never really grow up or mature all that much — we simply grow taller. O, to be sure, we laugh less and play less and wear uncomfortable disguises like adults, but beneath the costume is the child we always are, whose needs are simple, whose daily life is still best described by fairy tales."
> – Leo Rosten

> "Be not forgetful to entertain strangers for thereby some have entertained angels unawares."
> – Paul of Tarsus

Bridging Over the Underminers

> "Always in life an idea starts small, it is only a sapling idea, but the vines will come and they will try to choke your idea so it cannot grow and it will die and you will never know you had a big idea, an idea so big it could have grown thirty meters through the dark canopy of leaves and touched the face of the sky."
> – Bryce Courtenay

Recognize those people who may be takers of your time, energy, resources, and talents. You may see the takers placing an unreasonable amount of dependence on others. This may be done to the extent that they may keep others under control by working on deconstructing the self-esteem of those from whom they leach. There may be negative comments where compliments would be most helpful, impatience where patience would be most helpful, insults where kindness would be most helpful, cutting down where building up would be most helpful, and general undermining comments that work to confirm their superiority complex while belittling those around them. Once you have recognized these people in your life you will be able to start putting a stop to their vacuuming of your life energy. Not doing so is enabling them to continue their actions, cheating yourself out of your life force, neglecting your needs, devaluing your life, and undermining your strengths.

Not making changes to improve your life by not disconnecting parasitical people from your energy will be contributing to your victimization and an underutilization of your potential.

Many people have become conditioned to allowing themselves to be treated as if they are inferior to others; don't use their own power to get ahead in life; and are stuck in the circular motion of self-deceit. Many people have been in these types of degrading, people-pleasing, and belittled situations their entire lives. It has become their norm. Anything outside what is normal to them may become uncomfortable — even if it is more healthful. Even when they are faced with the truth and at a point where they can make a healthful decision, they may react harshly or angrily at the prospect. Their response may have to do with their unwillingness to accept that they were wronged by people they had been deluded into considering as admirable.

Many people are caught up in a circle of compulsive behaviors they formed as a way to cope with their undesirable situation. But often the way they spend their time is more of an escapism mechanism than a coping mechanism. Under these situations they become their own underminer. For instance, for many people, TV watching becomes a coping mechanism, and it is often a way to escape from thinking about how empty they have allowed their lives to become. This also may have to do with self-hate, being uncomfortable with their life, looking for a way out, and not dealing with their issues, while focusing on scandalous celebrities or the variety of fictional characters constantly presented in the mass media.

> "Real generosity toward the future lies in giving all to the present."
>
> – Albert Camus

If you want to improve your life, turn off your TV, stop paying attention to celebrity culture, don't buy into commercial nonsense, and stop trying to replicate corporate imagery.

Avoid placing blame on other people. It is unproductive to blame others for your situation and it focuses on energy that has already been spent. Focusing on blame is of the victimhood mentality. This is not to say that you are or are not a victim, or have or have not been harmed. But it is about using your power and resources to move onward toward better experiences and a brighter future. Also, realize that when you are overly critical of others, and accusing others of shortcomings, you may be accusing yourself of the very same. Instead of focusing on what others may have done wrong, move forward out of the train wreck and spend your time, energy, and resources on what you can do to improve your existence.

Recognize that you may be your own underminer, by allowing your life to be overtaken by the lives of others; by going into debt to replicate commercial imagery; by feeling you will only be happy if your life resembles corporate idealism; by using excuses and denial to rationalize your behavior; by consuming fried and junk foods; by not getting daily exercise; and/or by allowing yourself to be buried by various layers of unhealthfulness.

> "Be careful the environment you choose for it will shape you; be careful the friends you choose for you will become like them."
> – W. Clement Stone

Take an assessment of the people in your life. Identify the relationships that are wearing you down, which may be of your own making. Also, identify the relationships in your life that are healthful. Then, work to create more healthful relationships by either healing those that are damaged, ending those that are damaging, and beginning some that are nurturing and enriching. Also, consider spending some alone time to organize and structure your life to better reflect what it is you are striving for.

What many people do when they end one unhealthful relationship is that they jump right into another. Often they exhibit an amazing ability to find and associate with those who are at a certain level of dysfunction that is in tune with the same low qualities they've been wallowing in. Their new relationship will resemble those of the past, with similar difficulties but with a different mask and a new name.

If you have constantly been around people who put you down or otherwise undermine your life, it is likely that you have low self-esteem. Be aware that low self-esteem can be just as debilitating as an addiction to drugs or alcohol.

> "Your time is limited, so don't waste it living someone else's life."
> – Steve Jobs

Living a life conforming to the projections of others is one way to limit yourself to a small fraction of what you can be. If you have continually been around people who project negativity toward you, including through overly critical comments, name-calling, sarcasm, mockery, ridicule, or unrighteous dominion, it is likely you may not be living anywhere near your potential for satisfaction. It is likely that your talents and intellect have been muted. And it is a strong indication that you have a lot of work to do to get on a better path.

> "I don't want everyone to like me; I should think less of myself if some people did."
> – Henry James

You may be the type of person who has kept adjusting yourself to try to be what you think is most acceptable, to gain the favor of someone impossible to please, and/or to be the example of someone who has it together so that you gain favor with others, or to become the life of the party. You will never be liked by everyone on the spinning ball. Stop trying to compete for the most popular. Popularity contests ended in high school — where they were also ridiculous.

> "The willingness to accept responsibility for one's own life is the source from which self-respect springs."
> – Joan Didion

You may be playing a part in supporting someone else's life by subjecting yourself to their visions and dreams while living little of your own. If that is the way you want to live, that is your right. Maybe it works for you. But maybe you are cheating yourself, underestimating your abilities, and denying yourself the expression of your talents and intellect.

By conforming to the lives of others, what you may be doing is truly setting yourself up for deep regret when you realize that you have not established and worked toward the expression of your own talents, abilities, and intellect. These feelings can be greatly compounded if or when the person you lived for is found to have deceived you, and/or drops you from their life.

Stop allowing others to steal your life. Stop permitting yourself to be influenced by those who pull you down. And stop thinking about the damage their words and actions may have done to you. Instead, get busy in the present making the changes in your life that will improve your existence.

> "It is not because things are difficult that we do not dare; it is because we do not dare that they are difficult."
> – Lucius Annaeus Seneca

Improving your life may be as difficult or as easy as you make it, or that you allow it to be. But it is better to use your energy to achieve your goals and live your life — rather than cheating yourself by allowing others to rob you of the joy you could be experiencing.

> "We should not judge a man's merit by his great abilities, but by the use he makes of them."
> – François de la Rochefoucauld

Don't waste time trying to tell others what you are capable of doing. It is always more empowering to plan out, to work for, and to accomplish your goals. Whether others do or do not recognize your achievements does not devalue your work. Don't expect praise. Keep moving along toward accomplishment.

> "I was told, 'You can be anything you want, kid.' When you hear that often enough, you believe it."
> – Ed Bradley

Remember that getting through life is sometimes like walking down a street. When the dogs bark at you, don't stop to listen. Simply keep moving along.

Rather than permitting the negativity of others to undermine your life, allow the good of others to affect you. Reject the negative. Accept the positive. Acknowledge the good. Nurture beneficial qualities. Encourage betterment. Create situations that lead to satisfaction.

> "Life has been your art. You have set yourself to music. Your days are your sonnets."
> – Oscar Wilde

It is not productive to expect others to improve your life. Doing so weakens your power. It is up to you to make the changes in your life that you want. Of course having supportive relationships can play an important role in helping you attain your goals. But ideal relationship structures don't have to exist for you to advance in your life. You may not have made the best choices and have been key in damaging your relationships and in getting people to lose trust and faith in you. You may find that you will have to go it alone for a time because, for any number of reasons, including those due to your own unfortunate choices, you simply have no one in your life who nurtures you. Whatever the case, it is always invigorating to make positive changes in your life. The sooner you do it, the better.

"Trust in yourself, then you will know how to live."
– Johann Wolfgang von Goethe

Start improving your life now, and don't wait for anyone to do it for you.

Nurture yourself.

Refuse to be an underminer of others, or of yourself.

"One kind word can warm three winter months."
– Japanese proverb

"The great gift of human beings is that we have the power of empathy, we can all sense a mysterious connection to each other."
– Meryl Streep

"I've learned that people will forget what you said, people will forget what you did, but people will never forget how you made them feel."
– Maya Angelou

"It's all really very simple. You don't have to choose between being kind to yourself and others. It's one and the same."
– Piero Ferrucci

"The ideals that have lighted my way, and time after time have given me new courage to face life cheerfully, have been kindness, beauty, and truth."
– Albert Einstein

"Life is short and we have never too much time for gladdening the hearts of those who are traveling the dark journey with us. Oh be swift to love, make haste to be kind."
– Henri-Frederic Amiel

"I expect to pass through this world but once; any good thing therefore that I can do, or any kindness that I can show to any fellow creature, let me do it now; let me not defer or neglect it, for I shall not pass this way again."
– Etienne de Grellet

"I seek constantly to improve my manners and graces, for they are the sugar to which all are attracted."
– Og Mandino

"When I was young, I used to admire intelligent people; as I grow older, I admire kind people."
– Abraham Joshua Heschel

Instead of doing these things:
Negate
Criticize
Be mean
Insult
Belittle
Call names
Undermine
Devalue

Do these things:
Uplift
Compliment
Be kind
Nurture
Acknowledge good
Encourage good
Induce positive-thinking
Recognize the beauty in people, including you.

"No kind action ever stops with itself. One kind action leads to another. Good example is followed. A single act of kindness throws out roots in all directions, and the roots spring up and make new trees. The greatest work that kindness does to others is that it makes them kind themselves."
– Amelia Earhart

"A compliment is verbal sunshine."
– Robert Orben

"Leave each person you meet a little better than when you found them."
– Robin Sharma

"When you are kind to others, it not only changes you, it changes the world."
– Harold Kushner

"Each of us has a spark of life inside us, and our highest aspiration ought to be to set off that spark in one another."
– Mark Albion

Unison

"Life without love is like a tree without blossom and fruit."
– Kahlil Gibran

"Love is always open arms. If you close your arms about love you will find that you are left holding only yourself."
– Leo Buscaglia

"We're never so vulnerable as when we trust someone — but paradoxically, if we cannot trust, neither can we find love or joy."
– Walter Anderson

"Every man needs love, guys like romance. I do anyway."
– Paul McCartney

"Three keys to more abundant living: caring about others, daring for others, sharing with others."
– William A. Ward

"The scientific search for the basic building blocks of life has revealed a startling fact: there are none. The deeper that physicists peer into the nature of reality, the only thing they find is relationships. Even sub-atomic particles do not exist alone. One physicist described neutrons, electrons, etc. as '…a set of relationships that reach outward to other things.' Although physicists still name them as separate, these particles aren't ever visible until they're in relationship with other particles. Everything in the Universe is composed of these 'bundles of potentiality' that only manifest their potential in relationship."
– Margaret J. Wheatley

If any species is to carry on, there has to be relationship. Because we rely on other forms of life to keep living, all life on Earth is inter-connected relationship. Just as a plant cannot exist without water, we could not exist if it were not for other people. None of us would exist if it weren't for relationships.

> "It is in the shelter of each other that the people live."
> – Irish Proverb

It very much appears that we are wired to be in a close, intimate relationship with another person. The more complete, functional, nurturing, and satisfying that relationship is, the better it is for our health. Even our brains function better if we are in a healthful relationship. Science has shown that relationships and the interaction with others impact our brain neuron growth patterns and function, our hormone levels, and the function of our tissues — including our heart.

> "Only through our connectedness to others can we really know and enhance the self. And only through working on the self can we begin to enhance our connectedness to others."
> – Harriet Goldhor Lerner

On the other hand, an unhealthful relationship can do the opposite, increasing our stress and resulting in unhappiness and physical ailments. In an unhappy relationship, everything good that can be present in a happy relationship can exist in the direct opposite form.

> "Assumptions are the termites of relationships."
> – Henry Franklin Winkler

It seems that one of the most common elements of unhealthful relationships consists of assumptions. Some of us have been around those who assume in ways that are confrontational, accusational, and truly unhealthful. This is the projection of guilt, and it commonly has to do with the guilt and dysfunction of the people making the accusations, their lack of healthful communications skills, and their history of being in dysfunctional relationships where their trust may have been broken. They have decided that, rather than assuming good, they are going to assume bad. Rather than giving compliments, they are going to belittle. Rather than saying what is pleasant, they are going to mutter guilt. Rather than uplift, they are going to put down. Rather than accept individuality, they are going to be unaccepting. Rather than offer solutions, they are going to create problems. Rather than provide nurturing, they are going to project shame. Instead of being helpful in the relationship, their attitude creates damage.

"Much of the conflict of our lives can be explained by one simple but unhappy fact: We don't really listen to each other."
– Michael P. Nichols

"The greatest compliment that was ever paid me was when one asked what I thought, and attended to my answer."
– Henry David Thoreau

"So when you are listening to somebody, completely, attentively, then you are listening not only to the words, but also to the feeling of what is being conveyed, to the whole of it, not part of it."
– Jiddu Krishnamurti

People experiencing dissatisfaction in relationships often mention that their partner does not listen to them. In that situation the basic form of communication may have broken down to where every other part of the relationship is in disrepair. But the relationship doesn't have to remain in that condition.

"Listening is such a simple act. It requires us to be present, and that takes practice, but we don't have to do anything else. We don't have to advise, or coach, or sound wise. We just have to be willing to sit there and listen."
– Margaret J. Wheatley

For healthful communication in a relationship, there needs to be two active participants listening, sharing thoughts, and taking actions to move forward into improvement.

"Only that in you which is me can hear what I'm saying."
– Ram Dass

"If someone listens, or stretches out a hand, or whispers a kind word of encouragement, or attempts to understand a lonely person, extraordinary things begin to happen."
– Loretta Girzatlis

"An elementary particle is not an independently existing, unanalyzable entity. It is, in essence, a set of relationships that reach outward to other things."
– H. P. Stapp

Often one person in a dysfunctional relationship has an ego so large that the person drifts into selfish and narcissistic behavior. Concerns may focus on how everything should work in that person's favor, regardless of the needs of the other person. But, family conditioning may exist, wherein a person has only been permitted to display a certain aspect of their being, and hiding others in ways that may have more to do with shame and denial than about self-absorption.

> "Narcissism thus involves a withdrawal of instinctual energy and an investment of libido in the ego. This investment in the ego implies that the person is unable to love or relate with others and is self-absorbed."
> – Carl Gustav Jung

> "We're afraid of a lot of things in life. It's part of the human condition. What do we fear? Love? Failure? Telling the truth about ourselves? I think we don't show people all we truly are because we're afraid that if they actually know everything about us, they won't love us. I'm as guilty of that as anyone."
> – Kevin Coestner

> "When you are in a state of nonacceptance, it's difficult to learn. A clenched fist cannot receive a gift, and a clenched psyche — grasped tightly against the reality of what must not be accepted – cannot easily receive a lesson."
> – Roger John

> "People travel to faraway places to watch, in fascination, the kind of people they ignore at home."
> – Dagobert D. Runes

An easy way to determine if communication in a relationship is breaking down, or is kaput, is that people stop spending time together, make opposing plans, and are not interested in any sort of compromise or joint venture.

It is interesting how certain people conduct themselves in their relationships. Much of what they decide to do in a relationship may be related to behaviors they learned from childhood, and other decisions they make relating to how they treat their companion have to do with peer pressure, or what they interpret their relationship should be according to what they see in TV shows, commercials, and in celebrity gossip magazines. They can get so hung up in what their relationship is supposed to be according to the pop media, that they lose touch with what it is, and in how they can play a part in making it better.

> "Remember, we all stumble, every one of us. That's why it's a comfort to go hand-in-hand."
> – Emily Kimbrough

Very often people seem to separate from their partner when their partner isn't falling into a mold formed by peer, family, and societal pressures. One little mistake, or what is perceived as a flaw, can be the determining factor of whether or not the relationship ends. Under such conditions the relationship likely wasn't all that healthful from the get-go.

> "We often discover what will do, by finding out what will not do; and probably he who never made a mistake never made a discovery."
> – Samuel Smiles

All of us have made unwise decisions and all of us have issues. Just because someone has made bad choices, or has what you choose to define as flaws, is no reason to discard them like rubbish.

> "Whenever catching sight of others, look on them with an open, loving heart."
> – Patrul Rinpoche

Some people are truly a mess, and they need to spend some time getting their life together before they, and their problems, become a part of the life of someone else. Some may need a helping hand, a guide, a confidante, an advisor, a sponsor, a life coach, and a patient, kind, and forgiving someone to show them a better path in a way they may never have experienced. They may benefit from meeting with others who are also working to change from slothfully dysfunctional to intentionally healthful. One reason I wrote this book is so that it could be used in group settings for people to explore ways in which they can improve. Those who may need additional help, or healing, could turn to professional mind/body psychologists for help.

> "For a chunk of my life, I avoided shy people, assuming they had nothing to say. Then one day I realized that if I quit blabbering for a minute, they'd often utter something that would blow my mind."
> – Tara Somerville

"People can only hear you when they are moving toward you, and they are not likely to when your words are pursuing them. Even the choicest words lose their power when they are used to overpower. Attitudes are the real figures of speech."
– Edwin H. Friedman

All too often relationship storms turn into a blame game, with one topping the other. When there is a lack of love, gratitude, appreciation, and caring, the relationship becomes like an unfounded structure that will eventually come tumbling down as the weight added to it has no sure footing.

A sign that a relationship is starting to heal is that people start listening to each other, don't try to tell the other how to think, consider the other's point of view, and stop dictating the other person's life and feelings. When relationships heal, the caring, gratitude, and appreciation return.

"To learn through listening, practice it naively and actively. Naively means that you listen openly, ready to learn something, as opposed to listening defensively, ready to rebut. Listening actively means you acknowledge what you heard and act accordingly."
– Betsy Sanders

Quality of communication is a determining factor of the health of a relationship. The expression of the individuals through words is just one level of communication. People communicate through body language, through facial expressions, through movement, through thought, and through the activities in which they engage.

People also communicate by not communicating. It may be that one person simply came to a realization in their life, and that particular companion is no longer part of it.

One basic fact about people is that they tend to change. And they do so on many different levels.

"People change and forget to tell each other."
– Lillian Hellman

In healthful relationships, there is a dance between the people, how they change, and how the other person goes with it, against it, supports it, or otherwise adapts to it.

In controlling relationships, at least one of the partners expects the other to conform to a particular role. This is also where conflict can exist, and much of it in ways that can destroy happiness, self-expression, intellectual stimulation, social exchange, and sensual satisfaction.

> "Indeed, this need of individuals to be right is so great that they are willing to sacrifice themselves, their relationships, and even love for it."
>
> – Reuel Howe

What a certain level of unhappiness, or certain types of relationship traps, can lead to is escapism. Escapism may be through drugs, through food issues, through secretive behavior, through double lives, through obsessive fanaticism, through gambling, through the fake satisfaction and weakening influence of pornography, and through cheating and lies.

Under the conditions of a relationship that seems broken, people would likely benefit by getting together and figuring out if the relationship is salvageable, or if ending it would be the best maneuver. Carrying on with indifference to each other could be nothing but a waste of two lives that would be more satisfied with experiencing joy.

> "All the art of living lies in a fine mingling of letting go and holding on."
>
> – Havelock Ellis

> "If only I could throw away the urge to trace my patterns in your heart I could really see you."
>
> – David Brandon

> "Out beyond ideas of wrong-doing and right-doing, there is a field. I'll meet you there"
>
> – Rumi

Discovering the strengths and/or weaknesses of your relationship may come about when discussing what you both want from life, what makes you feel satisfied, and what areas you would like to change. And some are revealed through living, interacting, and everyday activities.

> "Seldom, or perhaps never, does a marriage develop into an individual relationship smoothly and without crisis; there is no coming to consciousness without pain."
>
> – Carl Gustav Jung

I have heard people say that they had to rediscover the person they were after their relationship became committed, and they also had to rediscover the person they were with. When the courting ends and the home life begins, each may discover many issues and traits about the other that they had not considered, may not have noticed, and may have ignored or overlooked. When this new discovery is made, a whole new level of the relationship can get underway — and with it, a level of openness and adjustment. Otherwise the closed-mindedness and stubbornness is bound to close doors, and bring about relationship traps, dysfunction, escapism, and unhappiness.

> "There is no greater weakness than stubbornness. If you cannot yield, if you cannot learn that there must be compromise in life — you lose."
> – Maxwell Maltz

Stubbornness and closed-mindedness introduce conflict. One person in the relationship may like the way things are going, and does not conceive of changing, even if the suggested changes will bring about a more healthful life. They also may have felt that they are being overrun, may not want to participate in the ideas of others, and are uncomfortable with change — even when they are encouraged to participate in designing the changes.

> "By mutual confidence and mutual aid — great deeds are done, and great discoveries made."
> – Homer

Work to create healthful relationships where respect and love are present. Listen to each other and collaborate on projects, giving one another a turn at what they do best. And allow others their opportuneities to learn and grow.

> "It takes more courage to reveal insecurities than to hide them, more strength to relate to people than to dominate them, more 'manhood' to abide by thought-out principles rather than blind reflex. Toughness is in the soul and spirit, not in muscles and an immature mind."
> – Alex Karras

Some of the people in your life may have played a key part in events that were not among your best experiences. You may need to heal those relationships. One way of doing so is to recommit to each other through working to improve both of your conditions, nurturing a better future for both of you.

"For him who confesses, shams are over and realities have begun; he has exteriorized his rottenness. If he has not actually got rid of it, he at least no longer smears it over with a hypocritical show of virtue."
– William James

"The fragrance always remains on the hand that gives the rose."
– Mahatma Gandhi

When the clouds of contesting behaviors have blown over and forgiveness has set in, that is when people have learned, and a renewed sweetness can begin — perhaps beyond what it had ever been. That is when relationships can be wonderful, strengthening, nurturing, and loving, in the good times, as well as the less than good.

"Shared joy is double joy, and shared sorrow is half-sorrow."
– Swedish proverb

"The meeting of two personalities is like the contact of two chemical substances. If there is any reaction, both are transformed."
– Carl Gustav Jung

There are times where persons in your life will shine brighter. But if relationships are to be healthful, it is more likely that they will be based on nurturing and respecting each other, and not on who is more prominent. Without a stem, the beautiful flower falls. The stem and the flower are each as important as the other in the structures of their existence.

"There are two ways of spreading light; to be the candle or the mirror that reflects it."
– Edith Wharton

"Maybe love is like luck. You have to go all the way to find it."
– Robert Mitchum

"I hold this to be the highest task for a bond between two people: that each protect the solitude of the other."
– Rainer Maria Rilke

Synergy in a relationship can be a tremendous force in accomplishing goals, in unburdening your life from clutter and conformity, and contributing to persistence in working toward a better life for both of you.

"In my friend, I find a second self."
– Isabel Norton

"Friendship is the marriage of the soul."
– François-Marie "Voltaire" Arouet

"It is not a lack of love, but a lack of friendship that makes unhappy marriages."
– Friedrich Wilhelm Nietzsche

"The best way to inspire people to superior performance is to convince them by everything you do and by your everyday attitude that you are wholeheartedly supporting them."
– Harold S. Geneen

When you have a partner, and you are both following a healthful diet and getting daily exercise, you become attuned to the same frequencies. Even couples that are not living healthfully often are able to finish each other's sentences, and may end up taking on the same physical characteristics. This is because they are living in sync, subsisting on the same nutrients, and often engaging in the same physical, sexual, and sleeping patterns. When two people are living healthfully, the bond can become very strong, including through the function of mirror neurons.

"Look at sex realistically and in a light mood. Sexual energy is needed to upgrade your brain cells. Sex, sweetness, and intimacy are good but you must also have a functional brain."
– Choa Kok Sui

When other areas of the relationship complement each other, the intimacy will also likely become more aligned. The simple act of intimacy relieves stress, triggers similar hormonal changes, creates mirrored neural connections, forms molecules of emotion, induces and releases fantasy, and adds to the healing and nurturing qualities of the relationship.

"Sexuality expresses God's intention that people find authentic humanness not in isolation but in relationship."
– James B. Nelson

Just as some types of wood will support four times the amount of weight if two beams are joined together, so also will a couple be able to become many times stronger living in unison than if they were living separately. The vibrational frequency of the couple will be tuned into much of the same energy. Thoughts, ideas, hopes, desires, and dreams harmonize. A synchronicity happens that can both astound and strengthen. When they are following a healthful, balanced, plant-based diet and getting regular exercise, a couple can become an amazing expression of synchronized energy.

> "I have spread my dreams under your feet. Tread softly because you tread on my dreams."
> – William Butler Yeats

> "We are one, after all, you and I. Together we suffer, together exist, and forever will recreate each other."
> – Pierre Teilhard de Chardin

Studies have shown that couples will follow and maintain an exercise regimen more regularly if they join each other in their agenda to become physically fit. Not that they have to be directly next to each other doing the same exercise, but simply knowing that their partner is involved in improving his or her health is a motivating factor in improving their own.

> "We are each of us angels with only one wing, and we can only fly embracing each other."
> – Luciano de Crescenzo

Equally, similar to succeeding at an exercise program, maintaining a healthful diet can be an easier goal to accomplish if you do so with the accompaniment of a lover, relative, or friend. In this way you can motivate each other to maintain the goal of eating healthfully, share in each other's experiences with recipes, and in locating and trying out unfamiliar foods, places, events, and activities. All of this can help bind a relationship.

> "The objectives of two lovers is almost always the same: to find meaning in their individual lives and in their life together."
> – Paul Pearsall

No matter how you are living, it could be an interesting exercise to make a list of things you want, things you want to do, and things you need to do to bring about the life that you would like to have. Ideally you would be able to work on this with the person with whom you are in a relationship, and then collaborate to align your goals, priorities, needs, and wants. Then work together to attain those things.

"Love lasts when the relationship comes first."
– Abraham Lincoln

"Love doesn't just sit there, like a stone; it has to be made, like bread, remade all the time, made new."
– Ursula K. Le Guin

"Underneath all the twists and turns of relationships, love is the only and ultimate truth between souls."
– Kathy Hearn

"We think sometimes that poverty is only being hungry, naked, and homeless. The poverty of being unwanted, unloved, and uncared for is the greatest poverty. We must start in our own homes to remedy this kind of poverty."
– Mother Teresa

"The time to be happy is now. The place to be happy is here. The way to be happy is to make others so."
– Robert Green Ingersoll

"Let us be grateful to people who make us happy; they are the charming gardeners who make our souls blossom."
– Marcel Proust

"Being in love shows a person who he should be."
– Anton Chekhov

"To love someone is to see a miracle invisible to others."
– François Mauriac

"There is, within each of us, a heart that is much larger than ordinary human affairs would normally reveal, a heart that can embrace the world because it overflows with love."
– Julie Redstone

"The unique personality which is the real life in me, I can not gain unless I search for the real life, the spiritual quality, in others. I am myself spiritually dead unless I reach out to the fine quality dormant in others. For it is only with the god enthroned in the

innermost shrine of the other, that the god hidden in me, will consent to appear."
– Felix Adler

"Relationship is surely the mirror in which you discover yourself."
– Jiddu Krishnamurti

"When we share — that is poetry in the prose of life."
– Sigmund Freud

"A positive attitude is perhaps more important at home than anywhere else. As spouses and parents, one of our most vital roles is to help those we love feel good about themselves."
– Keith Harrell

"Things derive their being and nature by mutual dependence and are nothing in themselves."
– Natgarjuna

"Let us love, since our heart is made for nothing else."
– St. Therese

Television

"Ralph Waldo Emerson once asked what we would do if the stars only came out once every thousand years. No one would sleep that night, of course. The world would become religious overnight. We would be ecstatic, delirious, made rapturous by the glory of God. Instead the stars come out every night, and we watch television."
– Paul Hawkin

"When people are free to do as they choose, they usually imitate each other."
– Eric Hoffer

"Time is a companion that goes with us on a journey. It reminds us to cherish each moment, because it will never come

again. What we leave behind is not as important as how we have lived."
– Jean Luc Picard

All of us have the same amount of time in our days. Some of us spend it wisely. Others of us give it away to frivolity. People in modern society most often waste their time away from jobs they dislike and relationships that are in need of healing by lounging into escapism. Often they are the very same people who complain about their jobs, are dissatisfied with their relationships, don't like their lives, and wish they could be experiencing more joy. One of the most common ways people waste their time is by spending it in front of a television. They would be better off if they spent this otherwise wasted time getting their life in order and creating the life they want.

"If you read a lot of books you are considered well read. But if you watch a lot of TV, you're not considered well viewed."
– Lily Tomlin

Television programming largely focuses on that which is energetically dark, such as greed, vanity, corruption, deception, crime, punishment, mistreatment, ridicule, and brash or vulgarized sexuality. By focusing your attention on this form of "entertainment" you are absorbing this unhealthful energy into your thoughts, life, and atmosphere.

"You can tell the ideals of a nation by its advertisements."
– Norman Douglass

Most TV programming is designed to keep you watching for as long as possible so that you watch as many commercials as possible with the goal of getting you to spend money on the products that are advertised. TV is the best way companies have found to sell low-quality, mass-produced, trendy products to the masses. It is also why municipalities have to spend so much money on trash management, which is created by all the stuff people purchase.

"The bitter taste of poor quality lingers long after the sweetness of low price is forgotten."
– John Ruskin

"Television is the first truly democratic culture — the first culture available to everybody and entirely governed by what the

people want. The most terrifying thing is what people do want."
– Clive Barnes

Many TV and film productions contain products that companies have paid producers to feature in TV shows and movies. This is called *product placement* and *product integration* and has to do with products being obvious in a scene or part of a show or story line. It may be as simple as having an actor hold a can of soda (product placement), or as involved as designing a certain type of car that will first be seen in a major movie production, such as cars used in the Bond films (product integration). It is a subtle form of advertising, but is effective enough to interest more and more companies in paying production companies to place products in TV episodes and films. Sometimes a large part of the cost of producing a TV show or film can be paid for by accepting money from product placement or integration agreements.

"Don't you wish there were a knob on the TV to turn up the intelligence? There's one marked 'brightness,' but it doesn't work."
– Leo Anthony Gallagher

Many people give no mind to saving for the future. Many spend their money on whimsy. All too many spend every penny as fast as they get it, and usually on purchases that do not hold a lasting value for the purchaser or the planet, but that make them appear more like the characters they see in advertisements, and especially the characters on TV commercials.

Unfortunately, many people use TV as a babysitter, which the advertising agencies are well aware of. While advertising aimed toward children is most present during daytime TV shows watched by children, some of it also airs during shows aimed toward adults. This is because advertisers know that children are watching TV at all hours of the day.

Some of the commercials will show that good parents buy certain products for their children. Children seeing those commercials who then do not get those products from their parents, even after asking and begging, can then reason that they are being denied, neglected, or mistreated. In this way, commercials sometimes play into the guilt factor.

Many parents who use the TV as a babysitter say they don't know what else to do with their children. Perhaps they'd like to consider that TV has been around only since the mid-1900s, and that babies have been around for many thousands of years. What do they think people did before TV?

Some parents keep their babies and toddlers in front of TVs with the belief that watching television will educate their children and/or develop their intelligence. I'm certain Albert Einstein, Leonardo da Vinci, Artemisia Gentileschi, Camille Saint-Saens, and Rumi were as smart as they were because they spent their developing years staring at television shows while consuming fried and other junk foods.

A study published in the August 2007 issue of *Pediatrics*, conducted by researchers at the University of Washington and the Seattle Children's Hospital Research Institute, concluded that infants who watched the most baby educational videos knew fewer words than children who did not watch educational videos.

According to a study published in the March 1, 2009, issue of *Pediatrics*, conducted by researchers at Boston's Children's Hospital and Harvard Medical School, having babies and toddlers watch educational DVDs and videos does not make them smarter. The study's authors wrote, "Contrary to parents' perceptions that TV viewing is beneficial to their children's brain development, we found no evidence of cognitive benefit from watching TV during the first two years of life." The study, which monitored more than 800 babies for their first three years of life, concluded that DVDs and videos tailored for children as young as three months had no benefits. By age three, the study subjects who watched the most TV scored lower on tests for language and visual motor skills.

The American Academy of Pediatrics advises that parents avoid exposing children under the age of two to TV or "screen media," which includes video games and computer screens.

The more children watch TV the more likely they are of having short attention spans and to eat unhealthful foods. Maybe that has something to do with the fact that an American watching the average amount of TV sees dozens of food commercials every day. A 2007 study conducted by researchers at Indiana University and the Kaiser Family Foundation reviewed over 8,000 TV advertisements and found that none of them were for fresh fruits or vegetables.

When it is taken into consideration that about the only thing many people know about nutrition is what they hear in the mass media, it is no wonder that obesity, diabetes, colon cancer, kidney stones, heart disease, and other commonly diet-related health conditions keep increasing in commercialized society. On average, people who watch TV are heavier and less healthy than those who don't watch TV. The more TV people watch the more likely they are to consume low-quality foods, fast foods, and junk foods, such as those that contain synthetic chemical dyes, preservatives, flavors, scents, and sweeteners; processed salt; monosodium glutamate (MSG); fried oils; trans fats; and processed sugars, including corn syrup. The foods containing these substances are the very same foods advertised on television.

"As long as people will accept crap, it will be financially profitable to dispense of it."
– Dick Cavett

"You can fool too much of the people too much of the time."
– James Thurber

TV is king of the media-saturated and commercial-driven society. The more TV adults watch the more likely they are to be in financial debt. It is not hard to figure that the debt may have something to do with the constant messages people get from television encouraging them to spend money on the advertised things.

By watching TV you are removed from relating to people. This is especially true within families. There are people who consider quality time with their family to be that which they spend watching TV together. They may become more emotionally connected to the characters on the TV shows than they are with the people in their lives. Then, as a family activity they spend their weekends wasting their money shopping for stuff they saw on TV commercials and eating at chain restaurants that sell the lowest-quality food. This scenario puts them further into debt, which means they have to rely more on the job they dislike so that they can attempt to keep up with their credit card payments, the result of spending sprees to purchase all the stuff they store in their garages, closets, attics, basements, and rented storage units.

"You are here to live, not to sit on the couch."
– Jon Krakauer

By watching TV you are removed from your self. When you are tuned-in to watching TV, you are not tuned-in to your talents, you are not developing your skills, you are not practicing your craft, you are not having meaningful conversations with people, and you are not involved in improving your life. When your TV is turned on, your life is turned off.

Stop being a spectator. If you have a TV, turn it off.

Watching TV is watching other people lead their lives. It is a waste of time and a waste of life.

If you own a TV, put it in a place that is out of the way, or place a cloth over it. Also, remove the batteries from the remote and store it away.

If you don't have a TV, don't get one.

By avoiding TV, you are excluding the invasive sensationalism and commercialism of television from your days and nights.

"If you wish to achieve worthwhile things in your personal and career life, you must become a worthwhile person in your own self-development."
– Brian Tracy

Make sure that the sensationalism and commercialism of television does not rule your emotions or relationships.

Stop trying to live your life as if you are stuck in a TV commercial. Instead, focus on your life. Realize that your life is worth living, your talents are worth developing, your intellect is worth using, and your relationships are more important than what is happening on TV.

Maybe the television is telling your vision too much, and you need to stop it. Consider that your life may be much better off without watching *tell a vision*, and instead, working to create your own vision. Many people have spent so much of their time watching TV their entire lives that their thought patterns are in lock-step with the patterns of nonsense spewing out of their TV. They have been paying so much attention to TV that their thoughts are no longer their own, but are the products of Hollywood, Madison Avenue, and Wall Street.

Instead of watching TV, spend time on and take actions aligned with developing your talents, your skills, your craft, and your intellect to improve your life, your surroundings, and your relationships.

Refuse to get caught up in pop nonsense and celebrity gossip, especially the garbage constantly flowing out of the electronic media, which is always an example of a distortion of values. Celebrity consciousness gives you a spiritual lobotomy.

"Turn off the TV, don't read the newspapers, listen to your own heart, and listen very tenderly to the hearts of those people who are within your circle of care and affection."
– John Robbins

"It's how we spend our time here and now, that really matters. If you are fed up with the way you have come to interact with time, change it."
– Marcia Wieder

Make your life real and based on your talents, abilities and intellect, and not on a commercially and celebrity-obsessed culture.

Make your life beautiful.

"Be glad of life because it gives you the chance to love and to work and to play and to look up at the stars."
– Henry Van Dyke

Take Charge of Change

"Most people never run far enough on their first wind to find out they've got a second. Give your dreams all you've got and you'll be amazed at the energy that comes out of you."
– William James

If you are going to get what you want, you need to be proactive in getting it. You are more likely to become what you wish to be by simply and continually becoming attuned to the change you want.

"Even the most deeply implanted habits of the heart learned in childhood can be reshaped. Emotional learning is lifelong."
– Daniel Goleman

"Happiness is not achieved by the conscious pursuit of happiness; it is generally the by-product of other activities."
– Aldous Huxley

Whatever it is that you are reflects the common patterns of your behavior, which are the patterns you have developed throughout your life according to what you have permitted combined with your intellect and to what you are naturally drawn. Your common patterns are your self-traditions, and they help determine where you go, what you do, what you agree to, and how you think and communicate. You can change your patterns.

"Character is the basis of happiness and happiness the sanction of character."
– George Santayana

Changing your life starts with the way you think and with what you conclude your life needs in relation to what you want it to be.

Once you understand the source of what has formed your life into what it is, you can begin to put the unhelpful things out of your life, and/or organize them in a way that is of your benefit. In your mind you can start to dispose of the clutter and damage forming the wall blocking you from experiencing the thoughts that would bring you the actions to create a better life. To improve your physical health and promote healing, you can follow a diet that is more healthful, and you can exercise every day.

> "Extreme measures are very appropriate for extreme disease."
> – Hippocrates

When the tissues of the body heal, they need nutrients. The better-quality of the nutrients that are consumed, the better the tissues can heal and function. In a similar manner, if you are healing your life from one that has injured your spirit, mind, and body, you need to start feeding your life with those things that will help it to heal, rehabilitate, and function on a healthful level.

Maybe the reason your life has not turned out the way you want it to be is that you have allowed others to take it over, or have thought others would create a good life for you. Under these conditions, you have given up your power.

> "Caring means doing."
> – Andre Agassi

If you want your life to improve, you need care about it. Your caring becomes evident through actions that take charge of your life. It is evident in what you permit yourself to participate in. It is you who can improve your life, you who can make it function, and you who can transform it to become more of the way you wish it to be.

> "Nothing is more revealing than movement. Actions do speak."
> – Martha Graham

How your life evolves largely depends on what you are permitting yourself to think, do, and say.

As negative thoughts lead to negative emotions, so too do positive thoughts lead to positive actions. Think about that while considering what you most desire to have in your life.

> "Be careful with the present you are creating — it should look like the future you dream of."
> – Mujeres Creando

Do you want positive emotions? Then continually focus on thoughts that will uplift you. This will illuminate your life because thinking positively changes the electric charges throughout your body cells and enlivens your tissues. You can't be focused on damaging thoughts as you are working to nurture thoughts that will bring positive change. By continuously entertaining intentional, goal-oriented, health-affirming thoughts, you are literally bathing the cells of your body in positive energy and in positive-thought chemicals that create positive emotions.

> "Live your life and forget your age."
> – Norman Vincent Peale

Do away with revolving thoughts that create negative emotions.

Do not get caught up in regrets, which are an enormous waste of time and energy and do not create anything worthwhile. Instead, focus on more healthful and helpful thoughts that bring about improvement in your life through intentional, goal-oriented actions.

As you work intentionally to set goals and attain them through actions you will learn to better control your thoughts to focus on the positive. As you do so you will notice positive changes in your life.

> "By thinking and acting affirmatively in this minute, you will influence the hour, the day, and the time, your entire life."
> – Denis Waitley

Begin to replace thoughts of unfortunate memories with thoughts of planning for a better future. Replace thoughts that make you feel drained with those that create good feelings. Choose to think of the life you want to have instead of thinking of the life you had — or the life you may feel that you missed out on. By working the power of your mind this way, you can bring positive thoughts to fuel your actions.

> "The important thing is not being afraid to take a chance. Remember, the greatest failure is to not try. Once you find something you love to do, be the best at doing it."
> – Debbi Fields

By continually harboring the thoughts that are in alignment with the life you want, you are planting the seeds that will grow into the actions that will create the life you want.

> "Go confidently in the direction of your dreams! Live the life you've imagined. As you simplify your life, the laws of the universe

will be simpler; solitude will not be solitude, poverty will not be poverty, nor weakness weakness."
– Henry David Thoreau

Those who are well nurtured, are encouraged, get adequate physical activity, have access to healthful food, and are provided for when they are growing up are more likely to succeed than those who experience an abusive and neglectful childhood. This is where the power of suggestion is evident. This does not mean that you will be a failure if you were not well nurtured as a child. At any time you can shed your past and begin to provide the nurturing you need not only to change your life, but also to radically transform it into something amazing. Many people have done this, and have succeeded far beyond what anyone would have predicted.

"It is not the strongest of the species that survive, nor the most intelligent, but the most responsive to change."
– Charles Darwin

You can work to deal with what the universe flows your way. Instead of fighting it, work with it.

Take your trials and work with them to get you where you want to be. Do so in the same way that a sailor works with the wind to get a boat to its destination.

"Any change, any loss, does not make us victims. Others can shake you, surprise you, disappoint you, but they can't prevent you from acting, from taking the situation you're presented with and moving on. No matter where you are in life, no matter what your situation, you can always do something. You always have a choice and the choice can be power."
– Blaine Lee

What may help you bring your life onto the level you wish to experience is the law of substitution.

Many people mention that the law of substitution is a concept written about by Brian Tracy in his book *Maximum Achievement.* The law of substitution works to exercise your mind so that it holds positive instead of negative thoughts in ways that crowd out the negative. Because your mind is always working, make it work in the best way to suit your desire to create a beautiful life.

This is the start of the power that can take over your life. The power will drive you to think, act, plan, and communicate more positively. To build upon this you will need to provide your body with what it needs to grow more healthfully. This involves partaking of the best nutrients available to you while eliminating low-quality foods; exercising your intellect by learning about and practicing new things; setting goals, making priorities, and acting on them every day; and by getting exercise every morning to make your body generate health. All these actions will work in symphony to drive your life forward toward your goals.

> "Happiness does not lie in happiness, but in the achievement of it."
> – Fyodor Dostoyevsky

What you become from now on is up to you. Focus on your goals, not your obstacles. Focus on the present, not the past. Do not engage in slothfulness, but do keep active doing what will create the life you want.

As you conduct your life in a more proactive, intentional, and goal-oriented manner, there is no more blaming others, there is no more self-loathing and droning on and on about the past. Instead, when living intentionally with continual actions aligned with your goals, there will be the creation of positive change in your life every single day.

> "Deep unspeakable suffering may well be called a baptism, a regeneration, the initiation into a new state."
> – George Eliot

Things will happen that you will not like. Whether you like it or not, they still are going to happen. So you may as well deal with them in ways that bring some benefit to you. Even when you feel as if you are taking a beating, look for ways to learn and grow while relentlessly remaining engaged in actions that bring about creating your vision. Take every situation you are presented with and somehow make it work as a benefit to you.

> "If we had no winter, the spring would not be so pleasant: if we did not sometimes taste of adversity, prosperity would not be so welcome."
> – Anne Bradstreet

> "Better to do something imperfectly than to do nothing flawlessly."
> – Robert H. Schuller

What you think of as your greatest failure may actually turn out to be your greatest success, or a doorway to it.

You can take charge of your life and force change to take place. You can change your character from one who is unhealthful to one who generates health.

No matter what happens, persevere!

Keep using your intellect, talent, abilities, energy, resources, spirit, and the power of your thoughts to work toward creating the life you desire.

Write yourself a note of declaration every single morning to remind and contract with yourself to be actively involved in improving all areas of your life that day.

> "I'd rather be a could-be if I cannot be an are; because a could-be is a maybe who is reaching for a star. I'd rather be a has-been than a might-have-been, by far; for a might-have-been has never been, but a has was once an are."
>
> – Milton Berle

Positive change happens at the present, and can be made in the future. Not in the past.

Positive life change comes through motivational and inspired thoughts that elicit actions, not in depressing thoughts that focus on the drama of former disastrous relationships, that create mental decay, and that bask in laziness.

Positive life change comes through providing the nutrients the body needs to function at a high level. These are the nutrients that are available in vibrant, alive plant substances containing the power of Nature. They are not available in a diet of deadened, commercialized, corporatized, overly processed, and otherwise junk foods containing fried oils, bleached grains, processed salts and sugars, MSG, and synthetic chemicals.

Positive life change comes through working toward established goals and from organized priorities set to guide a person toward betterment. Not in disorganized randomness.

Positive life change comes through daily exercise to enliven and strengthen the body. Not in sedentary slothfulness spent in front of a television, playing video games, or in surfing the Internet.

Positive life change comes by choice, which happens in your mind. The mind that you need to change if you are going to change your life.

> "You must be willing to do the things today others don't do in order to have the things tomorrow others won't have."
>
> – Les Brown

"He not busy being born is busy dying."
– Bob Dylan

"You don't have to be great to start — but you have to start to be great."
– John C. Maxwell

"If opportunity doesn't knock, build a door."
– Milton Berle

Awakening

"When one realizes one is asleep, at that moment one is already half-awake."
– P. D. Ouspensky

First you learn it is okay to breathe. Hopefully you learn how nice it is to be cuddled, feel safe, and hear loving words. You learn about movement and the senses. Then you learn about the satisfaction of food. You learn that when you cry you get attention. You learn that your vocal tones get you certain things. You learn your physical structure can be worked to get you things. From that point you learn all sorts of stuff, some of which may be beneficial and help you thrive in health, and other stuff that can put you in a state of despair and regret. As you become an adult you should know that at any moment on your path you could decide which direction to follow.

"One's mind, once stretched by a new idea, never regains its original dimensions."
– Oliver Wendell Holmes

Teachings do not give you intellect, talents, skill, or instinct. What you learn can only work with, awaken, and adjust what you already possess.

As you make your way through life, you will learn more, because you can't learn less, but you can use less of what you learn.

"I do not believe that the same God who has endowed us with sense, reason, and intellect has intended us to forgo their use."
– Galileo Galilei

It is easy to recognize those who are not living up to their potential. Look around you and see that there may be people in your everyday life who are living mundanely — stuck in a lifestyle they most likely would not have chosen. Also recognize that there are people who have allowed themselves to be positioned in a pattern of habitually going about their days in a perpetual path to dullness that is far beneath the level of life they could be living if they otherwise were proactive in creating a better life. Don't neglect to consider that you may be one of them.

> "We do not see things as they are. We see them as we are."
> – The Talmud

Consider that the absolute most important thing you need to change your life is the version of you that is continually focused on and engaging in actions of creating the life you wish to live.

> "Let us become the change we seek in this world."
> – Mohandas Gandhi

Just as some people were able to develop their talents and skill in their childhood, it is possible at any stage in life to begin working with whatever strengths and resources that exist within your fabric to change your life for the better.

> "I'll match my flops with anybody's, but I wouldn't have missed them. Flops are a part of life's menu and I've never been one to miss out on any of the courses."
> – Rosalind Russell

You have something to learn from your past. Using one single piece of paper, make a list of each year of your life since age ten. Using few words, list each thing you have done and/or each realization you had in each of those years that most impressed and/or changed you. Maybe some of the years will be blank, but that is okay. Recognize if there are any patterns of behavior in your life that brought about more satisfaction or less satisfaction. Realize that if something had not happened in your life that you wished for, you can still work to make things happen that you are currently wishing for.

> "You're never a loser until you quit trying."
> – Mike Ditka

Make a short list of things that would satisfy you if they were regularly present in your life. The simple act of writing these words on paper can help plant the seeds leading to the changes you wish for.

> "All the flowers of tomorrow are in the seeds of today."
> – Anonymous

> "Use every letter you write, every conversation you have, every meeting you attend, to express your fundamental beliefs and dreams. Affirm to others the vision of the world you want. You are a free, immensely powerful source of life and goodness. Affirm it. Spread it. Radiate it. Think day and night about it and you will see a miracle happen: the greatness of our own life."
> – Robert Muller

As you awaken each morning, read through the list of things you want to achieve. Remind yourself that you are worthy and capable of attaining these things a well as the health and success you desire. Nurture the seeds of attaining your goals by continually engaging in actions that will manifest achievement.

> "People often say that motivation doesn't last. Well, neither does bathing — that's why we recommend it daily."
> – Zig Ziglar

Reading your list of goals every morning is like fertilizing your thoughts and actions with focus and intention.

> "Every day we are engaged in a miracle which we don't even recognize: a blue sky, white clouds, green leaves, the black, curious eyes of a child — our own two eyes. All is a miracle."
> – Thich Nhat Hanh

Life is like a vine that can be trained to grow in a certain pattern. The way your life grows starts within your mind and continues into what you do with thoughts that propel actions. You can train your mind to think more healthfully just as you can train your body to perform a certain task. Provide the right seed thoughts that blossom into a complete set of manageable ideas to guide your actions. How your body works can be guided with the best nutrients combined with daily exercise. How your mind performs in conjunction with your actions depends on how you train it. It all has to do with practice.

As an athlete practices every day to win, be so engaged in training your mind with motivational thoughts that they form into actions bringing about triumphant satisfaction in your life.

Awaken your life from any slumber, rise up and be actively and continually engaged in making your life one of success and satisfaction.

"The temptation to quit will be greatest just before you are about to succeed."
– Chinese proverb

"Our greatest glory is not in never falling, but in rising every time we fall."
– Confucius

"I will waste not even a precious second today in anger or hate or jealousy or selfishness. I know that the seeds I sow I will harvest, because every action, good or bad, is always followed by an equal reaction. I will plant only good seeds this day."
– Og Mandino

Practice Improvement

"Everybody is nine years old."
– Jerry Lewis

Just as schooled children are exposed to the same tasks over and over so that they learn them, you can teach yourself how to do things by repeatedly doing them. It is through the practice of principles that the body, brain, and mind learn to perform them. By doing them repeatedly you learn to do them better, and you also learn how the principles and practice can become habits.

Just as a painter creates a picture with repeated brush strokes of colors that can be either dark or bright, so too can you create your life with repeated motivational thoughts that bring about goal-oriented, intentional actions.

"Life is painting a picture, not doing a sum."
– Oliver Wendell Holmes, Jr.

Think of your thoughts as a constant movie playing in your mind and you are the screenwriter, the producer, the set designer and décorator, the wardrobe department, the lighting technician, the camera operator, the sound mixer, the soundtrack composer, the script supervisor, the director, and the actor. You can write the script any way you wish. Begin writing the script the way you want it by thinking about ways you desire things to happen.

Your mind is the choreographer of your life. Think about your life circumstances continually arranging around you in ways that would best suit your needs, talents, skills, intellect, desires, and love.

> "To know what you prefer instead of humbly saying Amen to what the world tells you you ought to prefer, is to have kept your soul alive."
>
> – Robert Louis Stevenson

Prefer to focus on the things that you want in your life, not on the things that you don't desire. Recognize the substances of character you like to see in other people, and not on the qualities you don't like. Train yourself to be what you wish to be by continually being engaged in activities that formulate your life into what you want it to be. Always engage in thoughts, education, goal setting, and activities that will make your life prosper.

> "Education is the movement from darkness to light."
>
> – Allan Bloom

The power of believing is evident when little children get slightly hurt. They often will stop crying and seem to feel better once their parent says, "It's all better now." Nothing changed with the injury. The only thing that changed was the child's state of mind as it was guided by the power of suggestion to believe.

> "It's no accident that things are more likely to go your way when you stop worrying about whether you're going to win or lose, and focus your full attention on what is happening right this moment."
>
> – Phil Jackson

Perhaps your normal way of thinking is to allow yourself to think negatively. Negative thoughts create a pathway that leads to more negativity. You cannot experience positive growth if you are going to constantly entertain negative thoughts, which create negative emotions, which affect your actions, relations, atmosphere, and results. If you want to improve your life, it is always time to make your normal way of thinking a positive pathway, and to keep your body engaged in activities relating to your goals.

> "The problem is never how to get new, innovative thoughts into your mind, but how to get old ones out. Every mind is a building filled with archaic furniture. Clean out a corner of your mind and creativity will instantly fill it."
> – Dee Hock

No longer allow your way of thinking to destroy your potential of living the life you want to live. It is understandable that there are things in your life that are controlled by other factors. However, it is most likely that the life you have been leading is a result largely of your thought patterns. To create a different result, you have to think differently from the way you have been thinking. To take yourself out of the life you have been living, and into the life you want to live, you have to think and do things differently from the ways you have thought and done.

Think of any object or event created by man. If someone did not think that up, it would not exist. If ancient people did not think of building pyramids, the pyramids would not exist. If people did not think up war, there would not be war.

> "All that we are is the result of what we have thought."
> – Buddha

Investigate the possibility that your life is what it is simply because of the way you have thought, and the actions you have taken in alignment with those thoughts. If you are not satisfied with your life, ponder the likelihood that you have allowed yourself to conduct yourself in specific ways that have closed off your life to potentially experiencing a more satisfying life.

> "Find the seed at the bottom of your heart and bring forth a flower."
> – Shigenori Kameoka

It is not easy to recognize the colors and beauty of a flower that has not bloomed. Your beauty is manifested by working to use your talents and living up to your capabilities through taking care of yourself while working to attain your goals.

Open your life to your intellect and talents. Draw on the substances that are available to you to restructure your life. Look at yourself as capable, workable, and able. Believe and know that you can be better at what you do and that you can be more healthful and more satisfied with a stronger presence of love in your life.

> "The art of awareness is the art of learning how to wake up to the eternal miracle of life with its limitless possibilities."
> – Wilfred Peterson

Consider that your problems are actually your opportunities and lessons to learn what can be done better in your life. Look at what you perceive to be your disadvantages, and then work with them to your advantage.

> "Opportunities to find deeper powers within ourselves come when life seems most challenging."
> – Joseph Campbell

Use your energy to break through any boundaries between how you are living and how you want to live. Use your talents, intellect, instinct, and power to create the life you want. And do so regardless of any obstacles that may land in your way.

> "To maintain a skillful balance between the inner and outer aspects of our lives is an enormously challenging and continuously changing process. The objective is not to dogmatically live with less, but is a more demanding intention of living with balance in order to find a life of greater purpose, fulfillment, and satisfaction."
> – Duane Elgin

One of the first steps in building a beautiful life is to eliminate what prevents such an existence from becoming a reality. This could mean doing away with clutter in the living space, clearing up, healing, or ending fractured relationships while bringing into your life what it is you will need to attain a more satisfying state.

> "Take away the cause, and the effect ceases."
> – Miguel de Cervantes

One of the most powerful things people can do to improve their life is to identify and fix or eliminate that which is problematic.

Identify what may be stopping you from growth. Cautiously, responsibly, and strategically arrange your situation in a way that would be most helpful to propelling your life forward.

The key words in that last paragraph are *cautiously* and *responsibly*. Depending on the person's current life condition, it may take more time, energy, effort, focus, skill, and patience for some persons than for others to attain a most desirable state of being. Practice safety, respect, and responsibility when dealing with what may need to be aligned to attain a more healthful life — especially when your choices may impact the lives of others.

> "We don't receive wisdom; we must discover it for ourselves after a journey that no one can take for us or spare us."
> – Marcel Proust

While creating a healthful life involves truths that are universal, because of life complexities, each person may be dealing differently with them. While one person's life may be relatively easy to transform, others' may be more complex. Because of consequences too numerous to mention here, people will have to tally their own resources and factor their own solutions.

> "Wisdom is the principle thing; therefore get wisdom. And in all your getting, get understanding."
> – Proverbs 4:7

It is through examination, decisions, actions, and experience that wisdom is built. The challenge is to face the issues and objects bravely in ways that are beneficial.

Be smart in dealing with your circumstances in ways that will improve your condition. Your first thoughts on what to do may not be the most appreciated. Therefore, caution and responsibility in strategies and actions are keys to making changes that are most beneficial. Figure out the best possible and most timely manner of how to deal with each concern ways that will bring about and help maintain a vibrant life.

> "The secret of health for both mind and body is not to mourn for the past, worry about the future, or anticipate troubles but to live in the present moment wisely and earnestly."
> – Buddha

Even people who are leading the life that seems most desirable to others have to deal with the constant influx of things the universe presents to them.

Be diligent, brave, wise, and use any other trait, ability, and attribute needed to get you where you want to be.

"Never give up, for that is just the place and time that the tide will turn."
– Harriet Beecher Stowe

"Do you know what a big shot is? A little shot who keeps shooting."
– Norman Vincent Peale

"Act, and God will act."
– Joan of Arc

Break Free

"One concept we often impose on our experience is an assumption of permanence, which can put us at odds with the impermanence of all natural processes."
– Gil Fronsdale

"To ignore the power of paradigms to influence your judgment is to put yourself at risk when exploring the future. To be able to shape your future, you have to be ready to change your paradigm."
– Joel Arthur Barker

Those who discover an improved way of living may have to push themselves to eliminate stubborn patterns of thought and behavior. The level of their change likely will not only be driven by how badly they want it, but also by how badly they don't want their former life. Their self-improvement will likely also be driven by how strongly they grasp the knowledge that they are responsible for making the changes they want to see.

"Such is the irresistible nature of truth, that all it asks, and all it wants, is the liberty of appearing."
– Thomas Paine

There may be many things that people new to intentionally healthful living have to deal with in their early days of following a new path. What new behaviors and thought processes they may be experiencing through expression could appear as odd to those around them. It may leave them vulnerable to a whole new variety of observations, which may be spoken in the form of criticism and belittling comments from those who lack belief in themselves, or who are afraid to break away from local pop conformity, mundanity, or stagnation. But the more they stick to their truth, the more they will see the benefits through experiencing a life of health and satisfaction. The more they experience these, the more others are likely to recognize the improvement. The more they experience improvement, the less likely they are to give consideration to the naysayers, the ridiculers, the mockers, the critics, the haters, and anyone who may speak undermining comments.

> "Nothing would be done at all if a man waited until he could do it so well that no one could find fault with it."
> – John Henry Newman

People often expect things to happen in a certain way. They may do this deliberately, or they may be unaware of their expectations. Anything that goes outside the boundaries of what they are expecting to happen, or what they are accustomed to seeing happen, may cause them to display surprise, bliss, guffaws, regret, dismay, offense, protest, or even violence.

> "When you judge another, you do not define them, you define yourself."
> – Wayne Dyer

Those who try a new way of living, even if it is a much more healthful way than what is being lived by the people around them, are often criticized for their new way, even if the benefits are obvious. They may experience some undesirable attention from those around them who are not accustomed to seeing someone conduct themselves in a certain manner. This criticism can be what hampers many from attaining the advantages of living more healthfully. It is peer pressure and it can play a big part in the way you agree to conduct yourself to conform to what your local society considers to be normal and acceptable, but not necessarily the most healthful.

> "Don't be distracted by criticism. Remember the only taste of success some people have is when they take a bite out of you."
> – Zig Ziglar

> "You must constantly ask yourself these questions: Who am I around? What are they doing to me? What have they got me reading? What have they got me saying? Where do they have me going? What do they have me thinking? And most important, what do they have me becoming? Then ask yourself the big question: Is that okay?"
> – E. James Rohn

Those who discover a better way often find that they need to break free of peer pressure, which is often based on negativity, unfair criticism, disbelief, societal pressures, antiquated concepts, and low self-esteem. This depends on what is going on in the minds of the peers. The critics may think that those who are working to improve their lives think they are better than others. More than anything, this exposes the closed mindset of the critic. Words reveal the concepts in the mind.

> "Great spirits have always encountered violent opposition from mediocre minds."
> – Albert Einstein

Those who spend their time doubting others likely are doubting themselves. Those who do not believe in the capabilities of others likely do not believe their own capabilities. Those who focus on the negative things build on the negatives in their own life. Those who do such things shut down the opportunity for achieving good in their own life, as the flow of muck that is doubt and criticism creates an atmosphere of destruction and failure and of conforming to the mundane.

> "The truth is that there is nothing noble in being superior to somebody else. The only real nobility is in being superior to your former self."
> – Whitney Young

Improving your life is not about thinking you are better than other people, for we are all made of the same substances. It is not about comparing yourself to others, for we are all unique. It is not about competing with others, for there is no competition. It is about you, and not about anyone else, because you can only be you.

"Life is what we make of it, always has been, always will be."
– Anna Mary Robertson "Grandma" Moses

Improving your life is about thinking and working to be more healthful and satisfied in ways that complement your talents, intellect, skills, wisdom, and other graces.

"The greatest danger for most of us is not that our aim is too high and we miss it, but that it is too low and we reach it."
– Michelangelo di Lodovico Buonarroti Simoni

People may misinterpret your self-improvement, and they may think that you are detaching from them. What you are detaching from is slothfulness and from not living up to what you are capable of being. When you are improving your life through following a more healthful diet, getting daily exercise, and spending several hours a day focused on and engaging in activities in alignment with your goals, what you are attaching to is your potential, elegance, and beauty.

"Always aim high, work hard, and care deeply about what you believe in. And, when you stumble, keep faith. And when you're knocked down, get right back up and never listen to anyone who says you can't or shouldn't go on."
– Hillary Clinton

Consider those you find to be your strongest critics. If they are the people who are keeping you in an unhealthful situation, realize that the louder their criticism becomes may be a sign that they are not dealing with their own life in the best way. Consider that you may have agreed to allow them to keep you down. The agreement shows through in your role-playing, behaving in ways that correspond to those of one who is being harshly criticized, giving into the criticism, allowing belittling comments to define and limit you, and being shaded by low self-esteem.

"Tell not your dreams, but to your intimate friend."
– George Washington

Not only should you be careful about with whom you associate, you should also be careful about with whom you share your goals. This isn't because you are trying to be secretive or to hide something about yourself. It also isn't about competition. It is about your energy, and theirs.

"Do not reveal your thoughts to everyone, lest you drive away your good luck."
– Apocrypha, Ecclesiasticus 8:19

Explaining your goals to people disperses energy. It can also get those who don't believe in you to infuse you with their discouragement and/or otherwise work against you. People who don't like you, who don't believe that you are capable of succeeding, or who simply are negative, can consciously or unconsciously develop thought patterns that result in words and actions that aren't in your favor. It all falls under the definition of discouragement; it also has more to do with their own thoughts, beliefs, and esteem, and little to nothing to do with you. Thus, ignore discouragement that would stop you from being more healthful.

"A man who trims himself to suit everybody will soon whittle himself away."
– Charles Schwab

Don't feel as if you need to explain yourself to everyone who criticizes you. That type of defensive behavior disperses energy, robs you of your drive, weakens you, and is a waste of time. Those running a race do not slow down to explain their goals to the spectators. They simply stay focused on and remain confident in running the race the best they can.

"You have to believe in yourself when no one else does. That's what makes you a winner."
– Venus Williams

"Example is always more efficacious than precept."
– Samuel Johnson

I strongly suggest that you do this: Instead of slowing down to explain yourself, simply stay on course and live your life aiming toward improvement in all areas, and allow your healthful life, and not your words, to stand as the explanation.

"Well done is better than well said."
– Benjamin Franklin

"What you do speaks so loudly that no one will ever hear a word you are saying."
– Ralph Waldo Emerson

"I think one's feelings waste themselves in words; they ought all to be distilled into actions which bring results."
– Florence Nightingale

Through achievement you will experience satisfaction and self-validation, no matter what anyone else says or does.

When you distance yourself from the life you had been living, you may realize how unhealthful you were. You also may recognize how sensitive and susceptible you had been to the influence of peer pressure. You may also realize how you may have spent a lot of time trying to conform to the expectations of others. And you will likely experience a great relief by freeing yourself from all of the nonsense you were accepting.

"When patterns are broken, new worlds emerge."
– Tuli Kupferberg

"All the world's a stage, and all the men and women merely players: they have their exits and their entrances; and one man in his time plays many parts."
– William Shakespeare

People are sensitive to the expectations of those around them. They often get caught up in role-playing into what they are expected to do and say, or what they think they are expected to do and say. This type of behavior may also lead to not living up to one's potential. Some people call it living an undercover life. People go undercover to assimilate into their perceptions of what is socially acceptable, and under those conditions they may never break free of the shadow cast on them by the expectations of others. They may never lead their own lives to be the beauty they can be.

"If you do not express your own original ideas, if you do not listen to your own being, you will have betrayed yourself."
– Rollo May

There are many stories of those who came up with a plan to make something of themselves that nobody else had done, to go places nobody else had gone, to discover things nobody else had found, and to bring things about that others had not made happen. Often these people were laughed at, disowned, mocked, assaulted, or worse.

"Keep away from people who try to belittle your ambitions. Small people always do that, but the really great make you feel that you, too, can become great."
– Mark Twain

You do not need to tune into the negative, damaging thoughts of others. Instead, tune them out. Choose to focus on those thoughts, people, activities, and things that will help you reach your goals.

"Wanting to be someone you're not is a waste of the person you are."
– Kurt Cobain

Conforming to the lives of others is a sure way to fail when it ignores who you are and is less than what would bring out your best. Remain aware that choosing less vibrant foods and making choices that don't sustain the quality of life you desire puts you on the path to getting what you don't want.

Continually break free of that which holds you back. Stop compromising your self-awareness, your intellect, your wisdom, and your talents. Wake up from the personalities you created to assimilate into the perceived society in which you are living undercover. Work to advance your connection to your talents and intellect. Aim to experience your life out loud.

"Be who you are and say what you feel because those who mind don't matter and those who matter don't mind."
– Theodore Geisel

Be who you are, not the personality you created to assimilate into a life that is not yours, and not the personage you may have pretended to be to avoid criticism of what your beauty can be.

Open up your constricted perception. Get closer to your truths. Advance spiritually.

Enable yourself to become fluent in your higher consciousness and to maximize your life within that energy.

"My father didn't tell me how to live; he lived, and let me watch him do it."
– Clarence Budington Kelland

Understand that to improve the condition of your life you need to keep making better choices. As you remain on the path to self-improvement you are more likely to meet and associate with others who are doing the same. You may also find that you are the inspiration to those who haven't been inspired, who have not had a role model, and who have not otherwise tuned into what they can achieve by utilizing their most valuable aspects.

> "We're here for a reason. I believe a bit of the reason is to throw little torches out to lead people through the dark."
> – Whoopi Goldberg

Bring It On

> "Adversity introduces a man to himself."
> – Anonymous

An elderly woman once told me that wisdom comes with age because throughout life you learn from experience, and, she added, "Especially from the unfortunate experiences."

> "We don't receive wisdom; we must discover it for ourselves after a journey that no one can take for us or spare us."
> – Marcel Proust

> "Let us not look back in anger, nor forward in fear, but around in awareness."
> – James Thurber

Along that line of my friend's comment I am reminded of a story I heard about John F. Kennedy, Jr. When "John John" was a teenager he was mugged in New York City. When someone asked his mother about it she said that she thought it was probably good for him. That darkly comical comment holds truth. Having this experience of being mugged may have worked to make the teenager wiser.

We can constantly choose to take the unfortunate experiences and make them work for us.

> "Smooth seas do not create skillful sailors."
> – Anonymous

This brings me to suggest a mental exercise I've heard more than one person suggest. As the mind is like a garden where good thoughts can grow, it also, like a garden, has weeds that need to be tended to and combined into a compost pit where they can transform into fertile soil.

> "Heaven never helps the man who will not act."
> – Sophocles

Many of the problems of your life are not likely to simply vanish. You will benefit by facing them and dealing with them. Not doing so is similar to having an invisible force working against you, holding you back, and preventing you from dealing with the task of taking care of whatever your life problem may be.

Ignoring a life problem does not make it go away. If you have a rotting sack of garbage in your home it will not go away until you dispose of it.

> "Not everything that is faced can be changes. But nothing can be changed until it is faced."
> – James Baldwin

Rather than ignore a problem, it would be much more healthful to do what it takes to figure how to deal with the issue, then proceed to do what it takes to fix it so that the mind can be freed to think about more helpful things while using the wisdom gained from the past.

> "What we plant in the soil of contemplation, we shall reap in the harvest of action.
> – Meister Eckhart

Part of the issue at hand when people are not taking care of their life stems from not thinking they are strong enough, or worthy enough, to have such a life free of whatever problems they are not dealing with. They may be dwelling in self-inflicted shame, pity, and guilt, and in the ever-damaging issues of self-hate and self-defeat. These all can be most dreadful habits that they are not aware of.

> "Life can not give me joy and peace, it is up to me to will it.
> Life just gives me time and space, it is up to me to fill it."
> – William James

When a people grasp the concept that they don't have to settle for having problems overtake their life, and that they are worthy and strong enough to deal with their issues, they begin to factor solutions and bravely take the actions necessary to take care of whatever it is they need to do to improve their situation.

> "A good indignation brings out all one's powers."
> – Ralph Waldo Emerson

Allow yourself to realize that you can take actions necessary to fixing and polishing the things in your life that are fractured and tarnished. It is likely that you will find your problems easier to deal with than you thought, and will find that dealing with them was well worth the time, energy, and resources spent doing so.

> "Appreciate your learning process, for it is of equal value to have realized there is a need for change as for the change itself."
> – Beth Johnson

One mental exercise that can be practiced to help you prepare for cleaning up your life is to perform a task that clears your life in a smaller way. A way to do this is to take some time out of your day to go through the objects in your living quarters and get rid of something — or things — that you do not need. This may include giving something away to someone who can get better use from it, or simply cleaning and organizing your home. Focus specifically on an object — or objects — that cause clutter in your physical space. Use this as a representation of what your mind must be like with thoughts that are disorganized because you have not cleaned up other areas of your life — and this other clutter in your life is cluttering your mind.

> "Simplicity is the ultimate sophistication."
> – Leonardo da Vinci

A similar exercise is to rid your physical body of the things that it does not need to have. By this I mean excess weight, and/or foods that are not healthful. Unhealthful foods leave behind residues and intercellular plaque that add to physical ailments holding you back from experiencing vibrant health. This exercise involves cleaning out your diet.

> "If humans clear inner pollution, then they will also cease to create outer pollution."
> – Eckhart Tolle

Go into your kitchen. Get rid of all of the food items that are not healthful. Dispose of any item that contains artificial preservatives, dyes, flavorings, scents, and/or sweeteners. Eliminate all foods that contain monosodium glutamate (MSG). Look for items that contain white sugar, white flour, white rice, white bread, white potatoes, corn syrup, corn oil, soy margarine, margarine, shortening, lard, dairy products (milk, butter, cheese, yogurt, keifer, casein, and whey), and/or eggs (including mayonnaise), and identify foods that contain gelatin. Dispose of these items. Do away with any food items containing cooked oil. Get rid of all fried food. Make the commitment to keep your kitchen and body free of all these nonfood and low-quality food items. Allow only healthful foods to enter your home, including raw fruits, vegetables, nuts, seeds, herbs, natural spices, whole grains (such as freshly germinated quinoa and millet), and water vegetables.

I encourage people to eliminate all dairy from their diet. But if you consume dairy, please avoid dairy from factory farms, pasteurized dairy, dairy containing additives, homogenized dairy, and all heated dairy. Please research xanthine-oxidase, oxidized cholesterol, and neurotoxic amino acids in dairy. If you still consume dairy, choose only raw, unpasteurized, organic dairy from animals living outdoors and grazing in fields. One example is organic raw goats' milk keifer rich in probiotics. Find local organic family farmers, or natural foods co-ops. Check the Weston A. Price Foundation's Campaign for Real Milk (RealMilk.com)

> "Just as the material of the body that is ready for life has need of the psyche in order to be capable of life, so psyche presupposes the living body in order that its images may live."
> – Carl Gustav Jung

Following through on your commitment to improve your life, on cleaning out the clutter of your life, on getting daily exercise, on consuming the highest-quality foods available to you, on focusing on the positive, on reading through your priority list every morning, on continually taking goal-oriented actions, on nurturing your talents and intellect, and on communicating more healthfully with those around you, you will be better suited to deal with anything that may otherwise stumble you.

Additional reading material on these topics include my books, *Sunfood Living: Resource Guide for Global Health* and *Sunfood Traveler: Guide to Raw Food Culture*; Cherie Soria's book, *Raw Food Revolution Diet*; John Robbins's book, *The Food Revolution*; *Becoming Raw: The Essential Guide to Raw Vegan Diets*, by Brenda Davis, Vesanto Melina, and Rynne Berry; Terces Engelhart's and Orchid's book, *I Am Grateful: Recipes and Lifestyle of Café Gratitude*; Victoria Boutenko's book *Green Smoothie Revolution*; and other raw organic vegan books of your choice by exploring what has recently been published. Consider Brendan Brazier's *Thrive Diet.*

Also, seek out books that inspire you to live a more sustainable life that includes a plant-based diet. And please, get involved in growing some of your own food, and in supporting your regional organic family farmers. Learn about organic culinary gardening, community supported agriculture (CSA), feral wild land gardening (planting berry and fruiting tree forests), and wild food foraging.

> "The question isn't who is going to let me; it's who is going to stop me."
> – Ayn Rand

Collective Mind, Environment, and Society

> "We are like islands in the seas, separate on the surface, but connected in the deep."
> – William James

> "We don't accomplish anything in this world alone. And whatever happens is the result of the whole tapestry of one's life and all the weavings of individual threads from one to another that creates something."
> – Sandra Day O'Connor

> "The life I touch for good or ill will touch another life, and that in turn another, until who knows where the trembling stops or in what far place my touch will be felt."
> – Frederick Buechner

> "Act as if what you do makes a difference. It does."
> – William James

> "Let go of your attachment to being right, and suddenly your mind is more open. You're able to benefit from the unique viewpoints of others, without being crippled by your own judgment."
> – Ralph Marston

> "A hundred times every day I remind myself that my inner and outer life are based on the labor of others, living and dead, and that I must exert myself in order to give in the same measure as I have received and am receiving."
>
> – Albert Einstein

Look to those who surround you as part of your collective mind.

Not only are your thoughts part of a flow of the thoughts of others, the substances of your body are also part of the collective substances in your environment. This includes the substances that make up the people, animals, plants, gasses, liquids, ground, and objects around you.

There are a number of materials continually flowing in and out of you, including liquids, solids, gasses, bacteria, magnetic fields, and atomic particles. Each of these is vibrating at different frequencies. In this way the substances that make up you are continually communicating with your environment on many levels. Anyone who has studied quantum physics and sacred geometry has an understanding of these things.

The thoughts and actions of others often influence your thoughts and actions. In this way you are being tuned by the vibrational energy patterns carried by the minds of others. This is part of how you are a participant in the collective mind.

> "I have inherited a belief in community, the promise that a gathering of the spirit can both create and change culture. In the desert, change is nurtured even in stone by wind, by water, through time."
>
> – Terry Tempest Williams

> "I am of the opinion that my life belongs to the community, and as long as I live it is my privilege to do for it whatever I can."
>
> – George Bernard Shaw

What you think about and how you live your daily life help to guide the direction of society. The way each person lives impacts the environment. Collectively how each of us lives carries more weight and is of a much greater influence than the small number of politicians and other so-called world leaders.

> "Every man is more than just himself; he also represents the unique, the very special and always significant and remarkable point at which the world's phenomena intersect, only once in this way, and never again."
>
> – Hermann Hesse

"The whole idea of compassion is based on a keen awareness of the interdependence of all these living beings, which are all part of one another, and all involved in one another."
– Thomas Merton

"Every action in our lives touches on some chord that will vibrate in eternity."
– Edwin Hubbel Chapin

The collective mind is made up of the people in the society and region of the world where you live. It plays a part in the thinking of people around the planet. Because of the electronic and mass media, the collective mind is accelerating in its thought processes — unfortunately, not always in an ascending manner.

The collective mind, much like yours, can also be changed. For example, at one time a large number of people thought racial segregation and the killing of various types of people for petty or fabricated reasons were okay. As people became enlightened and began to understand the wrongs that were taking place, the attitude changed and society no longer accepted the former barbaric treatment. The collective mind changed.

"One little person, giving all of her time to peace, makes news. Many people, giving some of their time, can make history."
– Mildred "Peace Pilgrim" Norman

Another example of how the collective mind is changing is in the way that many people are becoming aware of environmental issues, and that the small decisions they make to improve their environment make a difference. For instance, millions of people have finally become aware of how much environmental damage is being done by the global community that uses billions of plastic bags and plastic bottles every month. Many people are now choosing to use instead long-term reusable, biodegradable fabric bags, and long-lasting, reusable drinking bottles.

"Nothing is more powerful than an individual acting out of his conscience, thus helping to bring the collective conscience to life."
– Norman Cousins

You are a part of the collective mind, collective environment, and collective society in which you live. What you think about matters. You matter and your choices are important to the health of society.

"Perhaps the most basic challenge humanity faces is to awaken our capacity for collective knowing, and conscious action so that we can respond successfully to the immense social and ecological difficulties that now confront us."
– Duane Elgin

"We ourselves feel that what we are doing is just a drop in the ocean. But the ocean would be less because of that missing drop."
– Mother Teresa

If you want society to improve and become more environmentally sustainable, you need to improve and live a more environmentally sustainable life. If you want there to be less pollution, you have to pollute less. If you want there to be fewer toxic chemicals and a world that is safer for wildlife, you have to use fewer toxic chemicals and work to protect wildlife. If you want people to be more healthful, you have to be more healthful. If you want people to be positive and to be part of the solution, you have to be more positive and you must be part of the solution.

"The people's good is the highest law."
– Marcus Tullius Cicero

Just as a rotten berry can ruin an entire box of berries, a person with a negative and damaging attitude can spread their energy among the people around them. Similarly, just as one pebble can change the flow of a stream, the positive attitude of just one person can sway an entire group of people toward a better way.

This also works on an individual level. Slight changes in your thinking pattern can lead you to a completely different situation from the one you were in had you not taken control of your thoughts.

If you notice that a situation you are in is on a course you don't like, realize that you can play a part in changing the current.

"As human beings we all want to be happy and free from misery. We have learned that the key to happiness is inner peace. The greatest obstacles to inner peace are disturbing emotions such as anger and attachment, fear and suspicion while love and compassion, a sense of universal responsibility are the sources of peace and happiness."
– Dalai Lama

Group dynamics can be an interesting phenomenon, given that the attitude of everyone in a group can be altered by the attitude of one person.

Sometimes when you are around a group of people you may notice one or two who are focused on what they don't like about someone else in the group. They may begin to say degrading, belittling, and otherwise slanderous things about that person, spreading the negative thoughts into others within the group. They offer no solutions while they centralize their thoughts on the negative things about the person instead of on the positive, helpful, and nurturing.

> "When you speak of someone or about someone, you should speak as though they were in the room with you. The ears that you speak to today are attached to the mouth that could relay the message tomorrow."
>
> – William Biddy Allen

The energy resonating from someone in a position of power can be especially communicable and can spread throughout an organization. This can work either positively or negatively. In the same way, the people who are not in the top positions of an organization can also be a major influence in creating change.

Many people have experienced tyrannical or otherwise unpleasant bosses. A boss who is unpleasant can wreak havoc on the nerves of the staff — creating an unfavorable work environment that leads to stress in the homes of the employees.

People in a position of coaching sporting teams work every day to guide the collective mind of the group of people for which they are responsible. Wise coaches know their attitude can quickly spread throughout the team and have a huge impact on their success. Therefore, a coach will constantly work to recognize when anything other than an attitude of success is present in the team, and work to adjust the views of anyone who is not being helpful.

There may be times that you will need to advise someone to be cautious of another person, but there is a tender balance between advising caution and promoting unfair attitudes and judgments, between warning and slandering, and between advising and requiring or expecting.

> "If we encourage and uphold our essential goodness and capacity for loving connection, we can nurture a society of people who are healthy and whole and whose lives will bring healing, peace, and joy to those they touch."
>
> – John Robbins

While you may not always be successful at it, work to be patient, kind, and forgiving, and others will likely conduct themselves in a similar manner. Bring a good energy with you wherever you go. By sending out positive energy, you are a positive influence on the people around you. By being confident, you can help those around you to become more confident. By working hard, you will likely inspire others to do the same.

> "Of all the things I have learned in my lifetime, the one with the greatest value is that unexpected kindness is the most powerful, least costly and most underrated agent of human change."
> – Bob Kerrey

Uplift, compliment, nurture, encourage, and guide people toward the better choices. Treat others as you would like to be treated. Watch it spread as if you are conducting the matter around you — because, you are.

> "Even if it's a little thing, do something for those who have need of help, something for which you get no pay but the privilege of doing it."
> – Albert Schweitzer

> "Few people know that they have the power to bless life. We bless the life in each other far more than we realize. Many simple, ordinary things that we do can affect those around us in profound ways."
> – Rachel Naomi Remen

Just as your mental health is important to your physical health, and your physical health is important to your spiritual health, and your diet is important to your body and environment, and the quality of your environment is important to your ability to live healthfully, you and all of the people around you are important to the well-being of each other.

> "The greatest good you can do for another is not just to share your riches but to reveal to him his own."
> – Benjamin Disraeli

Recognize that your thoughts and words can bring out the best qualities of people. Nurture the things you like about people. Complimenting, encouraging, and nurturing good in others is doing the same for yourself. Expressing gratitude for the little things people do is one way to bring about more of the same.

"Those who bring sunshine into the lives of others cannot keep it from themselves."
– James M. Barrie

"Some of the most significant problems of humankind can only be fundamentally approached as matters of conscience, commitments of the human spirit, and endeavors of whole communities, local and global."
– Thomas S. Inui

"Gratitude is something of which none of us can give too much. For on the smiles, the thanks we give, our little gestures of appreciation, our neighbors build their philosophy of life."
– A. J. Cronin

"This ongoing journey requires faith in the power of a single lamp to hold the darkness at bay. It demands confidence in the power of humble actions to act as an inspiration, or a magnet, and draw in greater energies. There is also a need for a certain agility and strategic planning that puts these positive energies a few steps ahead of the negative trends. And, above all, we need a constant awareness that the 'other' is not really different from the 'self.'"
– Rajni Bakshi

Treating others in a way that respects their intellect, talents, and abilities creates an atmosphere of respect within you. This is why it is good to acknowledge the positive aspects of those around you. It is in alignment with the concept that you should treat others as you would like to be treated. How you are treating others is how you are treating yourself.

"Happiness is a perfume you cannot pour on others without getting a few drops on yourself."
– Ralph Waldo Emerson

Your energy is swayed by the energy of those with whom you choose to associate. If you want to be more positive and successful, associate with those who are in alignment with those conditions. By conducting yourself in a certain manner you are more likely to meet and associate with others who are doing the same.

"It is one of the most beautiful compensations of this life that no one can sincerely try to help another without helping himself."
– Ralph Waldo Emerson

"We can not live only for ourselves. A thousand fibers connect us with our fellow men."
– Herman Melville

"Kindness is the golden chain by which society is bound together."
– Johann Wolfgang von Goethe

By first conducting ourselves in the best way we know how and doing what is right, we are becoming enlightened and allowing others in our realm to benefit from our enlightenment.

"Each time a person stands up for an ideal, or acts to improve the lot of others, or strikes out against injustice, he sends forth a tiny ripple of hope, and crossing each other from a million different centers of energy and daring, these ripples build a current that can sweep down the mightiest walls of oppression and resistance."
– Robert F. Kennedy

When you are involved in improving the situation of the environment, of wildlife, and of the human condition, such as by creating a more sustainable culture, you will find that the impact you have can be magnified greatly when you join others who are doing the same. More and more people are awakening to a life involved in correcting the wrongs and making better decisions that will bring better results than what we have been experiencing. This is a testament to the changing collective mind.

"So divinely is the world organized that every one of us, in our place and time, is in balance with everything else."
– Johann Wolfgang von Goethe

As mentioned, by doing what you like to do and going where you like to go, you are likely to meet others who share your interests.

"People are longing to rediscover true community. We have had enough of loneliness, independence, and competition."
– Jean Vanier

At this time, it is particularly important to associate with those who are involved with improving the condition of Earth. At this stage, it is crucial to the continuation of species that everyone participate in building a more sustainable culture that is protecting and restoring forests, wildlands, and wildlife habitat. As the situation for wildlife and the health of Earth improve, so too will the conditions of humanity.

> "It is worth reminding ourselves that what brings us the greatest joy and satisfaction in life are those actions we undertake out of concern for others. Indeed we can go further. For whereas the fundamental questions of human existence, such as why we are here, where we are going, and whether the universe had a beginning, have each elicited different responses in different philosophical traditions, it is self-evident that a generous heart and wholesome actions lead to greater peace."
> – Dalai Lama

> "With every deed you are sowing a seed, though the harvest you may not see."
> – Ella Wheeler Wilcox

> "If I have been of service, if I have glimpsed more of the nature and essence of ultimate good, if I am inspired to reach wider horizons of thought and action, if I am at peace with myself, it has been a successful day."
> – Alex Nobel

> "Sometimes it falls upon a generation to be great."
> – Nelson Mandela

> "The greatest discovery of my generation is that we are unique. The greatest discovery of the next generation, I pray, is that we are one."
> – Thomas Leonard

> "What you leave behind is not what is engraved in stone monuments, but what is woven into the lives of others."
> – Pericles

> "We have all known the long loneliness and we have learned that the only solution is love and that love comes with community."
> – Dorothy Day

"Today we are faced with the preeminent fact that, if civilization is to survive, we must cultivate the science of human relationships — the ability of all people, of all kinds, to live together and work together, in the same world at peace."
– Franklin D. Roosevelt

"So many people walk around with a meaningless life. They seem half-asleep, even when they're busy doing things they think are important. This is because they're chasing the wrong things. The way you get meaning into your life is to devote yourself to loving others, devote yourself to your community around you, and devote yourself to creating something that gives you purpose and meaning."
– Morrie Schwartz

Always remember that you can change the course of your community toward solutions, and that it is you who can change your world.

"We are participants in a vast communion of being, and if we open ourselves to its guidance, we can learn anew how to live in this great and gracious community of truth."
– Parker Palmer

"Life is divine, life is an extraordinary, incredible, miraculous phenomenon, our most precious gift. We must grow a global brain, a global heart, and global soul. That is our most pressing current evolutionary task."
– Robert Muller

"To appreciate beauty; to give of one's self, to leave the world a bit better, whether by a healthy child, a garden patch or a redeemed social condition; to have played and laughed with enthusiasm and sung with exultation; to know even one life has breathed easier because you have lived — that is to have succeeded."
– Ralph Waldo Emerson

"On this shrunken globe, men can no longer live as strangers."
– Adlai E. Stevenson

"We have a calling. We are the people who know what we need. What we need surrounds us. What we need is each other. And when we act together, we will find our way."
– John McKnight

"We are earth people on a spiritual journey to the stars. Our quest, our earth walk, is to look within, to know who we are, to see that we are connected to all things."
– Lakota seer

Artists

"The creative individual has the capacity to free himself from the web of social pressures in which the rest of us are caught. He is capable of questioning the assumptions that the rest of us accept."
– John W. Gardener

"A musician must make music, an artist must paint, a poet must write, if they are to be ultimately at peace with themselves. What a man can be, he must be."
– Abraham Maslow

"To the artist is sometimes granted a sudden, transient insight which serves in this matter for experience. A flash, and where previously the brain held a dead fact, the soul grasps a living truth! At moments we are all artists."
– Arnold Bennett

"An artist worthy of the name should express all the truth of nature, not only the exterior truth, but also, and above all, the inner truth."
– Auguste Rodin

"Every artist dips his brush in his own soul, and paints his own nature into his pictures."
– Henry Ward Beecher

Artists are often open-minded and find themselves having to sneak through the closed-mindedness of those around them to create their art and accomplish their goals. Doing this can also display both their creativity and determination to express their intellect.

"Art is literacy of the heart."
– Elliot Eisner

Artists often fall into the classifications of nonconformity. How they handle being in this classification can make or break them. This is especially so in the earlier parts of their lives.

Artists are also often sensitive and can be susceptible to losing themselves in and to being entrapped by peer pressure and conformity. Often this is done to protect against harsh criticism. When this happens they can become engulfed by self-deceptive and destructive behavior.

People who don't follow society's norms are often considered odd or eccentric. If this shows up in childhood, the child can be misunderstood. Instead of recognizing and working with the attributes of the child, it is becoming more likely that the child will be given pharmaceutical drugs to conform so that they fit in with the children who can sit for hours doing math and English lessons, memorizing things, and giving rehearsed answers to test questions.

> "Artmaking is making the invisible, visible."
> – Marcel Duchamp

Society suggests that we live our lives in a certain pattern, wearing particular styles of clothing and hair arrangements, eating common foods, and living in structures of a popular design. What much of society has transitioned into is the "norm" that is intellectually stifling and talent-strangling mundanity. You aren't supposed to stain your hair with beet juice and henna, and you aren't supposed to wear clothes that don't look like the mass-manufactured clothes that everyone else wears. You are supposed to conform to standard styles. And goodness help you if you should paint your house anything other than bland colors that blend in with the neighborhood landscaped with flowers, bushes, and trees approved by the design committee of the homeowners' association.

> "Be daring, be different, be impractical, be anything that will assert integrity of purpose and imaginative vision against the play-it-safers, the creatures of the commonplace, the slaves of the ordinary."
> – Cecil Beaton

In 1997 author, artist, and educator Sandra Cisneros went against the grain of the San Antonio, Texas, neighborhood where she lived and painted her house traditional Tejano colors, including violet. People reacted as if she had committed a crime. Suddenly there were news cameras and people swarming to take photos of her home. Her story made the international news.

Cisneros was out-of-line with the local homeowners who had painted their homes beige, grey, brown, Hawthorne green, or Sevres blue. Her rebellious act became the focus of the Historic Design and Review Committee, which gave her the option of repainting her home or going about the process of proving that her choice in colors for her home were historically appropriate. She argued that the Tejano people who formerly lived in the area did paint their homes in such colors, and they didn't have architects and review committees determining the colors of their homes. The Tejano history had been erased, their homes demolished, and their humble villages replaced by the modern city with its parking lots, government buildings, freeways, shopping centers, and homes with colors and designs approved by committees. In arguing her case, Cisneros wisely responded, "Color is a language. In essence, I am being asked to translate this language. For some who enter my home, these colors need no translation. However, why am I translating to the historical professionals? If they're not visually bilingual, what are they doing holding a historical post in a city with San Antonio's demographics?"

Cisneros won her case. After several years, the violet house faded in the sun to a blue. She then painted it Mexican pink with a backyard office painted marigold.

> "The core psychology of a social entrepreneur is someone who cannot come to rest, in a very deep sense, until he or she has changed the pattern in an area of social concern all across society."
> – Bill Drayton

Artists help define what society is and becomes. Therefore, they shouldn't underestimate their influence. They should also be aware of the good they can do.

> "Anyone who lives art knows that psychoanalysis has no monopoly on the power to heal. Art and poetry have always been altering our ways of sensing and feeling — that is to say, altering the human body."
> – Norman O. Brown

We have often heard someone start a sentence by saying, "That movie (or book, song, etc.) made me feel…" Those who create things should be aware that they are spreading their energy into other people through design, and that this guides society.

"Acknowledge all those who gave their lives in pursuit of the great human service, the service of the artist, transforming the sometimes unbearable discrepancy between the way things are and the way they ought to be, into something that makes us want to dance."
– Richard Berger

In the spring of 1968 there were riots and demonstrations in the streets of Paris, and later in other parts of France. This happened after the French minister of culture tried to oust Henri Langlois and close the Cinematheque Française. The crowds and well-known persons of the international film community rallied behind Langlois who was famous for endless screenings of films he had spent decades collecting from all over the world, including from war-torn countries. Langlois considered film to be its own country, and his theatre reigned over a large part of the art community of Paris. It was because of Langlois that the Cinematheque existed, and it is because of his dedication that many films from throughout the world have been preserved.

Among those attending Cinematheque Française was a group of passionate film fans and creators known as "the Rats of Cinematheque" or "Children of the Cinamatheque." The Rats, including New Wave film directors, such as Jean-Luc Godard, Francois Truffaut, and Jacques Rivette, spent many hours at the theatre and in social settings passionately discussing the films they watched at the Cinematheque.

The knowledge shared at Langlois' Cinematheque altered the film world forever because it strengthened the concept that film is a form of art and a way for filmmakers and society in general to express and to be expressed. The energy of the Rats of Cinematheque vibrates through the film community today. As film helps to formulate the thoughts of large numbers of people around the world, this part of film history is an example of how little things can affect much larger things.

"Respect yourself and others will respect you."
– Confucious

Society has a lack of value and respect for artists and creative types, often dismissing them as meaningless, yet there is a large dependency on artists to create the appearance of society. Artists help determine the types of clothing people wear, the type of structures they work and live in, and what they experience through all forms of entertainment.

No matter what stage of life you are in, it is never too late to recognize your talents and to practice your art.

> "It is later in the dark of life that you see forms, constellations. And it is the constellations that are philosophy."
> – Robert Frost

> "I am always doing that which I cannot do in order that I may learn how to do it."
> – Pablo Picasso

Some of those who have been considered to be the greatest artists went through decades of learning about and/or misunderstanding themselves before they created their most celebrated works.

> "There are some truths about life that can be expressed only as stories, or songs, or images. Art delights, instructs, consoles. It educates our emotions."
> – Dana Gioia

There are many examples of artists who created landmark works in their later years. For instance, Louise Bourgeois didn't create her famous steel and marble Maman spider sculpture until she was 87 years old. Another example is Anna Mary Robertson "Grandma" Moses, who didn't start painting until she was in her seventies. In the acting community, there are people like Estelle Parsons, who, at age 82 was on a national tour starring in the play, "August: Osage County," in which she appeared on Broadway when it won both the 2008 Tony Award and Pulitzer Prize for Best Play.

> "At the deepest level, the creative process and the healing process arise from a single source. When you are an artist, you are a healer; a wordless trust of the same mystery is the foundation of your work and its integrity."
> – Rachel Naomi Remen

> "It has been said that art is a tryst, for in the joy of it maker and beholder meet."
> – Kojiro Tomita

Films, television, plays, literature, music, and design can create various forms of energy. Art truly influences people to feel certain energies within their body tissues, which result in thoughts and emotions.

> "It is incontestable that music induces in us a sense of the

infinite and the contemplation of the invisible."
– Victor de LaPrade

"Healing is communication; and music, in its universal nature, is total communication. In the deepest mysteries of music are the inspirations, the pathways, and the healing which lead to one-ness and unity."
– Olivea Dewhurst-Maddock

"Music is the language of the spirit. It opens the secret of life bringing peace, abolishing strife."
– Kahlil Gibran

Artists may sometimes be eccentric types who have been misunderstood and mistreated at various times. Because of their sensitive nature they may have experienced things on a deeper level, including mental pain, which can become overwhelming and lead to unwise choices of how to relieve it. Artists don't need any more pain, nor do people need to contribute to their pain. What they need is a nurturing and safe environment; encouragement to steer their creativity into useful, helpful, and healthful projects; and, just like everyone else, dignity.

"When I'm trusting and being myself, everything in my life reflects this by falling into place easily, often miraculously."
– Shakti Gawain

Today we need a whole new set of artists dedicated to designing all levels of society to establish a more environmentally sustainable culture.

"The painter of the future will be a colorist such as has never been seen."
– Vincent Van Gogh

"I think raising consciousness, helping people see and understand how they're connected to these larger systems in the world around us, is an incredibly important thing. I think art can do this in ways that are provocative, meaningful and inspirational, deeply moving, beautiful, connected with history and culture and resonant. I think that's a big part of it. There's another part of it where I think artists have the opportunity to more than call attention to problems and preach, to really help solve problems. To help create things that work better, that are just more beautiful and right."

– Sam Bower

"Obstacles cannot crush me. Every obstacle yields to stern resolve. He who is fixed to a star does not change his mind."

– Leonardo da Vinci

"When we make a conscious decision to create — to make a painting for instance – we are opening the door to the pure source energy flowing through us and asking that we become able to interpret it in a way that we and others may understand it. Fasting is the greatest way that I know of to achieve ultimate clarity in this process — to tap directly into the source in order to bring back information via visual language that will inspire growth and awareness in others. Art is free to all without rules — how can anyone pass that up? Art is our responsibility — it is the essential catalyst for universal shift."

– Zito

If you are an artist, please become a part of the movement to create a more healthful, environmentally sustainable society that protects Nature and wildlife while following a plant-based diet.

"At the deepest level, the creative process and the healing process arise from a single source. When you are an artist, you are a healer; a wordless trust of the same mystery is the foundation of your work and its integrity."

– Rachel Naomi Remen

"I experience a period of frightening clarity in those moments when nature is so beautiful. I am no longer sure of myself, and the paintings appear as in a dream. An artist, under pain of oblivion, must have confidence in himself, and listen only to his real master: Nature."

– Auguste Renoir

"An artist is not a special kind of a person — every person is a special kind of an artist."

– Ananda Coomaraswami

"I am my own experiment. I am my own work of art."

– Madonna Ciccone

"Live your life from your heart. Share from your heart. And your story will touch and heal people's souls."
– Melody Beattie

"Where the needs of the world and your talents cross, there lies your vocation."
– Aristotle

"Every man's work, whether it be literature or music or pictures or architecture or anything else, is always a portrait of himself."
– Samuel Butler

"In art the hand can never execute anything higher than the heart can inspire."
– Ralph Waldo Emerson

"My art has led me into deeper relationship with the Earth. When I am outside painting the landscape I often feel part of it — not just a spectator, but a participant. Perception is participation. The more we perceive, the more we participate. The more we participate, the more we are connected. With connection comes caring."
– Adam Wolpert

"All children are artists. The problem is how to remain an artist once he grows up."
– Pablo Picasso

"The distribution of talents in this world should not be our concern. Our responsibility is to take the talents we have and ardently parlay them to the highest possible achievement."
– Alan Loy McGinnis

"No matter how old you get, if you can keep the desire to be creative, you're keeping the man-child alive."
– John Cassavetes

"I do know that craft, if you pursue craft, will return you again and again to this creative state. To pursue the craft means to endeavor to bring together the intention of the mind to the hand, and an invitation to feeling – an invitation to a new kind of feeling."
– Nicholas Hlobeczy

"When I stand before God at the end of my life, I would hope that I would not have a single bit of talent left, and could say: I used everything you gave me."
– Erma Bombeck

"There are no days in life so memorable as those which vibrated to some stroke of the imagination."
– Ralph Waldo Emerson

"Every artist makes herself born. You must bring the artist into the world yourself."
– Willa Cather

"When you do things from your soul, you feel a river moving in you, a joy."
– Rumi

"Your life is a work of art. You are the designer of your life, the paint brush is in your hands and with every beautiful picture you paint and every opportunity you cease, will one day form into your masterpiece."
– Adam Taste

Brain Plasticity

The key tool in creating a more sustainable human culture is the brain of a healthy human.

Brain nutrition begins before birth as tens of millions of brain cells are forming. Women who are planning on becoming pregnant, and those who are pregnant, would benefit their babies by striving for the most excellent nutritional foods available to them, especially in the form of a variety of raw fruits and vegetables.

Excellent prenatal nutrition is beneficial in many ways. Women who consume a variety of fresh fruits and vegetables during their pregnancy are found to have babies with more healthful lung function and with less susceptibility to asthma.

Substances in fresh fruits and vegetables are particularly beneficial to brain function. It is known that the neurotransmitter acetylcholine is key to cell communication and a healthful memory. That brain chemical tends to decline with age. Antioxidants in raw, dark-colored fruits and vegetables, and especially in apples, apricots, broccoli, cantaloupe, chard, kale, mangos, blueberries, goji berries, spinach, and watermelon help preserve a healthful level of acetylcholine.

As many people continue eating low-quality foods, their body tissues are not able to function at the most healthful level, and their brains are not functioning anywhere near their potential. Many people are consuming such unhealthful food while leading slothful and unsustainable lifestyles that their brains are not only neglected, but are in a state of dysfunction. They are deeply embedded in the problem.

The brain is highly reliant on quality nutrition. It especially needs raw plant substances containing high-quality nutrients. But the type of foods many modern-day people are consuming most often contain overly processed substances that no longer resemble what is found in Nature. And they are consuming fried and highly processed and heated, and otherwise low-quality fats, such as lard, mayonnaise, shortening, pasteurized dairy, unhealthful salad dressings, and trans fats. None of those fats are what the brain or body needs. In fact, these oils are so unhealthful to eat that they cause brain cell and whole body tissue dysfunction. Following a low-quality diet is degrading to all areas of the person's life — including brain function and neural growth.

> "The food you eat can either be the safest and most powerful form of medicine, or the slowest form of poison."
> – Ann Wigmore

It should be no surprise for anyone to find out that health suffers when a person follows a diet lacking in fresh fruits and vegetables while following a diet that consists of fried food, bleached grains, and the meat, dairy, and eggs from factory farms where animals live extremely unhealthful lives.

According to the National Institutes of Health, in the U.S. obesity increased in 23 states in 2008, and lowered in none.

Not only do people suffer from a number of common ailments when they become obese, their brains also suffer. According to a study that was published in the journal *Human Brain Mapping* in August, 2009 and funded by the National Institute on Aging, National Institute of Biomedical Imaging and Bioengineering, National Center for Research Resources, and the American Heart Association, the brains of obese people contain 8 percent less brain tissue and appear 16 years older than people of a healthful weight. The study involved studying the brains of 94 people in their seventies. The lead author of the study, Paul Thompson, a UCLA professor of neurology, was clear to explain that obesity interferes with cognitive function and increases the risk of Alzheimer's and other brain diseases. Brain scans detected that the brains of the study subjects appear to have lost tissue in many areas of the brain, includeing the frontal and temporal lobes (control memory and strategy), anterior congulate gyrus (controls attention and executive functions), hippocampus (long-term memory), parietal lobe (senses), and basal ganglia (control movement). The brains of obese people also showed a reduction in white matter composed of axons.

An unhealthful diet, lack of exercise, and being overweight clearly interferes with brain function, shrinks the brain, dulls the senses, increases the likelihood of stroke, Alzheimer's, diabetes, and cancer, reduces neural activity and sex drive, and is simply detrimental to any area of health.

According to the World Health Organization, in 2009 there were about 300 million people on the planet who could be classified as obese, and another billion were overweight.

Many people who feel they are not functioning healthfully go to an allopathic doctor who is likely to prescribe chemical drugs and/or surgery. There is no doubt that a growing number of surgeons are making a lot of money from an increasingly obese population. Any scan of today's media will turn up a number of advertisements seeking overweight people willing to undergo stomach reduction surgery. These advertisements often give the impression that the surgery is risk-free and simple. Anyone who knows anything about surgery knows that even simple surgeries can lead to serious complications, caused by anesthesia and possible infection. What would be better for obese people is for them to stop eating junk food, to follow a fresh-food, plant-based diet, and to get daily physical activity.

As the popularity of junk food has risen, so has the use of prescription antidepressant medication. According to the August 2009 issue of *Archives of General Psychiatry*, 27 million Americans were taking antidepressants in 2005. That was double the number of people on antidepressants in 1995.

What I strongly advise for those who feel they are experiencing mood swings, depression, emotional instability, and/or general brain fatigue is to eliminate all unhealthful fats, fried fats, bleached grains, processed sugars and salts, synthetic food chemicals, and MSG from their diet. Then, only allow in reasonable amounts of high-quality, raw plant fats while following a plant-based diet rich in fruits and vegetables. As they remain on a healthful diet while getting daily exercise and maintaining a regular sleeping pattern, they will likely experience a more stable state of mind.

Those experiencing or with a history of depression may benefit from reading a book by Gabriel Cousens and Mark Mayell titled *De-*

pression-free for Life: A Physician's All-natural, 5-step Plan. Gabriel Cousens founded the Tree of Life Rejuvenation Center, a raw foods health retreat in Arizona. Mark Mayell was the editor-in-chief of *Natural Health* magazine. Cleaning the diet, getting daily morning exercise, living intentionally with clear goals, and intellectual stimulation are all key.

I don't typically advise people to take supplements. However, to overcome depression, and especially if someone is transitioning from an unhealthful lifestyle and low-quality diet, there are certain supplements and superfoods that can help fuel the change toward better brain and neural function. This is why, in addition to following a fresh plant-based diet rich in green vegetables; getting daily morning exercise; following a list of goals; and getting into a habit of positive-thinking and intentional living, I also encourage those with a history of depression to research the following natural amino acids, berries, herbs, mushrooms, oils, foods, supplements, and vitamins to identify those that may be of benefit: ashwaganda herb; B-12 and other B-vitamins (from vegetarian sources); chlorella (a freshwater vegetable); vitamin D (in a vegetarian supplement form); digestive enzymes (in a vegetarian supplement form); dulse powder (a seaweed); essential fatty acids (they are contained in raw vegetables, fruits, berries, nuts, seeds, and water plants, and in germinated buckwheat and Chia seeds); 5-hydroxytryptophan, also known as 5-HTP (in veg caps); gamma-aminobutyric acid (also known as GABA); goji berries (and all edible and organically grown berries, including blueberries); hemp seeds (raw and organically grown); kelp powder (a seaweed); l-glutamine; lions mane mushrooms; mesquite powder; MSM powder; mucana prureins; phenylanine; pomegranate, probiotic powder (from a vegan source); pumpkin seeds (raw and organically grown); red cabbage; sesame seeds (raw and organically grown); spirulina; taurine; and tyrosine. Also, consider adding a green powder to your daily intake, such as Infinity Greens blended into a green smoothie.

By a plant-based diet, I mean one that consists of raw fruits, vegetables, and berries, sprouts, soaked raw nuts and seeds, seaweeds, and absolutely no meat, dairy, eggs, processed sugars (including corn syrup); processed salts; synthetic food chemicals, fried food, or MSG. If there is anything that people don't eat enough of, it is fresh, uncooked fruits, berries, and vegetables — especially green leafy vegetables.

It can be especially helpful to those suffering from depresssion to follow a lower-fat diet, with little or no bottled oils, and few nuts. Any fat should also be raw, from plant sources, and preferably organic, such as unheated organic walnuts, hemp seeds, sesame seeds, soaked raw almonds, seeded grapes, raw pumpkin seeds, sprouted sunflower seeds, germinated buckwheat and Chia seeds, and other high-quality sources of botanical fat, including raw green vegetables.

As I write this there are many millions of people taking prescription medications for sleep, mood, and psychological disorders while they are at the same time consuming the lowest-quality foods and trying to get more energy by consuming coffee, cola, soda, and caffeine "energy drinks." To experience better psychological health they should get their diet in order while following a daily exercise regimen.

How is society supposed to progress to a more healthful state if the brains of the people can't function at a healthful level because they are eating health-depleting, brain-numbing junk food and popping prescription chemical pills at every turn of the day to control their brain function while they stare at garbage they call "entertainment"?

All parts of you, including your brain, run on some sort of fuel. If your brain is bogged down by useless thought processes, stagnation, and clutter, you are not going to be able to function at your highest level. With the wrong brain and body fuel you will have limited use of your power. If you follow the typical lifestyle of low-quality foods and junk media thoughts you will not be able to accomplish the goals through intentional living that you would otherwise be capable of accomplishing if you thought better, exercised better, ate better, and communicated better.

The brain grows in a way consistent with the quality of our thoughts and actions, and the nutrients in our food choices. As a person remains focused on a certain thought or action over a period of time, the brain grows more neurons in the area of the brain that is being used more often. What a person does, says, sees, and otherwise experiences and anticipates, creates patterns of thoughts, which result in patterns of connections between neurons.

The processes involved with thoughts and actions trigger certain genes on the brain and other neurons to be turned on or off. The patterns of activities being conducted among the brain's hundred billion or so neurons, including how the synaptic connections between the neurons take place throughout the body, are what we call "thinking."

While not all your thinking can be controlled by you, a significant amount of it can, and you can think on a higher level if you feed your brain better-quality nutrients and engage in worthwhile activities that train your brain to act and respond more to your liking.

What you are doing, saying, seeing, hearing, and feeling, and what you are eating, is affecting the neurons in your brain. Your brain is continually either engaging already formed synapses, or creating new ones.

Activity, social interaction, and intellectual stimulation are good for the brain. Slothfulness is not. People who stare at the television, screen games, or Internet, and/or do not engage in daily activities that utilize their skills, talents, and intellect are doing their brain no favors. Isolating yourself from social and intellectual stimulation also degrades your brain.

Vigorous exercise is beneficial to the brain because it increases the flow of information through the neurons while also increasing blood flow and releasing endorphins, which relieve stress. Exercise works the brain to produce more cells, especially in the hippocampus region of the brain, which helps to manage retention and organization of information.

People who regularly exercise have more healthful amounts of gray matter in their brains. This is proof that exercise protects against age-related brain degeneration.

Anxiety and psychological stress have a negative effect on the brain. Regular exercise and quality nutrition are most effective in reducing stress and anxiety.

Physical activity along with intellectual and social stimulation engages the brain in ways that stimulates it to form new neural pathways. It also triggers the brain to release neurotrophin molecules, which are ben-eficial to maintaining cellular health.

Those who want to maintain brain health should remain active on several levels, including physically, socially, and intellectually while following a diet rich in raw plant matter. Everything you do and eat has an impact on the brain. If one part of the brain is not used as often, the activities of that part of the brain will diminish and a certain amount of atrophy will take place. Like a muscle, the brain needs activity combined with quality nutrients to stay strong. A diet consisting largely of raw, unheated plant matter is rich in biophotons, which are tiny fields of light that play a part in cellular communication. The brain is rich in photoreceptor proteins, which work as light sensors in the cells.

> "Each of us has that right, that possibility, to invent ourselves daily. If a person does not invent herself, she will be invented. So, to be bodacious enough to invent ourselves is wise."
>
> – Maya Angelou

You are continually forming new brain cells while also, through your thoughts, actions, relationships, and nutrition helping to form the way the brain is wired and rewired. Realize that you have some control over how your brain forms. You can build neural pathways that correspond to what you do want to think, feel, and do. Or you can build neural pathways that correspond to what you don't want to do. For these reasons, it is important to be involved with what you love — every day.

Sleeping and Arising

> "Within you right now is the power to do things you never dreamed possible. This power becomes available to you just as you can change your beliefs."
> – Maxwell Maltz

Understand that learning and action and daily exercise combined with a diet of high nutritional value keeps your brain healthful.

Considering that your brain wires iteself in correspondence to what you think, the intentions you agree to, the words you speak, the actions you take, the relations you make, and the nutrients you consume, it is easy to understand that it is important to be engaged in doing what you want to do while following a diet of the best nutrients available to you.

To get your brain to function the way you want it to, do things in correspondence with what you ideally see yourself doing; teach yourself about the things you need to learn to live the life you want to have; physically do things that correspond with what you see yourself doing; and eliminate low-quality foods from your life.

> "Energy is the essence of life. Every day you decide how you're going to use it by knowing what you want and what it takes to reach that goal, and by maintaining focus."
> – Oprah Winfrey

Align yourself with what you want. Whatever it is that you want to do, learn about it, and do it. Read books about it. Think about doing it. Plan on doing it. Do it mentally and physically. Doing these things will develop habits of behavior and thoughts that will construct physical and mental pathways and energy patterns in tune with the life you want to have.

> "When you arise in the morning, think of what a privilege it is to be alive: to breathe, to think, to enjoy, to love."
> – Marcus Aurelius

Two things you can do to help manifest your goals is to introduce thoughts and learning processes into your mind at the two times of day that highly influence your life: in the morning when you awake, and at night before you go to sleep. Adjusting your mind by guiding your thoughts and energy just before and after sleep will steer your life in the direction you want to go. These are the two times each day when your mind is in the alpha-wave zone. It is when your mind is open to suggestion and motivation. It is when your mind can be tuned in a way that will help continue your thought processes toward attaining your goals. It is when you should plug into your power and get your gears moving in the desired direction.

> "There are only two ways to live your life. One is as though nothing is a miracle. The other is as though everything is a miracle."
> – Albert Einstein

Saturate your mind with that which is aligned with the life you want. On awakening, spend at least several minutes engaged in reading, writing, drawing, or otherwise thinking about things that inspire you to attain your goals.

> "The secret of discipline is motivation. When a man is sufficiently motivated, discipline will take care of itself."
> – Alexander Paterson

Keep your list of goals and priorities near your bed so that you can review them every morning. This alone will be a significant tool in getting you to create the life you want to have because it will tune your mind energy to it.

> "There is between sleep and us something like a pact, a treaty with no secret clauses, and according to this convention it is agreed that, far from being a dangerous, bewitching force, sleep will become domesticated and serve as an instrument of our power to act. We surrender to sleep, but in the way that the master entrusts himself to the slave who serves him."
> – Maurice Blanchot

About one-third of your life is spent sleeping. High-quality sleep is very important in maintaining vibrant health, balancing the hormones, raising growth hormone levels, and resting the adrenal glands.

One thing that happens during healthful sleep is the occurrence of rapid eye movement (REM). Before and during REM the system experiences ponto-geniculo-occipital (PGO) spikes. During these REM/PGO phases the brain and body produce chemicals that counteract or work in alignment with and balance other chemicals the body has produced in sync with what has been experienced while awake. In other words, everything you go through, whether you are awake or asleep, produces some sort of chemical reaction in the cells throughout your body. Sleep helps you produce chemicals that balance out your body chemistry, including your hormones, blood sugar, digestive enzymes, and neurotransmitters, and these all play a role in your mood and immune function. Diet, exercise, and what you do with your time, energy, intellect, and talents are also important parts of this body chemical equation.

During sleep, and whether a person remembers or not, dreaming happens — and especially during the REM/PGO phase of sleep — which is when the most vivid dreams may occur. Dreams can help a person deal with unmet expectations, often through metaphorical imagery and thought patterns, helping to relieve stress and pent-up thoughts. The brain is always active in factoring solutions, including during sleep.

During sleep, the neural pathways go through testing patterns, and develop connections in tune with what people need for how they are choosing to spend their time and energy, and in how they are deciding to express their thoughts, talents, and intellect.

When a person does not get high-quality, restful sleep, stress and anxiety build and health is impacted. Both sleep and exercise help relieve stress. Vigorous exercise helps a person sleep better, and good quality sleep helps the body perform at a higher level. Sleep, exercise, and diet all impact the function of the digestive tract, which is where many of the neurotransmitter chemicals are produced, needed for a healthful nerve system, including within the brain.

It has been found that children who sleep in dark rooms sleep better, experience fewer mood swings, and get better grades. Sleeping in the dark also helps maintain healthful neural growth in the brain. This is one reason why babies that are born prematurely have dark eye masks put on them, so that their brains can benefit from the darkness. Sleeping in a dark room also helps to maintain healthful hormone levels.

The sensors within the eyes are light sensitive and play a role in controlling the body's internal clock. About 2 percent of the cells in the retina contain sensors that detect the presence and level of light. The molecule in the sensors is called a melanopsin. This molecule is active even in the eyes of those who have lost their vision. This means that sleeping in a dark room is also beneficial for blind people.

Billions of dollars are spent every year on sleep aid medications. This is evidence that people are searching for ways to get better sleep. There are other ways of getting better sleep than taking pills.

Avoiding coffee and caffeinated drinks is key to better sleep. Also, not eating for a few hours before sleep will allow the body to close down for the night and relax. Chocolate, spicy foods, and fried foods interfere with sleep. Foods that contain tyramine inhibit the body's natural neurochemicals, such as norepinephrine, and cause restless sleep or insomnia. These foods include bacon, cheese, chocolate, ham, potatoes, tomatoes, and sausage. I strongly advise people to completely eliminate all fried food, meat, sodas, and processed chocolate from their diet.

Even raw, organic, vegan, natural chocolate can interfere with sleep. If people are seeking the antioxidants and other nutrients in raw chocolate, it would be helpful to consume it early in the day. While some people in the raw food community tend to eat an abundance of raw chocolate, I tend to stay away from it because it makes my heart race and interferes with my sleep. But I'm not a pure angel, and do randomly eat some raw chocolate. I have found that raw carob is an excellent replacement for raw chocolate. While chocolate is stimulating, carob is calming — and also contains its own spectrum of nutrients.

One of the many things sleep does is balance the body's level of leptin, a hormone that plays a role in signaling the brain when you have eaten enough. Those who get quality sleep have been found to be of a more healthful weight. Being a healthful weight plays a part in all levels of well-being, including cardiovascular health, bone and joint health, and healthful levels of blood sugar.

Those who typically sleep during the day, such as people who work at jobs requiring them to be awake during the dark hours, would benefit from sleeping in a darkened room or wearing a dark eye mask to block light from their eyes.

One of the best things you can do for yourself is to create a sleeping environment that is pleasant, restful, organized, and clean. This is because what you are doing when you are in rest helps to determine what you will be doing when you are in motion.

Consider keeping a potted plant in your bedroom, such as mother-in-laws tongue, which is a plant that produces oxygen at night, and absorbs our exhaled gasses. Other houseplants, including the money tree plant, provide healthful air in the bedroom while absorbing pollutants. These plants will do better if they are exposed to outside air and sunlight. Rotating them every other week so that they have some exposure to sun can help them grow.

> "Keep the peace within yourself. Then you can also bring peace to others."
>
> – Thomas A. Kempis

Pay particular attention to what things you put into your mind before you go to sleep. Visualization before sleeping helps guide your dreams. It can be a powerful tool in accelerating the accomplishment of your goals. But at night, be sure to be calming and assuring rather than motivating and enlivening. Serenely drift into sleep with confidence that you are capable of obtaining the life you envision.

You can guide your sleep into calmness by thinking pleasant thoughts and visualizing beauty as you fall into sleep.

> "Music washes away from the soul the dust of everyday life."
> – Berthold Auerbach

It would be helpful if any music listened to before, during, or immediately after sleep is of a form that is positive, kind, and uplifting.

> "Joy, sorrow, tears, lamentation, laughter — to all these music gives voice, but in such a way that we are transported from the world of unrest to a world of peace, and see reality in a new way, as if we were sitting by a mountain lake and contemplating hills and woods and clouds in the tranquil and fathomless water."
> – Albert Schweitzer

Awake to pleasant sounds. Avoid waking up to loud, frantic sounds; to commercials; to the crass and exploitative attitudes that are often expressed on talk radio; and to news that immediately introduces your waking mind to negative stories that project fear for political and financial gain.

> "Music has the capacity to touch the innermost reaches of the soul and music gives flight to the imagination."
> – Plato

The music you wake up to, the thoughts you choose to have when you awake, your movements upon awaking, and the information you take in during the beginning of your day help tune your thoughts and energy patterns for the rest of the day. Bring it on stronger by reading things that inspire you, writing an intention that motivates you, doing physical exercises that tone you, and eating foods that nurture you at the highest level.

> "Take the breath of the new dawn and make it part of you. It will give you strength."
> – Hopi saying

Out of all the things you take on every morning, your attitude is the most important. The attitude you carry throughout the day can be established by what you tune your thoughts into during your first waking moments.

"Today is the tomorrow that you worried about yesterday."
– Dale Carnegie

Take a bit of time each morning to settle, meditate, and tune into the energy of your spirit. A good way to do this is by starting your day with meditative and intentional stretching and yoga. Anyone who has seen the way an animal awakens can get an idea of this. Take for instance the typical house pet, a cat or dog. When these animals awaken, they often take a few moments to stretch their limbs in a way that resembles yoga poses. This is one of the many lessons we can learn from animals — that waking up is a whole body experience. Do it gently and intentionally — taking time to really feel the stretch and feel your muscles, joints, and body tissues awaken.

"Make friends with your shower. If inspired to sing, maybe the song has an idea in it for you."
– Albert Einstein

After waking up, take a few moments to review your list of priorities. This will help you tune your mind and will place purpose and intention into the actions of that day. Make a separate list of things you want to accomplish that day. This way you will give your day a purpose with goals that you intend to achieve before you return to bed at the end of the day.

"Give to us clear vision that we may know where to stand and what to stand for — because unless we stand for something, we shall fall for anything."
– Peter Marshall

To further empower your intention, sometime during each morning write a short one-sentence, empowering, intentional belief statement. It doesn't matter if it is nearly the same as the statement you wrote the day before. The goal is to keep your mind and actions focused on your intentions of creating the life you want.

"Compose yourself in stillness, draw your attention inward and devote your mind to the Self. The wisdom you seek lies within."
– Bhagavad Gita

Be determined to awaken and start your day on a positive note. Begin by thinking and saying words that uplift, encourage good, and build belief in your talents. Tune into the positive energy of love and choose to keep it with you throughout the day.

Focus on uplifting not only your mind through positive thoughts and actions, but also those around you through encouragement, compliments, and words that uplift and build confidence rather than those that discourage, degrade, bully, doubt, criticize, slander, and deconstruct.

By keeping in a positive groove you will spread good energy. It may be rejected by some, but that is their decision to accept it or reject it just as it is your choice to focus either on the positive or the negative.

It is up to you to live a successful life. Today and every day you can position yourself closer to where you wish to be.

In all of your actions each day, make it a habit to strive in bringing your life closer to a sustainable, healthful existence.

> "Each day comes bearing its own gifts. Untie the ribbons."
> – Ruth Ann Schabacker

Dreaming

> "A man's dreams are an index to his greatness."
> – Zadok Rabinowitz

Sleep is equally as important to brain health as physical activity, nutrition, in-tellectual stimulation, and social interaction.

On many levels, sleep is important for the health of all of our body tissues, including providing time to rest the digestive tract and for the body to release toxins from the cell structures.

> "Dreams are the touchstones of our character."
> – Henry David Thoreau

Your mind is used during dreams, and is tuned by them. The mind chemicals that your body produces when you are awake do not stop when you are asleep. The chemicals keep sharing information, including that which deals with feelings you are experiencing in your dream. In this way, dreams are real. You experience them. Your communication system is involved in them. The difference between when you are awake and when you are asleep is that different levels of chemicals are being produced, and maybe at more healthful levels than when you are awake, particularly if you are in a stressful or otherwise unhealthful life situation.

Perhaps sleep also helps you to organize and file thoughts and memories into a more manageable arrangement while rewiring the brain to deal with things according to what you are focusing on in your life.

During sleep the neural pathways of the brain seem to go through testing patterns, rewiring, and reparation. This brings us to dream of things from the past and present, and often mixing these together into some sort of random story, thus the theatre of dreaming reflects our past and present, our imagination, fantasy, and reality, and our spiritual, physical, and sexual nature.

> "Dreams digest the meals that are our days."
> – Astrid Alauda

> "Let's not forget that the little emotions are the great captains of our lives and we obey them without realizing it."
> – Vincent Van Gogh

Because your body can store emotional energy from various experiences you have had in your life, some of what you are experiencing in your dreams may replicate the emotions from past experiences and expectations being released. This is why some dreams can be as intense as when you originally experienced those events in your awake life.

> "A dream is a microscope through which we look at the hidden occurrences in our soul."
> – Erich Fromm

> "Yet it is in our idleness, in our dreams, that the submerged truth sometimes comes to the top."
> – Virginia Woolf

Paying attention to your dreams can help you to heal. Just as talk or art therapy can help you release pent-up thoughts from life situations and deal with those situations, just as sex can help you release built-up sexual emotions and develop a close and healthful relationship, and just as exercise can help you release stress emotions and build a stronger body, dreams may help you to release clogged emotions that can play a part in your situations, relationships, and ailments.

Without being fanatical about it, write down some record of your sleep dreams, and remember to describe some of the colors, textures, and tonal qualities of things that you saw in your dreams, as well as the feelings you had during the dreams. There may be a message in there for you. And it may not be something you can fully, or even partially, interpret for many years. The longer you maintain the habit of writing down your dreams, the better you will become at understanding the language of your dreams.

> "Judge of your natural character by what you do in your dreams."
> – Ralph Waldo Emerson

> "Dreams are illustrations from the book your soul is writing about you."
> – Marsha Norman

The study and interpretation of dreams and what we may learn from them have always been a part of humanity. Dreams have influenced all areas of human expression, including the artistic expressions of dance, storytelling, theatre, writing, music, painting, drawing, and structural arts. Religious writings often mention dreams. Dreams and the fantasies and concepts springing from them help sculpt our lives and our culture.

Because of what is going on with your brain during sleep, it is healthful to end your day by reading a calming book, drawing a picture, writing an intentional statement, listening to gentle music, and kindly loving who you are with.

Some people will wake up in the middle of the night and watch trash TV, and/or listen to crass talk radio. If you do engage in activities when you awake in the middle of the night, work on accruing information that is more in tune with what you want in your life — instead of the people and characters on TV and radio that are representative of what you do not want.

Don't underestimate the importance of a healthful and regular sleeping pattern. It is key to restoring, maintaining, and building a healthful brain. Sleep also helps preserve the health of the entire body, regulates hormones, and balances the emotions. When combined with a life of intention to create the satisfaction you want, quality sleep is just as important as diet and exercise in maintaining vibrant health.

> "Dreams pass into the reality of action. From the actions stems the dream again; and this interdependence produces the highest form of living."
> – Anais Nin

While I was writing this chapter, I considered what the dreams of animals might be. It is obvious that cats, dogs, and horses dream — because they often physically engage or get fidgety when they are sleeping. I wondered what other animals dream about, including those that live far out in the wild. And I considered what bugs and insects dream about. I wondered what butterflies dream about. Later that day, I found this quotation:

> "I dreamed I was a butterfly, flitting around in the sky; then I awoke. Now I wonder: Am I a man who dreamt of being a butterfly, or am I a butterfly dreaming that I am a man?"
> – Zhuangzi

Exercise

> "I find, by experience, that the mind and the body are more than married, for they are most intimately united; and when one suffers, the other sympathizes."
> – Philip Dormer Stanhope

Movement plays a part in health. Similar to thoughts, food, and relationships, movement can also be healing or damaging.

> "Take care of your body. It's the only place you have to live."
> – E. James Rohn

Physical ailments are often related to bad diet, stressful working conditions, unhealthful relationships, lack of love, and destructive thought patterns. Illness can also be attributed to insufficient exercise, which results in pent-up, unreleased energy working against the person. Lack of movement and exercise also causes the accumulation of toxins and plaque in the tissues, and this degenerates the function and form of the body.

One of the many reasons it is good to exercise every morning is that exercise creates a pattern that releases stress and unexpressed thoughts from the body tissues. Exercise helps a body to become less acidic, more alkaline, and more attuned to experiencing health, which is in tune with happiness and success.

"The body is a sacred garment. It's your first and last garment; it is what you enter life in and what you depart life with, and it should be treated with honor."
– Martha Graham

Take care of your physical structure by getting daily exercise, such as swimming, running, biking, or doing yoga, calisthenics, and/or other full-body activities, such as gardening.

Daily exercise is essential to maintaining the health of body, mind, and spirit. It helps to maintain the health of all the various systems of the body, from the blood, lymph, and immune systems to the brain, digestive organs, bones, muscles, tendons, and skin.

"Take care of your body with steadfast fidelity. The soul must see through these eyes alone, and if they are dim, the whole world is clouded."
– Johann Wolfgang von Goethe

A 1986 study conducted by Ralph S. Paffenbarger at the Stanford University School of Medicine is often mentioned as key to proving that exercise boosts longevity. Paffenbarger's College Alumni Health Study tracked the life-long exercise patterns of 52,000 men who attended Harvard and the University of Pennsylvania between 1916 and 1950. His study found that those who exercised vigorously lived longer and experienced better health than those who did not engage in regular exercise. The study also found that those who did not engage in exercise had a higher incidence of heart disease and what are considered to be age-related disorders. The study has been used to form guidelines issued by both the Centers for Disease Control and Prevention and the American College of Sports Medicine. While Paffenbarger was conducting the study, which took many years, he took up jogging at the age of 45 because he recognized that exercise produces health benefits at any age. He went on to run the Boston Marathon 22 times, and participated in 150 marathons.

"The body is the soul's house. Shouldn't we therefore take care of our house so that it doesn't fall into ruin?"
– Philo Judaeus

It has been shown that those who exercise regularly have a clearer memory, a higher level of attention, have better decision-making and learning abilities, and are better at multitasking. They are less likely to experience depression, are more likely to be of a healthful body weight, are more likely to have a strong immune system, and are more likely to have healthful brain and neural function.

Getting daily exercise induces positive physical feelings that work in conjunction with positive thoughts. Exercise increases the neurotransmitters serotonin, epinephrine, and dopamine, helping to maintain a brighter outlook on life. Being physically fit increases the likelihood that you will experience elation, euphoria, exhilaration, delight, and bliss.

> "You cannot devalue the body and value the soul — or value anything else. The isolation of the body sets it into direct conflict with everything else in creation."
>
> – Wendell Berry

Those who exercise regularly have healthier tissues in every area of the body. Exercise helps both blood vessel and neuron growth (neurogenesis) within the brain because it boosts growth chemicals that nurture new nerve cells. Exercise also helps the brain to work more efficiently and adapt to both mental challenges and new experiences.

> "Physical fitness is not only one of the most important keys to a healthy body, it is the basis of dynamic and creative intellectual activity."
>
> – John F. Kennedy

Health professionals continually promote daily exercise, discourage overeating, advocate intellectual stimulation, and encourage people to deal with their daily stress by working to better manage and organize their days, improve their relationships, follow a plant-based diet, and get adequate sleep. This is because a large number of people do eat too much, don't get enough exercise, and don't face their problems. Managing your life involves not only eating healthfully, but also dealing with those four issues: movement, caloric intake equal to need, stress relief, and healthful sleep.

> "If exercise could be packaged into a pill, it would be the single most prescribed and beneficial medicine in the nation."
>
> – Robert Butler, M.D.

Not only does exercise help you to relieve stress, it also allows your mind to free itself and to concentrate on attaining workout goals — to run the extra mile, bike at a brisker pace, swim more laps, or to move with the yoga pose more intentionally and in tune with the breath. This focus on goals during exercise trains your mind into attaining goals in your daily life. For those who are less physically active, working in a garden can do the same because gardening involves both physical movement and the attainment of goals — to maintain and build a garden that produces in abundance.

Other benefits of exercise are that it works the physical system, increases the heart rate, triggers faster and deeper breathing, helps detoxify the system, and strengthens muscles and neural connections throughout the body.

When you are breathing deeply your lungs are moving the digestive organs in a way that is similar to giving them a massage. This assists the organs in releasing sediment, waste, and plaque.

The increased heart rate during exercise improves the flow of nutrients traveling through the tissues, while helping to collect and release waste products from the system.

The rise in body temperature experienced during exercise helps to detox the system through sweat, and through the need and ingestion of water to replace the water that is lost — thus helping to flush out toxins and waste products.

When you get regular exercise you are releasing stressful, acidic tensions from your system while you are strengthening bones and muscles.

An alkaline diet prevents acidic conditions. Meat, milk, and eggs promote an acidic condition in the body, and this weakens bones because it triggers the formation of osteoclast cells, which remove calcium from the bones to make the blood more alkaline. A plant-based diet rich in raw fruits, vegetables, and seaweeds promotes an alkaline condition, which strengthens bones because it triggers the production of osteoblasts, which are cells involved in bone growth and strengthening.

The combination of an alkaline diet and daily exercise will tune your body in a way that will benefit other areas of your life. When maintaining a regular exercise schedule with an alkaline diet, you will notice differences in your body, posture, confidence, relationships, and in how you approach tasks.

The advantages you will experience when you improve your levels of nutrition and fitness will prove that it is up to you to improve your life. This philosophy will carry over to how you address other issues in your life that need attention.

Overeating and the Medicine of Weight

Sticking to a fresh food diet, even if you occasionally overeat to try to get the feeling once provided by cooked and/or fried starches and protein, is vastly more healthful than the typical American diet.

When the amount of resources used to produce food are taken into consideration, it is easy to see why some people consider overconsumption to be disrespectful to the environment. Once into the habit of overeating, not only are people wasting their money, time, and health, they are also wasting resources used to produce the food.

> "For every mess of asparagus that you eat, a human back somewhere must ache."
> – Heny Louis Mencken

Overeating and lack of exercise lead to being overweight, which is damaging to the tissues of the body on a microscopic level. Overeating can be so damaging to the body that it can be easy to understand why some people consider it to be a form of self-hate, or self-violence. Putting too much food into your body overworks your system, stressing it and causing it to become less vibrant and more susceptible to degradation, distortion, weakness, and disease. On the other hand, eating just enough healthful foods while maintaining a daily exercise schedule creates a situation in which you are more likely to experience health.

Overeating is often associated with emotions. It is comparable to shoving the emotions down your throat in an attempt to block yourself from feeling them. Unfortunately, most people eat low-quality foods when they are stressed, which doubles the consequences.

Eating may be a natural response to stress because chewing increases serotonin, a natural body chemical that is a mood inhibitor and helps maintain liver health. Seratonin is naturally present in fruits and vegetables. It is also found in the gastrointestinal tract and is stored in the blood platelets. Seratonin is synthesized from substances found in food and the receptors for it are on nerve cells. Low levels of seratonin are associated with anger. Thus, a healthful, balanced live food diet containing plentiful amounts of fresh greens and fruits helps regulate mood and balance emotions. If you aren't eating quality fresh fruits and vegetables your body is also not getting the seratonin it is seeking from foods.

If you are reaching for food to help deal with emotions, select fresh fruits and vegetables, and not junk and processed foods. Sometimes a glass of water will help you deal with stress. Try squeezing lemon into it, or put slices of fennel or cucumber in the water. I know someone who chews on hardy green vegetables when he gets stressed, such as cilantro, parsley, chard, kale, or wild greens. This makes more sense than consuming junk foods.

A balanced diet with adequate, but not an abundance of calories also plays a part in cell health. An explanation of sirtuins and telomeres can help with an understanding of this.

When the mitochondria structure inside every one of your cells is provided with a responsible amount of nutrients, it releases the SIRT3 (sirtuin homologue 3) and SIRT4 (sirtuin homologue 4) enzymes that strengthen the energy of the cells. Under these conditions, on a responsible diet your cells live longer and are more healthful. This is one reason why people who eat a healthful, fresh foods diet and stay active appear younger than those who don't. They are literally biologically younger than people of the same age who eat low-quality foods, consume too many calories, and don't get adequate exercise.

David Sinclair, an assistant professor of pathology at Harvard Medical School, was involved in a study that revealed the presence of the SIRT3 and SIRT4 enzymes and how they protect the cells by preventing the mitochondria from releasing proteins that lead to cell death. This understanding helps to prove that reasonable calorie restriction rather than gluttonous calorie overload is key to health. (This is not to say that I am advocating the false concept of breatharianism, or the total elimination of food, which is something I would never support.)

Sinclair's lab released a number of studies based on the impact of caloric intake on cell health, and the study of sirtuins, which manage cell protein maintenance of intercellular structures. Sinclair's team concluded that low caloric intake rather than high caloric intake activates a cell gene that results in the production of the NAMPT (nicotinamide phosphoribosyltransferase) enzyme that signals for the production of the NAD (nicotinaminde adenine dinucleotide) molecule, which helps to maintain cellular metabolism. It is the increase in the NAD that triggers the SIRT3 and SIRT4 genes to release their enzymes.

The 2009 Nobel Prize in Physiology or Medicine was awarded to three American scientists, Elizabeth Blackburn, Carol Greider, and Jack Szostak, for their landmark work discovering key aspects of how telomeres and telomerase enzymes work in aging, in protecting chromosomes, and in disease mechanisms, including the development of cancer.

Telomeres are repetitive DNA buffer caps on the ends of chromosomes where the DNA molecules carrying genes are packed. The telomeres protect the chromosomes from degradation, which plays a major role in aging and disease prevention. Telomeres also prevent the chromosomes within cells from fusing together. The scientists also identified the enzyme that makes telomere DNA, naming it telomerase. When the cells divide, the telomeres are consumed, but are replenished by the telomerase enzyme, helping to complete the formation of the cell.

Understanding the way telomeres function helps in the understanding of cell life, and the length of human life. Each time the cells replicate, the telomere becomes shorter. Cells from a newborn will replicate nearly 100 times, while cells from an elderly person may replicate only about 25 times. But cancer cells have the ability to maintain their telomerase enzyme activity, which allows the cancer cells to preserve the telomere length on the ends of their chromosomes, and this allows for cancer cells to keep replicating many more times than a normal healthy cell.

People who follow a healthful lifestyle, including a nutritious, plant-based diet, and regular patterns of exercise and sleep, have been found to maintain longer telomeres than those who are lacking in health, through an unhealthful diet and lack of exercise. The length of the telomeres helps to determine how many times a cell can replicate. This is why it is said that those who follow a healthful lifestyle have younger cells, which means that their cells look younger on a microscopic level, and can replicate more times than those who do not lead a healthful lifestyle. In other words, those who take care of themselves are biologically younger when compared to those people of the same age who are leading an unhealthful lifestyle.

Situations found to reduce telomere length include lack of exercise and otherwise lack of adequate stress relief; substance abuse; a diet high in sugar, highly heated fats (such as in fried and sautéed foods), and other low-quality foods; a diet rich in acrylamides and glycotoxins, which are chemicals that form when food is cooked; an acidic diet; a diet lacking in the antioxidants contained in fresh fruits and vegetables; low levels of vitamin D; insulin intolerance; and obesity.

> "The doctor of the future will give no medicine but will interest his patients in the care of the human frame, in diet, and in the cause and prevention of disease."
>
> – Thomas Alva Edison

In 2008 Dr. Dean Ornish of the Preventative Medicine Research Institute in Sausalito, California, cooperated with doctors at the University of California, San Francisco, to conduct a study involving 30 men with low-risk prostate cancer. By placing them on a regular exercise program combined with a diet low in fat and refined sugars but rich in fruits, vegetables, and whole vegan foods, he was able to raise the telomerase enzyme levels in their blood by 29 percent.

A study conducted by researchers at Kings College London with colleagues from New Jersey Medical School and published in the February 2008 edition of the *Archives of Internal Medicine* concluded that exercise may have more to do with longevity than do genes. The study included more than 2,400 volunteers who were twins between the ages of 18 and 81. It found that those twins who were smokers, were overweight, and especially those who engaged in the least amount of exercise had telomeres that were shorter than those of their twin who lived a more healthful lifestyle. The telomeres were especially more prominent in those who remained physically active. When identical twins were studied, it showed that the identical twin that was more active had better telomere length on the chromosomes in their white blood cells. The researchers conclude: "Adults who partake in regular physical activity are biologically younger than sedentary individuals." Dr. Tim Spector of Kings College said, "A sedentary lifestyle appears to have an effect on telomere dynamics — thus providing a powerful message that could be used by clinicians to promote the potentially anti-aging effect of regular exercise."

In other words, you can maintain healthful telomerase enzyme levels and longer telomere caps by engaging in daily exercise, following a plant-based diet, maintaining a regular sleep schedule, a healthful weight, and by not smoking.

It is clear that taking in a healthful amount of calories is key to maintaining healthful weight and energy, and preventing such health situations as diabetes, cancer, organ disorders, and heart disease.

Avoid purchasing foods that would lead you to overeating. If you head to the produce section instead of the snack section, you know you made the right choice.

Many people overeat, or otherwise consume too many calories per day, because they eat before they go to bed. It is good to avoid eating within a few hours before bedtime. That is when the body should be shutting down for the night, and not for the organs to get busy digesting more food. Give your digestive system the rest it needs at night.

If food is desired before bedtime, consider an herbal tea. If cravings persist, snacking on half a piece of fruit, or on cut-up vegetables may help. Avoid getting into the habit of eating before bed. Simply drink water. Also, do mild yoga poses combined with calming visualization techniques to help you relax.

The August 2009 issue of the *Journal of the American Dietetic Association* contained a study conducted by researchers at the Fred Hutchinson Cancer Research Center and the University of Washington. The study found that people who practice yoga are thinner than those who do not. Those who practiced yoga for at least one hour per week were found to have an average body mass index (BMI) of 23.1. Those in the study who didn't practice yoga were found to have an average BMI of 25.8, which is considered overweight. The researchers concluded that those who practice yoga are less likely to overeat, are less likely to overeat when stressed, and are more likely to practice what they called "mindful eating," which is eating only until full. Researchers concluded that the mental focus involved in practicing yoga helps to have more control over eating.

The right choice is your choice, and can make all the difference every time you consider what you are going to eat or how you are going to deal with stress.

The Sunfood Diet

Sunfood is a term that has been used for at least a century. *Sunfoodist* describes someone who follows a mostly uncooked, plant-based, vegan diet that is free of all meat (including beef, pork, chicken, turkey, fish, and crustaceans), dairy (milk, butter, cheese, yogurt, keifer, ice cream, and products containing milk products, including casein and whey protein), and eggs (including any food containing eggs).

In their most natural state, soon after birth humans begin processsing raw, unprocessed food in the form of breast milk. As many people have said, you are already a raw foodist when you are born. As babies grow, they are naturally attracted to fruit, and as all mammals do, they stop breast feeding at a young age. It is only their parents and/or caretakers who introduce them to cooked food. Sadly, many parents today are feeding their children the lowest-quality foods from an early age. Rather than going from breast feeding to whole foods, the children are being fed fried foods, cola drinks, and things saturated with corn syrup, processed salts, MSG, and other ingredients that degrade health.

While babies do best on breast milk, and the human body functions best on a plant-based diet, it is unfortunate that people today eat a variety of low-quality foods, including pasteurized dairy from other animals. Milk is not for adults.

> "The human body has no more need for cows' milk than it does for dogs' milk, horses' milk, or giraffes' milk."
> – Michael Klaper

"A vegetable-based diet for children is generally more healthful than a diet containing the cholesterol, animal fat, and excessive protein found in meat and dairy products. Children and adolescents will get plenty of protein as long as they eat a variety of whole-grains, legumes, vegetables, fruits, and nuts."
– Benjamin Spock

Depending on personal preferences, the Sunfood diet may or may not contain bee products, such as honey, pollen, propolis, and royal jelly. Some people are opposed to consuming bee products because they believe that the bees are gathering food for their own communities, and taking their food is stealing. They also reason that when humans continually remove honey and pollen from a hive, the bees have to work harder to gather more food, which is tantamount to enslaving bees. Also, there are people opposed to consuming bee products because they know that some beekeepers kill wildlife, such as bears, to protect their hives.

If you choose to consume bee products, please seek out the products from beekeepers that don't kill other wildlife.

"Dietary contributors to disease are easily swept aside, as our culture assumes it's normal to be chronically medicated to regulate cholesterol, blood pressure, and blood sugar."
– Neal Barnard

The Sunfood diet promotes the detoxification of the body by unclogging the system through unadulterated, whole foods; rejuvenation of the cellular structure throughout all tissues by providing high-quality nutrients; and refinement of the body, mind, and spirit through nourishing and toning all three as the person tunes in to and flourishes on a higher frequency.

"At the root of all power and motion, there is music and rhythm, the play of patterned frequencies against the matrix of time. We know that every particle in the physical universe takes its characteristics from the pitch and pattern and overtones of its particular frequencies, its singing. Before we make music, music makes us."
– Joachim-Ernst Berendt

The Sunfood diet, combined with daily exercise and intentional, goal-oriented living that utilizes talents and intellect, rearranges the pitch of your being. It clears the garbage from your diet and eliminates the clutter in your body. It improves the communication between cells and the function of your entire system. While you may have been living under a slothful and struggling energy level that was the result of consuming deadening, low-quality, and junk foods, the Sunfood diet energizes you by eliminating the deadening foods and bringing in highly vibrant fresh fruits and vegetables with their living, biophoton-rich frequencies intact.

The Sunfood diet combined with daily exercise makes you biologically younger because it increases the amount of the telomerase enzyme in your blood, allowing the telomeres on your chromosomes to remain structurally longer. Cells containing longer telomeres can reproduce more times, which is what the cells of younger people do. Those who eat a low-quality diet, who do not get adequate exercise, and who are overweight have shorter telomeres on their chromosomes, and their cells divide fewer times, similar to the cells found in elderly persons. Many people who follow the Sunfood diet while staying physically active appear younger compared to people of the same age who are eating an unhealthful diet and who do not exercise, because the people who follow the Sunfood diet are biologically younger.

> "In science the credit goes to the man who convinces the world, not to the man to whom the idea first occurs."
> – William Osler

Obviously people and wildlife have been subsisting on uncooked plant substances forever. Humans are the only creatures on the planet that cook food. While the "Natural Hygiene" movement of the 1830s is often cited as the beginning of modern-day vegetarianism, the current popularity of a strictly or nearly completely raw vegan diet can be attributed to a variety of people throughout history. Some of them include Arnold Ehret, born in Germany in 1866, who wrote *The Mucusless Diet Healing System*, and who made the friendship of Albert Einstein; Max Gerson, born in German Poland in 1881, and who developed Gerson Therapy; Norman Wardhaugh Walker, born to a Scottish couple living in Italy in 1886, who invented the Norwalk Juicer and who wrote several books; Ann Wigmore, born in Lithuania in 1909, who promoted the healing aspects of wheatgrass juice and who wrote several books, including *Recipes for a Longer Life*; a Scottish man named Dugald Semple, who wrote *The Sunfood Way* in 1956; "Aterhov" Arshavir Ter Hovannissian, an Armenian man living in Iran, who wrote *Raw Eating* in the 1960s (which was plagiarized in the 1990s book titled *Nature's First Law: The Raw Food Diet*); and Viktoras Kulvinskas, born in Lithuania in the 1940s, who wrote a number of books, including *Survival into the 21st Century*.

Starting in the 1980s, there have been an increasing number of books about the raw food diet. Some are not of a very good quality, but standards are improving as more people are seeking information about this most healthful way of eating and its association with sustainable living, environmentalism, and the protection of animals.

Each raw foods teacher has his or her own dietary ideals, with some leaning toward a more fruit-based, low fat diet, and others advocating more greens and also "superfoods," such as seaweed powders, medicinal (not hallucinogenic) mushrooms, aloe vera, tropical berries, rare fruits, and high desert foods, such as maca root powder. Some raw food authors also seem more focused on money as they endorse and sell various products, while not always providing the best-quality of information or advice while blatantly promoting themselves as so-called authority figures. Others seem less concerned about selling packaged products while teaching that all you need are what grows out of Earth. Some advocate including raw, grass-fed goats' milk keifer in the diet, and others maintain a vegan diet, or one that includes bee products, but otherwise is vegan. Some include lightly steamed vegetables and simmered vegan soups that include beans but no oil or salt until the soup is in the serving bowl, and others advocate no heated foods whatsoever.

The Living Light Culinary Institute in Fort Bragg, California, has a growing history of being the top raw-food chef training school. It was founded by Cherie Soria, who is the author of *Angel Foods: Healthy Recipes for Heavenly Bodies*, and chief co-author of *Raw Food Revolution Diet.* Many of the world's top chefs have attended the institute, including Chef Ito of Au Lac restaurant in Orange County, California, and Chad Sarno, who has restaurants in England and Europe. Many top raw food restaurants, such as Café Gratitude in San Francisco, employ graduates of Soria's institute. The Hot Chefs Cool Kitchens event is held every year in Fort Bragg, and features many of the most popular sustainable diet authors and educators. (Sign-up for the eletter: RawFoodChef.com)

There are a number of other raw chef training programs, including Matthew Kenney's 105 Degrees in Oklahoma City; Sheridan Hammond's Samudra in Australia; and Angels Healthfood Institute in Oregon. Private chefs also offer raw chef classes. Many raw restaurants also offer chef classes and sminars with guest speakers, such as recipe book authors. Check my book, *Sunfood Traveler*, for more on this topic.

> "Man is the only creature that cooks his food, and he is more subject to disease than any wild creature that dines on unrefined food."
>
> – Dugald Semple

The Most Natural Diet

"People in modern society are going into stores that don't sell real food. They are shopping at supermarkets that sell boxed stuff that is so processed and preserved that it is essentially chemically embalmed. It's not food, it's just stuff. It's not healthful for them, for their spirit, for Earth, or for anything. It's self suicide sustenance."
– Chari Birnholz

Humans experience more diseases than their nonhuman counterparts. Humans also eat a diet that is much more diverse and far removed from the natural diets of animals living in the wild. Consider the connection.

Regionally, humans who follow a certain diet common in their community experience health conditions at rates not seen in regions where that type of diet is not followed. Those living in areas of the world where meat and dairy consumption is highest also have the most elevated rates of heart disease, colon cancer, arthritis, diabetes, certain types of kidney disease, and other diseases not experienced among people living in areas of the world where meat and dairy consumption is lower.

People in North America who consume the most meat are also more likely to consume the most pasteurized dairy, and the most corn syrup, synthetic food chemicals, and processed foods. These are the same people who are most likely to be obese, and who experience maladies common to those who are obese.

"To eat is a necessity, but to eat intelligently is an art."
– François de la Rochefoucauld

As you change your life and become different from what you used to be, you may find yourself getting attention that you had not been accustomed to receiving — including both compliments and perhaps cynical criticism. When people are accustomed to seeing you maintain a certain lifestyle and appear a certain way, and they then see that you have physically transformed, they also may feel uncomfortable. You will be breaking from the role that you had been playing. People will have to recast you in their mind as no longer being the person they thought you were, and maybe the person they thought you could never be.

"You can't turn back the clock. But you can wind it up again."
– Bonnie Prudden

Completely changing your diet to the most healthful way available to you will make a huge difference in many areas of your life. When provided with high-quality nutrition, the body will change to a state in tune with those nutrients. Within the body is an amazing power to heal, to detoxify the cells, to reform the tissues, and to reconfigure the shape of the organs. Providing the body with a diet that largely consists of vibrant, raw fruits and vegetables can fuel this power.

When you become more healthful, people notice. Your skin, shape, and movement change. Your confidence and energy improve. It is then that people may be interested in what you are doing that changed you.

> **In their excellent book, *Raw Food Revolution Diet*, Cherie Soria, Brenda Davis, and Vesanto Melina offer this advice to those with compromised health and who are switching to a raw food diet:**
>
> "Find out about your blood cholesterol, triglyceride, and blood sugar levels. Check your blood pressure and body weight. If you are on prescription medications, make sure that your health care provider knows about your diet plan. You will need to be closely monitored; when people embark on a raw food diet, medications commonly need to be adjusted or stopped completely. This must be done with the approval and assistance of your health care provider. Raw food diets commonly result in weight loss and normalization of blood pressure, blood cholesterol, and blood sugar levels. People who are on medications for high blood pressure, high cholesterol, or type 2 diabetes may notice rapid changes in their condition and their requirements for these medications. Those on insulin or oral hypoglycemic agents need to monitor their blood sugars closely, as blood sugars may drop too low. In this event, your health care provider may choose to prepare a new medication schedule for you. In any case, regular blood sugar monitoring is essential."

As you follow a fresh food diet your life will change. This is especially true if you had been eating devitalized, unhealthful, deadened, fried, and otherwise processed commercial foods. Opportunities will arise that you may never have considered. Things will happen that you didn't think were a possibility, or were not even in your conception of how things could happen. You will find yourself feeling and thinking differently from the way you had been. Your perceptions will change. Foods, music, and designs of things may seem different to you. Activities in which you may never have thought about participating may draw your attention. The way you eat, dress, think, and play, and the general way you participate in life may all go through radical changes. The higher frequency that you tune into by eating more vibrant foods can ignite your passions in intense ways you never thought possible.

"Through our soul is our contact with heaven."
– Sholem Asch

The power of your soul is what formulated your tissues and it is what is animating you. It is making you think. It is making your heart beat and your lungs breathe. It is making your cells function. It is what is making you seek your desires. It is pushing you to constantly work out your thoughts into actions. You can make it work for you. It is your power source. Honor it with rightful living, self-respect, intentional actions, and vibrant foods.

"The brain gives the heart its sight. The heart gives the brain its vision."
– Rob Kall

When you follow a plant-based diet that is rich in raw vegetables and fruits, and is free of fried oils, synthetic chemicals, refined sugars, processed salts, and MSG, the pineal gland, which is located at the center of your brain, functions at a higher level, as does your heart and brain.

Cells of the pineal gland resemble the photoreceptor cells in the eyes. It is known that a low-quality diet leads to degeneration of the eyes. Similarly, low-quality foods interfere with the function of the pineal gland. While the cells of the eyes allow you to see and interact with structures, the cells of the pineal gland allow you to interact with spirit, inspiration, and what motivates you in your visualizations. The pineal gland is not walled off behind the blood brain barrier. It receives large amounts of blood, thus it is directly connected to the function and feelings of the heart. For these reasons, the pineal gland is often referred to as *the third eye*. René Descartes called the pineal gland *the seat of the soul*. When your pineal gland is able to function at a high level, you are more likely to receive inspiration that triggers the use of your true talents and intellect emanating from your spirit.

"When you start using senses you neglected, your reward is to see the world with completely fresh eyes."
– Barbara Sher

A healthful diet and exercise program will get your body, heart, brain, and pineal gland to function at a higher level so that the rest of your life can function at an elevated level. Do not pollute your body with low-quality foods. Do not allow yourself to eat deadened or otherwise processed foods that lower your frequency and leave residues of toxins in your tissues, clogging your system. Follow a diet of high-quality foods that enliven your body, bring about the beauty of health, and improve your level of consciousness. Partake in the living power of Nature that is contained in vibrantly alive, organic foods. Let these ignite your health, intellect, passions, talents, confidence, and love.

> "And the time came when the risk to remain tight in a bud was more painful than the risk it took to blossom."
> – Anais Nin

State of Your Being

> "The pursuit of truth and beauty is a sphere of activity in which we are permitted to remain children all our lives."
> – Albert Einstein

> "Now I truly believe that we in this generation must come to terms with nature, and I think we're challenged, as mankind has never been challenged before, to prove our maturity and our mastery, not of nature but of ourselves."
> – Rachel Carson

Your thoughts lead to actions that create an atmosphere in alignment with what it is you have been thinking.

As you think in a way that is respectful of life, you will begin to be more respectful of your life. You will place more value in the person you truly are, including the intellect, instinct, talents, skills, and other graces you hold.

When you are living the way you want to live, you automatically attract others who are aligned with the energy you are conducting in your mind.

Be willing to be vulnerable, to live, to allow yourself to love, and to free yourself of that which has disallowed you from living your life the way you wish.

In their quest to feel better, many people get lost in the escapism of drugs. What they may not realize is that the drug may be bringing out something that they already have, a mind that is capable of working in a way that makes them feel and live better in alignment with their liking. There are ways to work through their blockages so that they can experience the splendor of life that they are trying to find through drugs.

It isn't only street drugs that people seek out in a hunt to feel better. Consider that in 2006 there was an average of more than one new corporate pharmacy opening in the U.S. every single day. That may give you an idea of how many people are taking prescription drugs to try to improve or maintain some aspect of their health. A large number of these very same people are consuming low-quality foods that lead to a decline in health. In the same way, people who are consuming harsh street drugs are having thoughts that lead to less vibrant health, and often to many levels of horrible health problems.

Many of the so-called "legal" drugs are used in an attempt to feel better in a way that sidesteps ways in which people really will feel better. Instead of improving their diet and relationships, and getting into the practice of daily exercise and goal-oriented living in which they use their intellect and talent, they rely on some form of mass-marketed chemical drug to feel better.

A large number of the drugs people are taking have to do with trying to get to a more comfortable state of mind. Their lives are so off-kilter that they think pills will be some sort of answer to their problems. Perhaps the pills will offer a type of answer. But there is a possibility that they are also cheating themselves by really not changing their lifestyle to become truly healthful.

The body naturally creates substances that alter consciousness. These self-produced, natural psychoactive drugs are manufactured within the cells of the brain and body. Perhaps the most commonly known of these substances is the endorphin peptide that produces the "runner's high" people experience when they exercise regularly. These chemicals that can be produced within the tissues of a healthful person are called *endogenous drugs*. When these drugs are produced, they are received on the receptors of cell membranes, altering the function of the cells. This happens both in the brain and throughout the body, and it involves many millions of chemical reactions throughout the brain and body every minute.

The same type of reaction that endogenous drugs produce can occur when a person takes street or prescription drugs, which are *exogenous drugs*. The synthetic drugs are treated by the body in much the same manner as the drugs the body naturally produces. The drug molecules bind with the receptors on the cell membranes. Over time, the body system can be weakened and damaged by synthetic drugs because the drugs are competing for receptors with which the body's own chemicals dock. When there is an overabundance of chemicals that dock with the cell membrane receptors, the cells may start to produce fewer receptors. The opposite may also be true, wherein the body cells start to produce more receptors to deal with all of the chemicals. Either of these situations can throw the body out of balance, especially when a synthetic drug prevents the body from producing chemicals that naturally dock with cell receptors that also connect with the synthetic chemicals. Addictions and body tissue damage can occur, including in the brain, and within all parts of the body. Use of certain drugs can result in organ malfunction, and even organ failure or death.

The longer a former drug abuser stays away from the substance and follows a healthful diet and exercise program combined with goal-oriented living while working to have healthful relationships, the better their health will be. As the person stops taking the drugs and lives more healthfully, the liver begins to produce a healthful amount of enzymes, and the person's physical and psychological/emotional health improves. Depending on the level of abuse and addiction that was experienced, it can take awhile for the cell structures throughout the body to come back into balance with producing a healthful amount of receptors and peptides.

If you are a person with a history of drug abuse, I strongly encourage you to follow a plant-based diet that is free of fried oils, bleached grains, processed salt, white sugar, corn syrup and other processed sugars, and that is completely free of MSG, artificial dyes, flavors, scents, and sweeteners. I encourage you to follow a diet that contains an abundance and variety of fresh green vegetables along with fresh fruits, sprouts, and some seaweeds. It is also good to include a reasonable amount of raw, unheated, unsalted nuts and seeds that have been soaked in water for a few hours. It is especially good if you become involved in growing some of your own food, and/or get your food from farmers' markets and natural foods stores; follow more of an organic, whole foods diet; get regular daily exercise, especially at the start of your day; and work to stimulate your mind with literature and music, and by practicing your talent, craft, or abilities. The goal is to function completely without the drug stimulation, and allow the body's natural chemistry to come into play.

While some people randomly use drugs for recreational or personal discovery purposes, other people often take and abuse mind-altering substances to deal with issues or situations that they don't feel they can deal with otherwise. These emotions may involve trauma, unhealed relationships, anger, fear, disgust, frustration, sadness, and other such emotions with which we find difficult to cope. In other words, drugs help us to ignore our feelings, remain in denial, and halt personal progression and healing.

What people really need to do is to stop putting artificial food and synthetic drug substances into their bodies, and to eat a more natural diet while getting in shape so their bodies and brains can function better. When your body and brain function better, so too does your life.

It is amazing how much sedation is going on among people in Western society. Many millions of people are taking prescription sedatives that their doctors say will help them. They feel eager or anxious, unable to suppress their urge for something that they can't define. Their body is trying to tell them something, trying to get a message across. But instead of working through and discovering what the message is, they suppress it by using some sort of drug from which pharmaceutical companies are making millions and billions by selling them through toxic stores we call "the drug store," or "the pharmacy."

> "We have become so drug-oriented, that the idea of changing anything just through diet is kind of preposterous to a lot of people. It's almost like old medicine, like a witch doctor."
> – Morgan Spurlock

It has been well documented that doctors often prescribe medications of all varieties without sufficient information on patient health, and without knowing what other drugs a patient may be taking that could counteract the prescription drug, or that may interact with another drug the patient is taking, which might cause the patient to suffer grave consequences. We also don't know how a lot of these prescription drugs react with the variety of synthetic food chemicals found in mass-marketed foods, or with the chemicals after the food has been cooked.

When a person goes to a pharmacy to have a prescription filled, the person they deal with at many drug stores may be an employee with no formal medical training and who may be as young as 16. There is an ongoing problem of misfilled prescriptions resulting in patient injuries, which have led to overdoses, comas, strokes, and deaths. Additionally, many prescription drugs carry serious risks even when taken as directed. Thousands of patients die or suffer horrible consequences after being misdiagnosed, or after taking drugs that are misprescribed. Many more die or are left disabled by surgeries that should never have taken place.

One clue to the level of health wisdom contained in a typical pharmacy store can be seen on the shelves. In the U.S., the pharmacy is often at the back of a large store filled with aisles containing products that are damaging to health. They sell candy, milk chocolate, fried chips, bleached grain snacks, junk foods, sodas, artificial sweeteners, and those certain destroyers of health: cigarettes and brewed and distilled alcohol. What is it that these pharmacies are promoting? It isn't health.

Many people have become so unhealthful because they have been living unhealthful lives on many different levels. They are filled with toxic thoughts, tarnished emotions, and an acidic system fed with low-quality foods that clog the system with junk food residues. They rarely, if ever, get adequate exercise.

An acidic body can be alkalized by a diet that consists largely of unheated leafy greens, green vegetables, sprouts, some sea vegetables, and alkaline fruits. An alkaline diet combined with daily exercise will bring the system more in tune with a higher and more healthful frequency. It is the good part of the high that people strive to experience with drugs.

> "We lift ourselves by our thought. If you want to enlarge your life, you must first enlarge your thought of it and of yourself. Hold the ideal of yourself as you long to be, always everywhere."
> – Orison Swett Marden

To begin being the healthful, satisfied person you wish to be, begin to act the part. Conduct your being in a way that is in alignment with the quality of life that you wish to have. Think in a way that nurtures actions that use your talents to bring you happiness. Carry yourself with an attitude and posture that is of confidence and satisfaction. Follow a diet and exercise regimen that brings about physical health. Communicate in a way that is kind, respectful, clear, nurtures loving relationships, and encourages vigorous growth toward good. Breathe in a way that calms your spirit and mind, but that energizes you to fulfill your intentions. Flow your intentions into your words, hands, feet, and life as you visualize manifesting what you desire to be.

This may all sound pleasant and nice, but you also have to live in the community of humans who surround you and with whom you must interact. However, you may be surprised at how people respond to you when you carry yourself in a way that is intentionally focused on improving and becoming part of the solution. Not allowing the emotions and drama of others to control your thought patterns, or to affect your state of being, can build confidence and respect both within yourself and within others. Staying focused when others are experiencing emotional upset can bring a spirit of dignity into any situation.

> "Each person has inside a basic decency and goodness. If he listens to it and acts on it, he is giving a great deal of what it is the world needs most. It is not complicated but it takes courage. It takes

courage for a person to listen to his own goodness and act on it."
– Pablo Casals

You are worthy of vibrant health. You are worthy of love. Your intellect and talents are worthy of being developed and used. Your life and the lives of those around you are worthy of being respected and nurtured. You deserve and are capable of maintaining a healthful diet and of working to improve all areas of your life.

> "Never forget the importance of living with unbridled exhilaration. Never neglect to see the exquisite beauty in all living things. Today, and this very moment, is a gift. Stay focused on your purpose."
> – Robin Sharma

Whatever you do, do it well. Be the best in whatever it is you choose to be. Wherever you are and whatever you are doing, work to bring out your best qualities.

> "Start by doing what's necessary; then do what's possible; and suddenly you are doing the impossible."
> – St. Francis of Assisi

Do whatever it takes to self-coach your transition into a vibrant life.

Feed your mind with intellectually stimulating information that nurtures your life to become better. Feed your body with a biophoton-rich fresh plant-based diet that will generate stronger intercellular vibrations. Have faith in the power of your mind, in the power of your diet, in the power of daily exercise, in the power of intentional, goal-oriented living, and in the power of tuning into the frequency of Nature.

> "There is a basic law that like attracts like. Negative-thinking definitely attracts negative results. Conversely, if a person habitually thinks optimistically and hopefully his positive-thinking sets in motion creative forces — and success instead of eluding him flows toward him."
> – Norman Vincent Peale

Believe in the power of your intellect and talents. Believe that you can use them to formulate your life the way you would like it to be. You can do this in the same way that your spirit formed your physical structure. This power can be accessed by rejecting the unspiritual and by doing away with non-nurturing thoughts, non-nutritious foods, and activities that waste your time, energy, resources, health, and love.

Become a being in tune with vibrant health.

"Keep your dreams alive. Understand to achieve anything requires faith and belief in yourself, vision, hard work, determination, and dedication. Remember all things are possible for those who believe."

– Gail Devers

"Life is a gift of nature; but beautiful living is the gift of wisdom."

– Greek adage

The Self Revolution

"A great revolution in just one single individual will help achieve a change in the destiny of a society and, further, will enable a change in the destiny of humankind."

– Daisaku Ikeda

"It is indulgent to sink down into states in which your own vibration and healing power is diminished. With it, your own capacity to act with exuberance, vitality, creativity, and passion and joy is also drained. What is needed is for a lot of us to become more fully alive."

– John Robbins

"I am only one; but still I am one. I cannot do everything, but still I can do something; I will not refuse to do something I can do."

– Helen Keller

We are all playing a role here on Earth. Some are aware of this. Some are not. Some people seem to be completely unaware of their power, and glide through life taking care of only the bare necessities. Some people work to participate in a way that uplifts others. Some people work in a selfish way by doing nothing for anyone while living selfishly and unsustainably. Some people bring down others through demeaning and undermining words and actions. But selfishness is even more destructive than being self-serving; it works against the person, and against everyone. The opposite of being selfish is being selfless, being so engaged in generating good and helpful things that there is no room for anything else.

> "Life is a gift, and it offers us the privilege, opportunity, and responsibility to give something back by becoming more.
> – Anthony Robbins

When we do what is naturally good for us, by keeping ourselves healthful through a plant-based diet; by keeping ourselves fit through daily exercise; by keeping our thoughts focused on improvement; by using our intellect and practicing our natural talents and abilities; by choosing to live more sustainably; and by working to protect the planet and animals, we are doing what is good for all, and are not living selfishly.

> "Happiness depends, as Nature shows, less on exterior things than most suppose."
> – William Cowper

> "The best things in life aren't things."
> – Art Buchwald

Selfish behavior involves having the biggest, and so-called "best," and living by the false concept of competition. It is likely that we all know someone who works to have the biggest, the most, and more than anyone else. That game of "he who has the most toys wins" tells its own story. If anything, the people who are obsessed with being wealthy are likely to carry a specific lack of satisfaction, or even a particular kind of sadness. Being caught up in accumulating and hoarding all that could possibly be gathered is likely to be more of a spiritually disintegrating indulgence than anything that ever benefits the person, or anyone else.

> "It all depends on whether you have things, or they have you."
> – Robert Cook

Just as drugs, alcohol, and poverty can distort a person's view of life, so can wealth. The whole concept that wealth equals happiness is a distortion. Some people place so much focus on wealth, on getting wealthy, and on projecting the image of being wealthy, that it is practically their religion. This is all so telling in a day when the banks and governments controlling money are in buildings resembling temples.

In ancient times, the larger buildings were for ceremonial purposes to honor life and Divinity. In today's commercial society, the stores are the larger buildings, and it seems that buying stuff and accumulating things to replicate images presented in corporate advertising has taken the place of living simple, honorable, respectful lives. In doing so, people have lost touch with their instinct, intellect, spirit, and their very nature.

> "The whole culture is one unified field of bought, sold, market researched everything. It used to be that people fermented their own culture. It took hundreds of years and it evolved over time. That's gone in America. People now don't have any concept that there ever was a culture outside this thing that's created to make money. Whatever is the biggest, latest thing, they're into it. You just get disgusted after a while for not having more of a kind of like intellectual curiosity about what's behind all this jive bullshit."
> – Robert Dennis Crumb

Large numbers of people today are leading spiritually impotent lives in which they have given up their hope and replaced it with monetary desires. Many have also given up their goals and lead lives in which they rely on surrogates of TV show personalities to define their desired successes. Instead of practicing their talents or being engaged in hobby, in craft, or in volunteering for worthwhile causes, people spend their time watching TV, playing screen games, and shopping for things. The items they accumulate are a congealment of their wasted energy that could have been spent doing something worthwhile for the planet. Their strongest belief appears to be one of trusting in the words and seductive distortions of advertising. The people they know most about are the delusionally self-important celebrities on whom the media focuses. A growing number of people are most engaged in is working to pay off debts created by replicating commercial imagery, an activity that produces a life of waste and absolute nonsense.

> "The more we accumulate wealth, the more it leads to a breakdown of community."
> – Mark Boyle

Riding my bike one day I was shouted at by a man driving alone in a big SUV. He told me that I should stay off the road. I was riding on the part of the road marked as a bike path. But that didn't appear good enough for him. It was as if he believed that he had more rights than I because he was driving a gas-guzzling monstrosity likely owned by a finance company. Many of the very same type of people are working at jobs they dislike, but which they need if they are to pay off the parasitic debts they have allowed themselves to accumulate, and the largest part of their days are spent counting the minutes before they can go home for the day. Their jobs do not nurture them, their deadened and processed diets do not give them nutrition, many of their relationships are as shallow as skin, and their lives do not fulfill them. Everything that dissatisfies them is the other person's fault. Personal responsibility for the state of degradation they are lost in is a concept not under consideration as they are too busy working to appear hip and cool, as if they are still working to be the center of attention at the high school dance.

> "Know thyself? If I knew myself, I'd run away."
> – Johann Wolfgang von Goethe

An astounding number of people are caught up in the image parade. They have become lost in the concept that the accumulation of the latest trendy things validates their lives. They fit in with the others who have conformed to the advertising imagery. Many of them have gone into debt to maintain the façade. Their lives are inauthentic and they have become lost in the power of greed and covetousness. They've bought into and have become slaves to the corporate system. They keep buying things and buying things, but seem to lack an understanding that nothing they own or purchase can fill the void of a life in which their most beneficial qualities are being ignored to the point of atrophy.

> "Realize that true happiness lies within you. Waste no time and effort searching for peace and contentment and joy in the world outside. Remember that there is no happiness in having or in getting, but only in giving. Reach out. Share. Smile. Hug."
> – Og Mandino

> "To do more for the world than the world does for you. That is success."
> – Henry Ford

No matter our financial status, we all have abilities, talents, and intellect that can bring us to participate in improving our situation, and in being a part of the solution to the issues facing us.

The more natural way in which we live, the more naturally our natural instincts will become pronounced in the way we live. As we do so we become closer to the way we are naturally meant to live: more in tune with Nature.

"It is not God's will merely that we should be happy, but that we should make ourselves happy."
– Immanuel Kant

"Happiness is a continuous creative activity."
– Baba Amte

"If you want your life to be a magnificent story, then begin by realizing that you are the author and everyday you have the opportunity to write a new page."
– Mark Houlahan

We all are capable in some manner of uplifting our lives as well as the lives of others; capable of achieving something good; and capable of learning from and using the substances and energies to gain the knowledge we need to improve our situation. All we have to do is tune into this process and act on it.

"The heart is the chief feature of a functioning mind."
– Frank Lloyd Wright

"If you expect the best, you will be the best. Learn to use one of the most powerful laws in this world; change your mental habits to belief instead of disbelief. Learn to expect, not to doubt. In so doing, you bring everything into the realm of possibility."
– Norman Vincent Peale

I believe that everyone is capable of participating in a lifestyle that is more respectful to the web of life on Earth than the less respectful way many of us have been living. I also believe that like seeds, thoughts create after their own kind. In this way, the more that people are active in thinking and working toward living in a natural way, the more it helps others to live naturally. By doing more naturally we are truly showing kindness to and love for our fellow beings, for Earth, and for ourselves.

"Don't ask what the world needs. Ask what makes you come alive, and go do it. Because what the world needs is people who have come alive."
– Howard Thurman

"He who lives in harmony with himself lives in harmony with the universe."
– Marcus Aurelius

Many people speak of a feeling within themselves that they know has something to do with what they desire to be doing. They may not know what it is, and they may fluctuate in life not knowing how to satisfy this feeling. But once they find its meaning, it is powerful and drives them to focus on accomplishing what they feel they should be doing. But I don't think it is necessarily one thing that most people can do or feel satisfied in doing. It can be a variety of things within a range of a certain occupation, talent, skill, ability, hobby, craft, or interest.

> "Every decision you make — every decision — is not a decision about what to do. It's a decision about who you are. When you see this, when you understand it, everything changes. You begin to see life in a new way. All events, occurrences, and situations turn into opportunities to do what you came here to do."
> – Neale Donald Walsch

> "If you don't live it, it won't come out of your horn."
> – Charlie Parker

Some people get caught up in trying to find the meaning to their life by focusing on things outside themselves. Perhaps they would be better off to simply start living their life with intention driving their talents and passions to accomplish set goals, then they will find their lives inside themselves.

> "I've come to believe that each of us has a personal calling that's as unique as a fingerprint — and that the best way to succeed is to discover what you love and then find a way to offer it to others in the form of service, working hard, and also allowing the energy of the universe to lead you."
> – Oprah Winfrey

Instead of listening to discouragement, listen to encouragement. As you do so, you will realize the value of each, and that encouragement is the more helpful, valuable, worthwhile, and powerful of the two.

The world is full of discouragement, which stumbles many on their way to otherwise succeed at using their intellect, in practicing their talents, in exercising their skills, and in loving those around them.

> "Creativity is a flower that praise brings to bloom, but discouragement often nips in the bud."
> – Alex F. Osborn

"My mother has always been unhappy with what I do. She would much rather I do something nice, like be a bricklayer.
– Mick Jagger

Much of the discouragement you experience may come directly from the people who should be encouraging you the most. Some of this may be that they are afraid you are wasting your time, and they believe you should be looking to succeed at something else. Or they may think that you are incapable of succeeding at anything, which may be a case of not believing in their own power, and could be a display of their devalued self-worth. It may have something to do with their refusal to open their mind to the possibilities and beauty of life. It may have to do with their wanting you to remain playing the same role they are accustomed to seeing you play, which may allow them to carry on certain low-grade behaviors — thus using you as their enabler. This may be because they are typically underminers, takers, users, and abusers.

The discouraging words of others have more to do with what they have been fed in their lives, and with what is going on in their minds, and less to do with who you are.

"Only by having faith in ourselves can we be faithful to others."
– Erich Fromm

Listening to discouragement, including from others and from ourselves, may have to do with not wanting to go outside our familiar comfort zones, but perhaps our comfort zones are the things that are making us uncomfortable.

"It takes a lot of courage to release the familiar and seemingly secure, to embrace the new. But there is no real security in what is no longer meaningful. There is more security in the adventurous and exciting, for in movement there is life, and in change there is power."
– Alan Cohen

In any situation all you can do is believe in your power and take action to manifest that power through intentional planning, actions, and success.

"If we did the things we are capable of, we would astound ourselves."
– Thomas Alva Edison

You may talk about leading a better life, and talking about it can make a lot of noise. But sitting around talking about it can also squander a lot of the energy that would be more helpful for you to spend on accomplishing your goals.

Perhaps it is time to cast yourself in a new role with a whole new cast of supporting characters.

> "Don't be afraid to take a big step when one is indicated. You can't cross a chasm in two small jumps."
> – Richard Buckminster Fuller

> "Every worthwhile accomplishment has a price tag attached to it. The question is always whether you are willing to pay the price to attain it — in hard work, sacrifice, patience, faith, and endurance."
> – John C. Maxwell

People may not be able to believe in your words, but they sure can believe in your accomplishments. Don't waste your time in explaining to others that you are capable of doing something; it is always more empowering to go out and accomplish your goals. Then you will recognize that you are capable of accomplishment. It is through your accomplishments that you will feel satisfaction, and you can allow yourself to feel and enjoy it regardless of the response, or lack thereof, that you get from those around you.

> "Every production of genius must be the production of enthusiasm."
> – Benjamin Disraeli

If the people around you are not providing you with the encouragement you need to hear, use your own encouraging thoughts and goal setting to motivate your actions. And do so every day, with clarity and intention, starting at the moment you awake.

If you want to hear encouraging words from others, perhaps what you will find helpful is to encourage them. The energy of this will likely produce more of the same.

> "Most people live, whether physically, intellectually or morally, in a very restricted circle of their potential being. They make very small use of their possible consciousness, and of their soul's resources in general, much like a man who, out of his whole bodily

organism, should get into a habit of using and moving only his little finger."

– William James

People who are catering to a healthful mind will be constantly working to improve their situation without degrading their family, friends, co-workers, neighbors, associates, or acquaintances. They will dwell in an energy that is both nurturing to them while also being encouraging and uplifting to those with whom they interact.

"To accomplish great things, we must not only act but also dream, not only plan but also believe."

– Anatole France

There is power in knowing you have talents and abilities you can use to improve your life. There is power in recognizing your spiritual essence that can guide you toward doing what is right for you. There is power in creating motivational thoughts in your mind that trigger goal-setting and intentional actions of self-improvement. There is inspiration to be had by succeeding at taking actions that turn your goals into accomplishments.

"Change and growth take place when a person has risked himself and dares to become involved with experimenting with his own life."

– Herbert Otto

Everyone has a spiritual tool that helps them realize when they are spending their time and energy wisely. While some people may choose to ignore this, they still have it. Recognizing it and using it to guide you to do what is right is a very good thing. The tool may be best described as your inner compass. It is controlled by an invisible field of energy that has formulated your physical structure, and with which you can connect for creating the thoughts leading to the actions that build the life you desire.

"The mind should dance with the body, and the whole universe is your stage. Try to feel that whatever you are doing is the most beautiful thing, the prettiest dance, because you are dancing with the whole universe. Don't resent anything. Let your heart guide you, free of all regimentation."

– Yogi Bhajan

If you are not actively working toward improving your life, you either are stagnant, are stumbling, or are going backward.

"One's destination is never a place, but a new way of seeing things."
– Henry Miller

"Life is a pilgrimage. The wise man does not rest by the roadside inns. He marches direct to the illimitable domain of eternal bliss, his ultimate destination."
– Oscar Wilde

You can start today to use all the tools naturally available to you for improving your life. This includes writing down your goals and making a priority list to work out how you are going to make your goals come true. It involves eating healthfully, exercising daily, communicating helpfully, organizing and detoxifying your life, and approaching your life with thoughts of intention that drive your actions to improve your self.

"Victory is won not in miles but in inches. Win a little now, hold your ground, and later win a little more."
– Louis L'Amour

One of the key ways to improve your life is to do what comes naturally in regard to your talents and abilities. Figure out, recognize, and work with what comes naturally to you.

"There are only 3 colors, 10 digits, and 7 notes; it's what we do with them that's important."
– Ruth Ross

If you are not constructing your life with what comes naturally to you, you are out of harmony with your spirit — and you likely have a strong feeling that this is happening. This shows up in frustration, in dissatisfaction, in regret, in depression, in choosing low-quality foods, in dysfunctional and damaged relationships, in lack of love, and perhaps as anger and misspoken thoughts, and in a life that is unfulfilling.

"A thought is an act of creation. It is what we are here for, to create, to bring into being ourself by means of thinking."
– Marcel Vogel

"I like projecting positivity. I believe that we are all fields of energy and you have the choice whether to be a positive or negative field of energy. I know that sounds hippie-ish but it's what I believe fundamentally. So you could be a bag of toxicity, or you could be a happy, good person that spreads joy. I believe in spreading joy."
– Drew Barrymore

Nurture your life with good things. Recognize that you are worthy and capable of improving your life. Work with visualization techniques to understand what you want and how to get it. Keep a journal to help you build and journey toward a better life. Act daily to achieve your list of goals. Adjust your standards to those that will bring about satisfaction. Allow yourself to be inspired. Build your life by using your intellect, talents, abilities, and energy to work for you. Surround yourself and associate yourself with the sounds, literature, food, actions, and people that will work to uplift you and propel you into a better life. Experience joy, respect, satisfaction, kindness, and love in your life. Let this be your normal comfort zone.

"Books are the carriers of civilization. Without books, history is silent, literature dumb, science crippled, thought and speculation at a standstill."
– Barbara Tuchman

"Education is not the piling on of learning, information, data, facts, skills, or abilities — that's training or instruction — but is rather making visible what is hidden as a seed."
– Thomas Moore

Read books that motivate and teach you. Listen to the music that inspires you. Plant the thoughts in your mind that activate positive change. Put in what you want to get out. Create a piloting consciousness that glides you toward realizing the goals you set.

"Nobody can go back and start a new beginning, but anyone can start today and make a new ending."
– Maria Robinson

"Every moment of every day we can bring this consciousness to our choices about our money, our time and our talents to take a stand for what we believe in."
– Lynne Twist

Be brave in taking control of your talents and intellect. Take command of what you think about and what you do. Force yourself to prosper in ways that bring about health and happiness at levels you had not experienced.

> "Things may come to those who wait, but only the things left by those who hustle."
> – Abraham Lincoln

> "If there is one thing I say to those who use me as their example, it's that if you ever get a second chance in life, you've got to go all the way."
> – Lance Armstrong

Improving your life can become so desirable to you that it will be the driving force behind self-discipline. Your desire can become stronger as you learn the benefits of working to create satisfaction. You will be willing to pay the price of living healthfully. The fee is giving up unhealthful foods and activities while living intentionally. It will be a fee well spent.

> "Happiness is the meaning and the purpose of life, the whole aim and end of human existence."
> – Aristotle

Work to change your life while believing that you can do it. Conceptualize and know that your mindpower, talents, and what you can teach yourself through study can bring about the changes you like. Bring all the useful tools into your life to make the changes in tune with what you desire. Improve your learning. Improve your way of thinking. Improve your diet. Improve your physical structure. Improve your atmosphere. Improve the way you spend your time. Improve the way you think of yourself as well as the way you think of others. Believe in your power and that you can shape your future into one of brilliant health, sustainable living, and satisfaction.

> "Live with intention. Walk to the edge. Listen hard. Practice wellness. Play with abandon. Laugh. Choose with no regret. Appreciate your friends. Continue to learn. Do what you love. Live as if this is all there is."
> – Mary Ann Radmacher

Do away with negative-thinking. Dispose of unkind words. Avoid slander. Conquer any tendencies that prevent you from organizing your life into the best it can be. Communicate better with those around you. Build a nurturing environment that propagates health, respect, kindness, and love.

> "Kindness is more important than wisdom, and the recognition of this is the beginning of wisdom."
> – Theodore Isaac Rubin

Refuse to detach from your strengths. Continually take action to propel yourself forward toward happiness. Respond in the direction of health and command through your thoughts, actions, and food choices that health be present in your life.

> "The height of your accomplishments will equal the depth of your convictions."
> – William F. Scolavino

> "It's time for greatness — not for greed. It's a time for idealism — not ideology. It is a time not just for compassionate words, but compassionate action."
> – Marian Wright Edelman

Think, visualize, plan, act, live, grow, and love toward the solution.

Provide the terrain and atmosphere, the illumination and the enlightenment, the nutrients and the activity, and the intention and drive for a better life.

Commit to breaking the limits under which you previously lived. Realize that your limits may have been of your making as you dwelled in a lack of faith in your abilities, talents, and intellect, and especially in a lack in your power of love.

> "Our thoughts, our feelings, our dreams, our ideas are physical in the universe. If we dream something, if we picture something, if we commit ourselves to it — that is a physical thrust towards realization that we can put into the universe."
> – Will Smith

Choose to be around people who believe in you, nurture you, and uplift you. Choose to listen to things, read things, and have things around you that inspire you. Organize your surroundings so they better suit what you want. Make these all play a part in your success.

Dip into the ether of your life, your spirit, to settle your mind and place yourself more in tune with your talents, and with what you can achieve in your life.

Make yourself into an instrument that will weave the fabric of your existence into a beautiful symphony in tune with Nature, health, and spiritual awareness.

> "Health is a state of complete physical, mental, and social well-being and not merely the absence of disease or infirmity."
> – World Health Organization

> "In terms of being late or not starting at all, then it's never too late."
> – Alison Headley

Begin right now to respect your life. Do it by refusing to allow junk foods and damaging substances into your system. Do it by allowing your body to begin detoxifying the residues from the unhealthful foods you have eaten. Do it by recognizing that you are an amazing and beautiful being. Do it by showing that your life has value. Do it by allowing yourself to become more healthful. Do it by following a high-quality plant-based diet. Start right now to visualize the power of Nature and nutrients of those biophoton-rich living foods streaming through all the cells that make up your physical being and infusing you with health as you engage in goal-oriented activities.

> "Do the things you want to see."
> – Russell Simmons

> "Fear is what prevents the flowering of the mind."
> – Jiddu Krishnamurti

Know that you are worthy of love. Understand that you should continually live accompanied by love and not by fear. Know that love is the strongest power on, in, and through the universe. Rule and blossom your life by and through love.

> "When we are motivated by goals that have deep meaning, by dreams that need completion, by pure love that needs expressing — then we truly live life."
> – Greg Anderson

Focusing a magnifying glass to project light onto paper can start the paper on fire. Focusing your mind on what you want can enliven your powers to transform your situation.

You are magnetically drawn to what you desire and what best suits you in alignment with your spirit.

When your focus utilizes the magnetic powers of your talents, intellect, instinct, skills, experience, essence, and love, you will be igniting your life.

"Be happy. It's one way of being wise."
– Sidonie-Gabrielle Colette

"Personal transformation can and does have global affects. As we go, so goes the world, for the world is us. The revolution that will save the world is ultimately a personal one."
– Marianne Williamson

Make every day noble with the elegance of your spirit.
Become fluent in the language of the love within your heart.
Begin it now.

"There is no moment of delight in any pilgrimage like the beginning of it."
– Charles Dudley Warner

"We live in a wonderful world that is full of beauty, charm and adventure. There is no end to the adventures that we can have if only we seek them with our eyes open."
– Jawaharlal Nehru

"Start living now. Stop saving the good china for that special occasion. Stop withholding your love until that special person materializes. Every day you are alive is a special occasion. Every minute, every breath, is a gift from God."
– Mary Manin Morrisse

"When you reach the heart of life, you shall find beauty in all things."
– Kahlil Gibran

The Symphony of Self

"The world is not to be put in order; the world is order incarnate. It is for us to harmonize with this order."
– Henry Miller

Body: soft (skin, muscles, fascia, tendons, eyes, nerves, brain, and other organs), hard (bones and teeth), and liquid (blood, lymph, cerebrospinal, respiratory, digestive, and reproductive fluids).

Feed your body with high-quality food consisting of a variety of raw plant substances, preferably some from your own garden; with natural water; with exercise that strengthens and relieves stress and maintains muscle and bone structures; with healing touch, and by keeping your mind and spirit healthful. Maintain a regular sleeping pattern. By doing these things you will have a more prominent base of the telomerase enzyme in the blood, which helps to maintain longer telomeres on your chromosomes, keeping your cells young.

Mind: mental, emotional, intellect, talents, craft, skills, and passions.

Feed your mind with positive thoughts and by managing your emotions; developing your talents, working with your passions in ways that uplift and edify; and keeping your body and spirit healthful through high-quality food, exercise, information, relationships, and intentions.

Energy: electrical charge being created within, entering, emanating from, and passing through you.

Feed your energy by generating positive and proactive intentional thoughts, and by creating a healthful environment that nurtures and protects wildlife and Nature. Stimulate your intellect with learning and reading, and by practicing your talents, skills, and abilities. Stay physically active through daily exercise. Consume raw, organic plant substances, which are rich in antioxidants and the light nutrients, biophotons.

Spirit: vibrational essence of being, instinct, infinite intelligence, and love.

Feed your spirit by practicing kindness and love, and by keeping a healthful body and mind through a fresh food diet, through daily exercise, through intellectual stimulation, through uplifting relationships, through using your talents, and through living intentionally. Associate with people and activities that strengthen your resolve to live true to your talents and intellect by using the power of Nature fueling you.

Community: all that is in and surrounds you.

Feed it by nurturing good things to happen; by working toward living a sustainable lifestyle; by following a natural, plant-based diet; by planting some of your own food; by composting your kitchen scraps; by supporting local organic farmers; by being involved with restoring forests, rivers, lands, and natural habitat; by planting native plants; by protecting wildlands and wildlife; and by working with your talent and craft to bring about an enlightened culture.

"Love abhors waste, especially waste of human potential."
– Leo Buscaglia

"Man's main task in life is to give birth to himself."
– Erich Fromm

"Once you have flown, you will walk the earth with your eyes turned skyward; for there you have been, there you long to return."
– Leonardo Da Vinci

"I am a little pencil in the hand of God who is writing a love letter to the world."
– Mother Teresa

Wherever you are there is an opportunity for directing the change you want to see.

Do not concern yourself with gaining the honor and respect of other people. Work from within to be honorable and respectable. The true respect and real honor comes from within.

Be your potential.

"What is a soul? It's like electricity - we don't really know what it is, but it's a force that can light a room."
– Ray Charles

"If you concentrate on yourself, you can change the world."
– Victoria Boutenko

Igniting Your Life Points of Intention

Inspire yourself to live your intellect and to express your talents, manifesting your spirit, refusing to be conquered by the bombardment of what you may have allowed to beat you down.

> "There are some people who live in a dream world, and there are some who face reality; and then there are those who turn one into the other."
> – Douglas Everett

> "As an irrigator guides water to his fields, as an archer aims an arrow, as a carpenter carves wood, the wise shape their lives."
> – Buddha

The subconscious mind tends to connect more with words that are written in longhand rather than typed out on a computer.

Using pen and paper, write down some notes in relation to the following points. Pay special mind to defining how you can make each point take place or become present in your life.

1. Connect with your intellect and talents. Your essence is there.

2. Live with purpose.

3. Make a strategic short list of goals. Read and adjust it every morning to align your intention.

4. Write an intentional statement every morning declaring what you will focus on.

5. Organize and unclutter your living environment.

6. Break a sweat every day through exercise, preferably in the morning.

7. Read or re-read at least one book every month that will help fuel personal growth.

8. Spend little, accumulate less, shop less, and save more.

9. State no untrue, slanderous, exaggerated, backbiting, undermining, or unfounded comments that would contribute to pain, fear, dishonor, or troubles in the lives of others, or of yourself.

10. Be inspired and inspiring, uplifted and uplifting, loving and lovable.

11. Do not buy into other people's self-created drama.

12. Live your own truth.

13. Do not participate in the myth and false concept of competition. There is no competition.

14. Do not participate in self-hate, self-sabotage, and other self-deceiving thoughts.

15. Do not dwell in victimhood or blame. Don't get stuck in the past. Focus on the present. Choose and work toward your future.

16. Forgive, let go, and move on with your life, away from your past, and into your future. No matter what happened, it is past.

17. Finish projects and experience satisfaction.

18. Eat a variety of locally grown organic live foods, especially green vegetables. Check out CenterForFoodSafety.org.

18. Grow some of your own food.

20. Refrain from purchasing or consuming junk food, fast food, fried food, foods that contain white sugar, corn syrup, processed salt, MSG, or synthetic chemicals, including dyes, flavors, scents, and preservatives.

21. Explore some of the raw and vegan books, such as Cherie Soria's *Raw Food Revolution Diet*, and the recipe book by Terces Engelhart and Orchid of Café Gratitude, *I Are Grateful.* Also reference *The Complete Book of Raw Foods*, which contains recipes from a number of chefs. Read John Robbins' *The Food Revolution* and Howard Lyman's *No More Bull.* For atheletic performance, read *Thrive Diet*, by Brendan Brazier, and Douglas Graham's *80/10/10 Diet.* Read *Becoming Raw* by Vesanto and Melina. And my books, *Sunfood Traveler: Guide to Raw Food Culture*, and *Sunfood Diet Infusion.*

22. Plant at least 12 locally native trees and a variety of native flowering plants someplace in the surrounding region every year. And/or donate to organizations involved in doing the same. Earth needs more trees.

23. Work to protect wildlife and to restore its habitat. Support environmental and wildlife protection organizations. Consider the Natural Resources Defense Council, Earth Island Institute, Earth First, and the Green World Campaign.

24. Live a more environmentally sustainable life. Study up on permaculture and Food Not Lawns.

25. The most important part of the planet is right where you are living. What will you do to improve it?

26. Visualize your life the way you want it to be. Then live toward that image.

27. Ask yourself: What would love do if love were the only power fueling your life?

> "Be yourself. Everyone else is already taken."
> – Oscar Wilde

> "I don't care what color you are, what sexual orientation you are, what nationality, what religion you are – if you operate out of a place of love, that's a family."
> – Sandra Bullock

> "I have a personal philosophy in life: kindness begets kindness."
> – Drew Johnson

> "Be kind, for everyone you meet is fighting a hard battle."
> – Philo Judaeus

> "If you want others to be happy, practice compassion. If you want to be happy, practice compassion."
> – Dalai Lama

> "Let it never be said that I was silent when they needed me."
> – William Wilberforce

> "When it comes to living your purpose, every day is the day, every time is the time, and everywhere is the place."
> – Harley "Durianrider" Johnstone

Glossary of Names

A: Glossary of names

B: Glossary of names

C: Glossary of names

D: Glossary of names

E: Glossary of names

F: Glossary of names

G: Glossary of names

H: Glossary of names

I: Glossary of names

J: Glossary of names

K: Glossary of names

L: Glossary of names

M: Glossary of names

N: Glossary of names

O: Glossary of names

P: Glossary of names

Q: Glossary of names

R: Glossary of names

S: Glossary of names

T: Glossary of names

U: Glossary of names

V: Glossary of names

W: Glossary of names

Y: Glossary of names

Z: Glossary of names

INDEX and TOPICAL GUIDE

A: Index and Topical Guide

B: Index and Topical Guide

C: Index and Topical Guide

D: Index and Topical Guide

E: Index and Topical Guide

F: Index and Topical Guide

G: Index and Topical Guide

H: Index and Topical Guide

I: Index and Topical Guide

J: Index and Topical Guide

K: Index and Topical Guide

L: Index and Topical Guide

M: Index and Topical Guide

N: Index and Topical Guide

O: Index and Topical Guide

P: Index and Topical Guide

Q: Index and Topical Guide

R: Index and Topical Guide

S: Index and Topical Guide

T: Index and Topical Guide

U: Index and Topical Guide

V: Index and Topical Guide

W: Index and Topical Guide

X: Index and Topical Guide

Y: Index and Topical Guide

Z: Index and Topical Guide

About the Author

"I've lost track of the number of people who want to be writers but never actually write anything. Talking about writing, dreaming about writing, can be very fun, but it won't get a book written. You've got to write."
– Laurell K. Hamilton

"I do not have superior intelligence or faultless looks. I do not captivate a room or run a mile in under six minutes. I only succeeded because I was still working after everyone else went to sleep."
– Greg Evans

"What is in my heart must come out, so I write it down."
– Ludwig Van Beethoven

"For business reasons, I must preserve the outward sign of sanity."
– Mark Twain

John McCabe's first book was *Surgery Electives: What to Know Before the Doctor Operates*. First published in 1994, and now out of print, it was an exposé of the financial ties of the medical school, hospital, pharmaceutical, and health insurance industries whose unethical business practices result in the deaths of tens of thousands of people in the U.S. every year. The book was endorsed by some congresspersons and by all of the patients' rights groups in North America.

McCabe also wrote a similar book specific for those considering cosmetic surgery. *Plastic Surgery Hopscotch* was published in 1995 and detailed many of the risks involved with the various surgeries, and in dealing with the medical industry in general.

In 2007 McCabe's *Sunfood Living: Resource Guide to Global Health* was published as a companion book to David Wolfe's *The Sunfood Diet Success System*. McCabe did research for and had helped compose the first edition of *The Sunfood Diet Success System*. He worked as a content and research editor to overhaul the manuscript for the succeeding five revised editions. He did the same on the first two editions of Wolfe's book *Eating for Beauty*.

In the 1990s, McCabe overhauled the manuscript of a book titled *Nature's First Law: The Raw Food Diet*, for its second edition. Wolfe and two co-authors were presenting this irreverent book as an original work.

However, McCabe did not know until 2007 that the material in it was largely plagiarized from a book titled *Raw Eating*, which was written by an Armenian man, "Aterhov" Arshavir Ter Hovannissian, living in Iran in the 1960s.

McCabe was the ghost co-author on Frederic Patenaude's recipe book, *Sunfood Cuisine*, which is out of print.

McCabe is also the author of the reference book *Sunfood Traveler: Guide to Raw Food Culture, Restaurants, Recipes, Nutrition, Sustainable Living, and the Restoration of Nature.*

McCabe is the author of *Hemp: What the World Needs Now*, which details the history and uses of the world's most useful plant, and how corrupt politicians worked with corporate leaders to outlaw industrial hemp farming.

McCabe has been a content and research editor, and a ghost co-writer on books by other authors. He also has been involved in fostering writers, including screenplay writers. He is a screenplay consultant, polishing scripts in preparation for sale and/or filming.

McCabe encourages people to plant and protect trees and forests; to protect animals and wildlife habitat; to protect the environment; to practice yoga; to walk or to ride a bike instead of driving a car; to use cloth shopping bags instead of "paper or plastic"; to use biodegradable cleaning and otherwise environmentally safe household products; to work against the genetic engineering of food; to stop the spread of nuclear energy and creation of nuclear weaponry; to work to legalize industrial hemp farming so it can be made into paper, clothing, food, building materials, energy, and other materials while supporting family farmers; to disconnect from the corporate food chain by planting organic food gardens and supporting local organic farmers; and to live close to Nature by following a plant-based diet consisting of organically grown, non-GMO foods free of synthetic food additives, MSG (monosodium glutamate), corn syrup and other processed sugars; and low-quality salt.

IgnitingYourLife.com
SunfoodLiving.com
SunfoodTraveler.com

To write the author:

John McCabe
C/O: Carmania Books
POB 1272
Santa Monica, CA 90406-1272, USA

"The real meaning of enlightenment is to gaze with undimmed eyes on all darkness."
– Nikos Kazantzakis

"A billion people sitting watching their TV in the room that they call living. But as for me, I see living as loving. And since there is no loving room, I sit on the grass under a tree dreaming of the way things use to be, pre-industrial revolution."
– Woody Harrelson

"Your profession is not what brings home your paycheck. Your profession is what you were put on earth to do."
– Publius Vergillus "Virgil" Maro

"People are unreasonable, illogical, and self-centered. Love them anyway. If you do good, people may accuse you of selfish motives. Do good anyway. If you are successful, you may win false friends and true enemies. Succeed anyway. The good you do today may be forgotten tomorrow. Do good anyway. Honesty and transparency make you vulnerable. Be honest and transparent anyway. What you spend years building may be destroyed overnight. Build anyway. People who really want help may attack you if you help them. Help them anyway. Give the world the best you have and you may get hurt. Give the world your best anyway."
– Mother Teresa

"The aim of life is to live, and to live means to be aware, joyously, drunkenly, serenely, divinely aware."
– Henry Miller

"Believe with all your heart that how you live your life makes a difference."
– Colin Beavan

"Walk tall like the trees, live your life as strong as the mountains, be as soft as the spring breezes, keep the warmth of the sun in your heart and the Great Spirit will always be with you."
– Navajo wisdom

"No more words. Hear only the voice within."
– Rumi

CPSIA information can be obtained at www.ICGtesting.com
Printed in the USA
LVOW071752060412

276519LV00018B/98/P

9 781884 702150